TO THE MONKS

OF

SAINT MEINRAD ARCHABBEY

WHO HAVE GONE BEFORE US

AND MADE THIS PLACE

A HOUSE OF PRAYER

The Tradition of Catholic Prayer

The Monks of Saint Meinrad Archabbey

Christian Raab, O.S.B.
Harry Hagan, O.S.B.
Editors

LITURGICAL PRESS
Collegeville, Minnesota

www.litpress.org

Nihil Obstat: Rev. Robert C. Harren, J.C.L., *Censor deputatis.*
Imprimatur: ✠ Most Rev. John F. Kinney, J.C.D., D.D., Bishop of St. Cloud, Minnesota, August 24, 2007.

Cover illustration: Detail from *Crucifixion* by Br. Martin Erspamer, O.S.B. Cover design by Ann Blattner.

1   2   3   4   5   6   7   8

Library of Congress Cataloging-in-Publication Data

The tradition of Catholic prayer : the Monks of St. Meinrad.
     p.   cm.
   Includes bibliographical references and index.
   ISBN-13: 978-0-8146-3184-3 (alk. paper)
   1. Prayer—Catholic Church.   2. Benedictines.   3. St. Meinrad Archabbey.
I. Benedictines.   II. St. Meinrad Archabbey.

BV213.T68   2007
248.3'2088282—dc22

                                                      2007006977

Contents

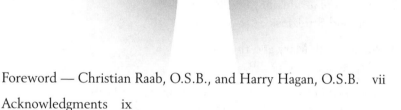

Foreword

This book grew out of the regular conversations between the novice master, Father Harry, and Brother Christian, at that time a novice. For several years Father Harry had been thinking of asking various monks to write chapters for a book on prayer. As their conversations continued to return to the tradition of prayer, Father Harry presented the idea of the book to Brother Christian, who himself had a broad knowledge of the history of Catholic prayer. Together they put together a plan for the project, and after Brother Christian's profession, they approached some monks of Saint Meinrad who had the scholarly expertise about a period or topic in Catholic spirituality. A generous response by their confreres made the work go quickly, and two years later the book has become a reality.

For Benedictines, tradition is a way of life that depends on those who have gone before us. Their way of life both guides and challenges us to make the tradition our own so that it may live in us today. Our prayer, then, depends on their prayer, and so we have devoted much of this book to exploring how others have lived a life of prayer. The first section surveys the history of Catholic prayer, the second section focuses on liturgical prayer, and the third section deals with special topics that, for the most part, span the whole of Church history. Since there is too much to say on each topic, we consciously limited the scope of each chapter and asked the authors to write an accessible introduction to their topic, focusing on three or four main people or ideas. This has not been easy, since the tradition is such a rich patchwork quilt. We have also limited the book to the Catholic tradition. The Protestant and Jewish traditions would each require hundreds of pages and not a chapter. Only part of Eastern Christianity finds a place here. We have left those and other topics for other people. Some will also find this person or that movement missing from this overview. Clearly our decisions have been colored by the fact that we are a group of Benedictine monks living in the Midwest. Still, that is who we are.

We want to thank Peter Dwyer, Mary Stommes, and Susan Sink of Liturgical Press for their dedication to this project. Thanks also to Dr. Joseph Raab and Father Raymond Studzinski, O.S.B., for their guidance as readers of this text, and to Prior Tobias Colgan, O.S.B., Brother Fidelis Mary von Hazmburg, O.S.B., Novice Craig Wagner, O.S.B., and Mary Jeanne Schumacher for looking over individual chapters. We appreciate the careful attention of Brother Matthew Mattingly, O.S.B., to details in the final stages. We also want to thank Saint Meinrad School of Theology for monies from the Adrian Fuerst Fund to obtain the rights to publish the color images used in this book, and we are grateful for the work of John Farless, who tended to the permissions and technical matters so that could happen. Finally, we thank our confreres who daily re-create this tradition of prayer as together we seek to prefer nothing to the work of God and to the love of Christ (RB 4:21; 43:3; 72:11).[1]

Brother Christian Raab, O.S.B.
Father Harry Hagan, O.S.B.
Coeditors
Feast of All Saints, 2006
Saint Meinrad Archabbey

---

[1] Throughout this collection, the Rule of Benedict is abbreviated as RB and quotations are taken from Timothy Fry, O.S.B., *RB 1980: The Rule of St. Benedict in Latin and English with Notes* (Collegeville, MN: Liturgical Press, 1981).

Acknowledgments

Excerpts from the English translation of *The Roman Missal* © 1973, International Committee on English in the Liturgy, Inc. (ICEL); excerpts from the English translation of *The Liturgy of the Hours* © 1974, ICEL; excerpts from the English translation of *The General Instruction of the Roman Missal (Third Typical Edition)* © 2002, ICEL. All rights reserved.

Excerpts from documents of the Second Vatican Council are from *Vatican Council II: The Basic Sixteen Documents*, by Austin Flannery, O.P. © 1996 (Costello Publishing Company, Inc.). Used with permission.

Excerpts from The Rule of Benedict are from Timothy Fry, O.S.B., *RB 1980: The Rule of St. Benedict in Latin and English with Notes* (Collegeville, MN: Liturgical Press, 1981).

Excerpts from *Pseudo-Dionysius: The Complete Works*, trans. Colm Luibheid and Paul Rorem, © 1987, Paulist Press, New York, Mahwah, N.J. Used with permission. www.paulistpress.com.

Texts from *Francis of Assisi: Early Documents*, Volume 1: *The Saint*, Volume 2: *The Founder*, Volume 3: *The Prophet* are used with permission.

Introduction

WARNING: This book may be hazardous to your spiritual health.

A book on prayer is a dangerous thing, every bit as dangerous as a book on love. Prayer, like love, withers under the microscope of the objective observer, and the reader of this present volume might be tempted to think it examines in a distanced way the tradition of Catholic prayer. The danger for the reader lies in believing that the book will offer some as yet unrealized insights into how to pray.

The Tradition of Catholic Prayer does offer insights, not as a how-to book, but as a from-where book. It looks at the great tradition in Catholicism that has been shaped by the prayer of real people over the centuries. They opened their hearts and minds to God in prayer and came away changed by the living God whom they encountered. They did this with others in the liturgical assembly, they did it alone behind closed doors in the privacy of their rooms as Jesus commanded his followers (Matt 6:6), they did it on fields of battle, they did it in monasteries and religious houses, they did it on trains and planes as they traveled, and they did it with their children at their knees. The present generation of Catholic Christians continues to pray, encountering the God whose loving kindness extends from generation to generation. Their life of prayer contributes to the living tradition of Catholicism, which is a legacy to generations yet to come.

Early on in the tradition a man known as Prosper of Aquitaine, who wrote in the first quarter of the fourth century, coined a phrase that succinctly states the right relationship between how we pray and what we believe. He wrote, "The law of praying founds the law of believing." Prayer, or encounter with the living God, establishes a foundation for what we come to believe about God, Christ, the Church, and how they relate to the created world in which we live. Prosper's pithy summary offers us a guide for negotiating the danger that a book on prayer poses to the reader by keeping before our mind's eye the primacy of prayer as the indispensable component of the Christian life. It gives rise to the living tradition that sustains each succeeding generation of Catholic Christians.

All the authors of the chapters in this volume are Catholics. They are also Benedictine monks. The reader might well wonder if the title of the book should not be *The Tradition of Benedictine Prayer*! While that might be an interesting book, it would be a far more focused book. Benedictine monasticism provides the authors with a particular vantage point from which they examine the larger tradition within which they are situated. As Benedictines they practice prayer day in and day out, with their brothers in choir, alone in their cells, using formal rites and wordless sighs of the heart. They pray for the Church, for the world, and for themselves. The bulletin board of our monastery is never without requests from many other people—Catholics and non-Catholics alike—requesting the prayers of the monks for particular intentions and daily needs ranging from the health of a loved one to the success of a job search. These people recognize the place prayer has in the life of the community and they entrust their cares to the prayers of the monks. It is an awesome responsibility for us.

The authors approach the tradition of Catholic prayer as practitioners of prayer themselves. They know that this tradition, while it has a fairly wide breadth, also has definite boundaries. From their vantage point, they look out at the wider tradition with one eye on the road of history and another on some particular landscapes along the way.

The first seven chapters trace the historical development of the tradition, beginning with the Old Testament and moving up to the present era. Father Cyprian Davis's chapter on "Prayer as Battle" takes an explicit monastic point of view, but shows how it makes a contribution to the greater tradition. The road is wide and includes room for the monastic lane as well as others. The historical section closes with the chapter on "Prayer in the Modern Period." The several contributors to this chapter lay out quite a selection of contemporary methods that have become familiar in the lives of Catholics and so take their place in the tradition of Catholic prayer.

The second part of the book examines more specifically the practices of liturgical prayer. Father Godfrey Mullen's and Father Harry Hagan's chapters on the liturgical year and the Liturgy of the Hours explore this backbone of Catholic spirituality. Father Kurt Stasiak's chapter on the Eucharist walks through the elements of the Mass and its prayers to demonstrate how corporate prayer joins us together and to Christ.

The third section of this book takes a look at some of the scenic landscapes that lie along the road that the tradition has followed. These special topics in the history of Catholic prayer give the reader the opportunity to enjoy some of the sights that have delighted—and continue to delight—the people who practice prayer. With the chapter on *lectio divina*, Father Raymond Studzinski puts the monastic lens back in place, although the method of prayer has its origins prior to its promotion in monastic circles. The cultural shift to a preference for the visual lies at the heart of Father Guerric DeBona's chapter on images of Jesus. Building on the approach of *lectio*, he moves on to a contemporary "video" way of praying. With his treatment of Mary and the saints in the great tradition of prayer, Brother Silas Henderson deals with perhaps the prayers most popularly identified as "Catholic." Rather than a peculiar deviation, Brother Silas shows how this form of prayer is solidly planted within the mainstream of the tradition. Prayer touches every aspect of our Christian life, so Father Mark O'Keefe looks at the life of virtue as it relates to prayer in the effort of conversion.

As noted above, the authors of all the chapters are Benedictine monks for whom prayer is daily fare, and not merely the subject of research. I know this because each day, four times a day, I pray with them. They are my brothers in Christ and in monastic profession. We together join the whole monastic community of prayers whose ages stretch from 106 to 23, covering several generations who have seen lots of change in the world and in the Church. This diversity enriches our prayer and our life together and allows the authors of this book to write from experience, so that they can give witness to Prosper of Aquitaine's maxim, "The law of praying founds the law of believing."

As Catholic Christians who pray, the authors gladly offer this book to the reader out of love for God and the Church, and in solidarity with their fellow travelers who brave the dangers along the way of the great tradition of Catholic prayer.

As Benedictine monks whose lives are spent seeking this same God, they humbly offer this book *ut in omnibus glorificetur Deus*, "so that in all things God may be glorified" (RB 57:9; 1 Pet 4:11).

Archabbot Justin DuVall, O.S.B.
21 March 2007
Feast of Saint Benedict
Saint Meinrad Archabbey

> [18] But we will bless the LORD
> > from this time on and forevermore. Praise the LORD!

When we speak, we not only live, but we also act as God acts—this God in whose image we have been made.

Psalms of Praise and Thanksgiving

Prayer can be divided into two large categories: praise and petition.

Praise is basically the making of statements about God. We can make statements about God's qualities:

> God is good, just, kind, merciful, etc.

Or we can make statements about what God has done:

> God has created the world.
>
> God has brought Israel out of Egypt.
>
> God has sent his only Son to save us.

By making statements about God, we describe the most important realities in our lives. We reaffirm the order of reality, particularly the reality that God is God and we are his creatures and not gods. In this sense, praise is an act of humility because humility is truth. However this is a truth that should be celebrated and proclaimed to all the world. So praise is always an act of celebration. It tells the story once again of the history of our salvation.

When we make statements about what God has done particularly for us, then we move toward thanksgiving which is essentially an acknowledgment of what another has done for us. So thanks and praise are intimately related and cannot be neatly separated. In a sense, every reason that we have for praise is also a reason to give thanks.

The psalms of praise typically have two basic elements:

1. a call to praise

2. statement/reason: a statement of praise which also serves as the reason for praise

The first element calls the community to praise. The other element has two functions. On the one hand it is the reason that people should praise. At the same time, it is also what people should say, the statement that they should make about God. We see this in Psalm 117.

call:

> ¹ Praise the LORD, all you nations!
>   Extol him, all you peoples!

statement/reason:

> ² For great is his steadfast love toward us,
>   and the faithfulness of the LORD endures forever.

The first two lines call all nations and people to praise the Lord. The next two lines give the reason, introduced by "for," that they should praise God. This is also exactly what people should say in order to praise God. These words are the very hymn itself.

> ² For great is his steadfast love toward us,
>   and the faithfulness of the LORD endures forever.

This same pattern appears in many psalms and elsewhere as well.
  Psalm 148 divides into two large sections:

148:1-5a   calls the heavens to praise God;

148:7-12   calls the earth and all people to praise God.

This psalm celebrates the greatness of God the creator who is above everything created, but it ends by stating that this exalted God is also near to "the people of Israel who are close to him" (148:14). Likewise praise brings us near to God. Human beings need to praise God in order to acknowledge God as creator and savior and to declare that we are creatures and servants of God.

  Two important hymns of praise found in the Liturgy of the Hours are the Canticle of Zachary (Luke 1:68-79) used at morning prayer and the Canticle of Mary (Luke 1:46-55) used at evening prayer. These two hymns restate both what God has done for the people of Israel and also for these two individuals. As such they are models of praise for us all.

Psalms of Petition

  Often when we think of prayer, we think of asking God for something, and many of the psalms focus on petition. Just as the praise psalms have a pattern, so also do the psalms of petition, and the pattern is rooted in our human experience of asking someone for something.

invocation	Typically we call the person by name.
description	Then we explain the problem. We talk about our need for something or for help, and we explain why the person would be able to meet this need.
petition	Then we ask the person.
so that	Sometimes we explain what we hope for as an outcome or result; this may be introduced also by "in order to."

This pattern shapes the prayers of the Roman Missal used at Mass with the addition of a final element called the doxology, which celebrates the Trinity. The prayers of the Roman Missal typically ask God to grant something through Christ in union with the Father and Holy Spirit, or makes prayers through Christ. Here is the opening prayer for the Vigil of Pentecost Sunday:[1]

invocation	Almighty and ever-living God,
description	you fulfilled the Easter promise by sending us your Holy Spirit.
petition	May that Spirit unite the races and nations on earth,
so that	[in order] to proclaim your glory.
doxology	Grant this through our Lord who lives and reigns with you and the Holy Spirit, one God, forever and ever. Amen.

In these prayers, the description typically focuses on what God has done, so it is a statement of praise and thanks. The elements may be expanded and repeated and rearranged in various ways as is seen in the Prayer before Meals:

petition and invocation	Bless us, O Lord, and these thy gifts

---

[1] *The Sacramentary of the Roman Missal*, English translation by the International Commission on English in the Liturgy (New York: Catholic Book Publishing Co., 1974), 270.

description of us	which we are about to receive
description of God	from thy bountiful hands
doxology	through Christ our Lord. Amen.

The opening of Psalm 61 shows the basic elements:

petition for God to hear	[1] Hear my cry, O God; listen to my prayer.
description of the psalmist	[2] From the end of the earth I call to you, when my heart is faint.
petition	[2c] Lead me to the rock that is higher than I;
description of God	[3] for you are my refuge, a strong tower against the enemy.
second petition	[4] Let me abide in your tent forever, find refuge under the shelter of your wings.

The psalms are different from the prayers of the Roman Missal, which are great universal prayers for the whole Church and tend to be rather formal and restrained. In contrast, the prayers of petition found in the book of Psalms are mainly by an individual in an immediate and great need. As a result these psalms can be very personal, rather emotional, and extremely frank. Often people beginning to read the psalms think that these prayers should express "my own" personal prayer, and instead they find the psalms filled with emotions and ideas that are very different, even shocking. It is important to remember that these were originally the prayers of other people. Therefore we must begin by trying to see what this other person was saying to God and why.

Central to these psalms is the description of the psalmist's need. Some psalmists are sick; some have been falsely accused; others are suffering from the weight of their own sin or feel abandoned by friends and even by God. From what the psalmist says, we must piece together the story of what has happened. Unlike a traditional narrative in which the actions unfold sequentially, the psalmist's story must be reconstructed from various parts of the text.

The psalms add to the basic elements found in Roman prayer form. The first is a statement of trust. In Psalm 31:14 the psalmist says:

[14] But I trust in you, O Lᴏʀᴅ; I say, "You are my God."

And in Psalm 56:4 we hear:

> [4] In God, whose word I praise, in God I trust;
> I am not afraid; what can flesh do to me?

In these psalms trust becomes the basis for prayer.

The other new element is the rhetorical question directed at God. Typically it is full of frustration, and even despair. Surely the most famous example opens Psalm 22:

> [1] My God, my God, why have you forsaken me?
> Why are you so far from helping me,
> from the words of my groaning?

This psalm moves back and forth between this sense of abandonment and a search for hope. The psalmist recounts the trust of Israel's ancestors as a basis for hope and later recounts his or perhaps her own experience of birth as a ground for hope. This search is punctuated by images of what is near and far away until it reaches a climax in the final petition of 22:21a: "Save me from the mouth of the lion!" After this, the psalm shifts radically.

The next line states that the psalmist has been rescued: "From the horns of the wild oxen you have rescued me" (22:21b). There follows an affirmation of praise (22:22) and then a call for all Israel to praise (22:23), and then a statement of praise (22:24).

Psalm 22 divides into a psalm of petition in the midst of conflict and a thanksgiving psalm celebrating God's rescue of the psalmist. A number of psalms contain these two different moments: e.g., Psalm 6:1-7, 8-10; Psalm 13:1-5, 6; Psalm 28:1-5, 6-9. Some scholars explain the two moments of the psalm by creating a liturgical context for it. They see someone who has survived an illness or false accusation coming to the temple and reliving the experience by reciting the first part of the psalm. Then a priest would have pronounced an oracle of salvation telling of God's deliverance. The person would then have recited the second part of the psalm, a thanksgiving hymn stating what God has done for the psalmist.

In the book of Psalms we find a number of thanksgiving hymns added as a second element to the prayer psalms. There are also examples where the whole psalm offers thanks: Psalms 30, 32, 118, and 138.

This double movement of petition and thanks can be seen very clearly in some of the narratives. Exodus 14 tells of the escape from Pharaoh at the Red Sea, and Exodus 15 gives Moses' triumphal hymn of thanks. Deborah sings a hymn of triumph (Judg 5) after Jael defeats Sisera (Judg 4). These hymns are two of the oldest texts in the Old Testament. In 1 Samuel 1–2, Hannah pours out her heart to God because she is barren. The priest Eli mistakes her ecstatic prayer and weeping for drunkenness, but she explains that it is because of her grief that she prays with such emotion. Eli sends her away in peace with either the assurance or the prayer that God grant her desire. The Hebrew is ambiguous. Hannah gives birth to Samuel and then in 1 Samuel 2 celebrates the gift of the child with a long hymn of praise which forms a foundation for Mary's hymn of praise, the Magnificat, in Luke 1:46-55. Likewise Judith makes her prayer of petition to God before going to meet the Assyrian general Holofernes (Judg 9). After her triumph, Judith sings a great hymn of thanksgiving (Judg 16). For Christians, this double movement reflects the cross and resurrection.

Not all the psalms end with everything resolved. In Psalm 58 the psalmist cries out against unjust judges whose mouths cause violence like poisonous snakes. The psalmist asks that these unjust judges vanish like water, wither like grass, dissolve like a snail, or be like a miscarriage (Ps 58:7-8). The psalmist has violent images for these purveyors of violence. Some people are scandalized by the sentiments, but as was stated earlier, the psalms were originally other people's prayers. They are not necessarily what I would say. The psalmists do not hold back. They pour out their hearts; they tell God exactly what they feel. In Psalm 137 we see the anger of an exile in Babylon who had seen the destruction of the temple in Jerusalem. Psalm 137 reaches its climax in the call for the children of Babylon to be dashed on the rocks. The psalm asks us to confront these feelings of violence. It may be that we will discover such feelings within ourselves, or the psalm may only remind us that there were people then and there are people today who feel such hurt and anger. Only by confronting such strong emotion can it be dealt with, and the psalm invites us to such a confrontation.

Even God comes in for harsh criticism in some of the psalms. We have already seen how Psalm 22 begins by asking God: "Why have you forsaken me?" Psalms 38, 39, and 88 are some of the darkest, reflecting the desperation of the sick. In Psalm 38 the psalmist sees sickness as the result of his own sin—a common theological understanding during this period. The psalmist confesses his sin and begs: "Make haste to help me, O Lord, my salvation" (Ps 38:22). Psalm 39 presents a darker picture still. Seeing God as the cause of this suffering, the psalmist asks God to turn away from him. Finally Psalm 88 presents us with a psalmist who seems completely in despair except for the fact that he has spoken this psalm; it even seems to end in despair: "You have caused friend and neighbor to shun me; my companions are in darkness" (Ps 88:18).

Again these psalms teach us that anything can be said in prayer. Too often people think that prayer must only be "pious" and good, but this is not what we find in the psalms. They have the raw emotion of country music, pop, and blues. They lay it on the line and show that anything can be said. They give us permission to say anything we want or feel to God. At the same time these psalms invite us to hear the hope and trust.

In conclusion, the prayer of petition has a basic pattern which these psalms develop to meet the needs of the psalmist. At the heart of petition is simply telling God what is wrong and asking for what we need. These psalms show us that we can say anything to God. God wants us to be real.

The Psalms and Christ

In the early monastic tradition, each psalm was followed by a short period of silence. This gave people a moment to react to the psalm and then to make their own prayer. The psalms are both mirrors and windows. They are mirrors in the sense that they sometimes, but not always, reflect our situation. Sometimes a line, if not a whole psalm, puts our experience into words. More often, the psalms are windows into the human experience. They let us see both the hurt and joy of life in this world, and they look for the God of salvation to play a part.

Many of the psalms tell of an enemy and oppression, of violence and the fight for goodness. Other psalms identify the king as the hero of this battle. The early Church identifies these motifs with the struggle of Christ crucified and risen. Whatever the historical and external reality of the psalms, the early Church understands them as a description of a spiritual and eternal reality bound up with Christ. This Christocentric interpretation is found already on the road to Emmaus with the risen Lord explaining to the disciples how to interpret the Old Testament in terms of the events taking place in their midst. The early Church follows this approach and understands the Old Testament in terms of Christ.

Saint Augustine, for instance, sees two levels of meaning in the Scriptures. First is the literal meaning which is particular and historical. The spiritual meaning transcends the particular and historical in order to speak to the universal reality of Christ. Augustine, therefore, is able to find links to the mysteries of Christ throughout the psalms. He also sees the psalms as the prayers of "the whole Christ"—*totus Christus*, a term which appears throughout his commentary on the psalms.[2] The "whole Christ" is made up of two dimensions: Christ the Head, who died and rose for us, and Christ the Body, that is, the Church. Augustine interprets the psalms either as the words of Christ the Head or as the words of the Church with its many emotions, struggles, and hopes. Because some psalms seem strange in the mouth of Christ, later commentators have tended to interpret the psalms as the prayers of the whole Body of Christ.

The history of interpretation, to some extent, is a movement back and forth between an emphasis on literal and spiritual meaning. The School of Antioch and the Scholastic tradition have emphasized a respect for the literal meaning, lest readers become too much enamored of and misled by their own imaginations. The modern historical approach has also emphasized the literal and historical meaning. Its concerns were shaped by the Enlightenment's rejection of the Scriptures as a credible historical witness, and modern historical scholarship has helped to clarify and answer those objections. However, historical scholarship can focus too narrowly on the literal, which tends to isolate the many pieces making up the Scriptures and create a sense of fragmentation. Some scholars have compounded the problem with a rejection of patristic interpretation as "allegorical," meaning naïve and fanciful, but that judgment is itself naïve.[3] The new emphasis on Scripture as literature has helped readers see the connections that unify and

---

[2] Cf. Agostino Trapè, "St. Augustine," in *Patrology*, ed. Angelo di Berardino, trans. Placid Solari, O.S.B. (Westminster, MD: Christian Classics, Inc., 1986), 342–462, esp. 397.

[3] For a defense of patristic scholarship, see John J. O'Keefe and R. R. Reno, *Sanctified Vision: An Introduction to Early Christian Interpretation of the Bible* (Baltimore: Johns Hopkins University Press, 2005). See also Robert M. Grant with David Tracy, *A Short History of the Interpretation of the Bible*, 2d ed. (Philadelphia: Fortress Press, 1984).

create a sense of universality. Literary studies provide a way to understand the interpretation of Augustine, Origen, and others, as well as the use of the Scriptures in the liturgy. However, the Scriptures are more than literature. They are documents of faith read in faith as the Word of God.

The primary reading of these texts in faith takes place during the liturgy. Here a spiritual understanding is primary, because faith allows us to see the necessary interconnection between Christ and all the Scriptures. Whether at the Eucharist or in the Liturgy of the Hours, the psalms become the many prayers of the Church past and present. Here the Body of Christ recites the psalms in the belief that these prayers give expression to the many situations and feelings of the Body of Christ before the face of God. By praying the psalms we join ourselves to the many and diverse prayers of the Church, and we pray the psalms for the whole Church and not just for our individual selves. Here the prayer of the Church becomes the prayer of Christ himself.

The Actions of Prayer

In part we carry on our relationships with other people by what we do for and with them. These actions communicate our thoughts and intentions and make them present in a very concrete way.

Postures of Prayer

The postures of prayer orient us toward God. In Psalm 95:6 the psalmist calls:

> ⁶ O come, let us worship and bow down,
>   let us kneel before the LORD, our Maker!

Prostration, bowing, and kneeling bring the body low and show an attitude of lowliness and obeisance which was typically shown to rulers in the ancient Near East. The word "to prostrate" is used extensively in the Old Testament and takes on the more general meaning "to worship." Prostration is a radical gesture and is maintained today only in the liturgy for Good Friday, ordination, and monastic profession. Early in the monastic tradition, prostration was used between psalms with the warning that it should not go on too long lest people fall asleep. The bow displays reverence; it is used particularly in the Byzantine liturgy as the main gesture of reverence, accompanied by the sign of the cross. Kneeling acknowledges sovereignty, and in Isaiah 45:23, the Lord commands: "To me every knee shall bow; every tongue shall swear." Therefore Philippians 2:10 states "so that at the name of Jesus every knee should bend, in heaven and on earth and under the earth." In the Western Church, kneeling becomes a basic posture at liturgy, particularly before the Real Presence.

In the Old Testament the basic posture of prayer seems to be standing with hands outstretched. When Solomon made his great prayer at the dedication of the temple, he stood before the altar and "spread out his hands to heaven" (1 Kgs 8:22; also Pss 28:2; 63:4; 134:2). The raising of hands suggests lifting of oneself to God and so raising one's prayer to God as found in the famous verse from Psalm 141:2:

> [2] Let my prayer be counted as incense before you,
>   and the lifting up of my hands as an evening sacrifice.

With hands extended, a person becomes vulnerable because the hands are so far from the body. Therefore this stance suggests surrender and openness—appropriate for prayer. Christians, of course, saw in this gesture an image of the cross, and it became a basic stance of prayer for the early Church as seen in the famous fresco of a widow from the Catacombs of Santa Priscilla (see fig. 1, pg. 251).[4]

Fasting

Fasting creates a kind of sacred time for a person and so both physically intensifies and expresses a person's prayer. During the period of the Second Temple, the Mosaic law commanded fasting only for the Day of Atonement, but there are numerous references indicating that fasting was a common practice to express grief in the face of death and sorrow for sin. Though Moses and Elijah fast forty days and David, seven, the usual length seems to have been only a fast of one day from all food except water. Fasting involves the body integrally in prayer.

Offering Sacrifice

Ancient peoples of the Near East understood their deities in human terms, as if they were very powerful beings capable of doing good or evil

---

[4] Such pictures are called an *orant* or *orans*. Although the gesture has become identified with the priest, it was not so originally.

for human beings. The temple was the house where deities lived, and sacrifices were a way of feeding them and making them happy.

Israel's understanding of God transforms these rituals. Though very foreign to our world, the offering of animals, grain, drink, and incense played an integral role for Israel in acting out their relationship to God.

The English word "sacrifice" comes from the Latin and means "to make holy" (*sacer* + *facere*). The Hebrew word for "holy," *qadosh*, means "set apart" and refers to that which has been "set apart" as belonging to God. To sacrifice something is to acknowledge explicitly that it belongs to God. Three types of sacrifice help us to understand the implications.

First was the holocaust, an offering in which everything was burned in the fire to show that it belonged wholly and entirely to God. A second type was called the *sh*e*lamîm:* a word related to *shalom*, meaning peace, prosperity, wholeness. This sacrifice sought to express the peace and prosperity received by the one making the sacrifice, so it often had a dimension of thanksgiving. Here only part of the animal was burned and given back to God. Another part was eaten as a meal by the one making the sacrifice with his family and friends, so it is sometimes called a communion sacrifice because those involved share a kind of meal with God and are joined in communion with the divine. A third type was a sin offering in which those making the sacrifice acknowledged their sin and sought forgiveness. In different ways all sacrifices sought to maintain or reestablish a person's relationship to God.

The importance of the sacrifice cannot be overstated. Still, there is another tradition that emphasizes interior disposition. In Isaiah 1:10-17, the Lord rejects the ritual of sacrifices and feasts and demands instead goodness and justice as prerequisites for any ritual. Psalm 51:17 likewise demands as sacrifice "a broken and contrite heart." All ritual must express a person's interior state; otherwise it becomes a kind of magic that seeks to manipulate the divine. Therefore, the external ritual must express the interior heart. At the same time we, as human beings, need actions and not just words to express our inmost heart.

Even with the destruction of the First Temple in 586 B.C. and certainly with the destruction of the Second Temple in 70 A.D., the understanding of sacrifice becomes more and more interior and spiritual.

Celebrating Feasts and Making the Pilgrimage

Likewise feast days were important rituals for celebrating the basic stories and beliefs of Israel. During the time of the First Temple before the fall of Jerusalem in 586 B.C., the autumn Festival of Booths played a central role because it celebrated the Lord's kingship. After the fall of Jerusalem, Passover and its springtime celebration of the Exodus became the central feast of cultic life.

For these feasts, the people were required to make a pilgrimage to Jerusalem. This journey was more than travel; it involved the whole body in remembering the many journeys of Israel's history: the expulsion of Adam and Eve from the garden, Abraham's journey to the promised land, Joseph's journey to Egypt, then the Exodus that brought them back, and finally the journey into the Babylonian exile and the return. Journey takes people into a new world, asks them to mature, and brings them home. Life is like a journey, so the pilgrimage to Jerusalem was a multilayered experience, and psalms of pilgrimage (Pss 120–134) explore some of these themes. Pilgrimage became a core experience for Christians particularly during the Middle Ages.

Keeping the Sabbath: Torah and the Synagogue

Keeping the Sabbath is one of the Ten Commandments. During the time of the Second Temple, the importance of keeping the Sabbath grew and became a hallmark of Israel's identity. The priestly tradition saw the Sabbath as established by God as part of creation, for God rested on the seventh day (Gen 2:2-3). In Exodus 31:16-17 the Sabbath became the sign of the Sinai covenant as was the rainbow for Noah's covenant and circumcision for Abraham's. To keep the Sabbath then was to participate week by week in God's covenant.

The laws for keeping the covenant restricted activity in order to promote rest, yet there was also a call to gather in a "holy convocation" (Lev 23:3). This gathering became the synagogue. With sacrifice strictly limited to Jerusalem by Deuteronomy and with the dispersal of Israel and Judah to Babylon, Egypt, and farther, the need grew for a new gathering of prayer. Although it is not clear exactly how it developed, the synagogue emerged as a place where Rabbinic Judaism gathered both to pray and to study. The great gift of the Second Temple was the gift of the Bible itself, for it was during this time that the Torah along with the prophets and other writings were written down and gathered into a recognizable body of literature. The people now had a book that brought them the word of God. For Rabbinic Judaism the study of the Scriptures went hand in hand with prayer. The Scriptures became a source of prayer. The importance of this is inestimable.

Prayer and the Presence of God

Sometimes in a relationship nothing needs to be said or done. It is enough to be with the other person and experience that person's presence. This too is a type of prayer and in some ways the most profound form of prayer. While Moses and Elijah on Mount Sinai are archetypal images of this experience, there are many stories about meeting God in various ways.

The Temple and Being with God

In the ancient Near East, a temple was the house where a deity lived, and the statue of the deity was the main focal point. Solomon builds the first temple in Jerusalem with a cherubim throne in the holy of holies where the Lord as king could sit and dwell, but there is no image of God. In fact, the first two Commandments forbid this: The first commandment prohibits the worship of any god but the Lord alone, and the second prohibits any image of God. Every image of God is necessarily inadequate and so forbidden. In this way, the Israelite tradition preserves the transcendence of God, and later traditions would put more emphasis on the transcendent by making the temple the place not for God to dwell but for YHWH's name or glory to dwell. Even so, the temple becomes the special place where one is connected to God, and we find in the psalms a desire to be in the temple in order to be with God as seen in Psalm 27:4.

> [4] One thing I asked of the LORD, that will I seek after:
> to live in the house of the LORD all the days of my life,
> to behold the beauty of the LORD, and to inquire in his temple.

While it is possible to pray anywhere at any time, we all need sacred spaces, whether they be spaces consecrated by generations who have come to some specific place to pray, a public building dedicated to the worship of God, or a private space made holy by one's own experience of God.

Sexuality and Relationship

In the ancient Near East, infertility was a serious problem, and much energy was devoted to assuring the good order and fertility of the earth. The peoples around Israel had fertility cults in which men and women played the roles of the god and goddess; by their sexual union they expected to cause their deities to be fertile and so to promote the fertility of the earth. This was a type of sympathetic magic in which a person does something that forces something else to happen. It was a way of trying to control the fickle deities.

Hosea in his prophecy makes clear that in Yahwism sexuality is fundamentally an issue of relationship defined by God's covenant of love and fidelity. From this relationship flows fertility as a gift from God. This theological context becomes crucial for an understanding of the Song of Songs which celebrates the sexual love of a man and woman. The rabbis questioned whether this poem of human, sexual love should be included in the Scriptures, but in the end they embraced it because sexuality cannot be separated from the divine, and many Christian writers have followed their lead. If the Song of Songs is literally about the love of a man and woman, the tradition affirms that it is also a metaphor about the love between God and Israel, the love between Christ and the Church, and between the love of God and the soul. If prayer is about relationship, then sexuality is necessarily a dimension that must not be forgotten or ignored. Moreover, the intense experience of the love of God becomes a privileged way of being with God as affirmed most dramatically in the mystical tradition.

The Face of God

The face of God appears throughout the Old Testament as one of the great images of God's presence, and so the psalmist says in Psalm 27:8:

> "Come," my heart says, "seek his face!"
> Your face, LORD, do I seek.

However, the presence of God was dangerous, and seeing the face of God could bring death.

In Exodus 33:18-23, Moses asks to see God's glory, but the Lord tells Moses that he cannot see the face of God and live. Still, the Lord is willing to put Moses in the cleft of a rock and protect him with the divine hand so that Moses may see God's back, but Moses is not allowed to see the face of God. In another tradition, however, both Moses and Jacob are celebrated for having seen God face-to-face (Deut 34:10; Gen 32:31), and the surly Gideon and foolish Manoa are amazed that they have seen God face-to-face and are not dead (Judg 6:22; 13:22). To see God face-to-face is an extraordinary and dangerous event, and much desired. Elijah, however, does not see God at all but meets him on Mount Sinai, not in the wind or in the earthquake or in the fire, but in "a sound of sheer silence" (1 Kgs 19:12). Such is the mystery of this God who is powerful but nonetheless comes near to us.

Conclusion

The Old Testament holds many prayers and many ways to pray. So many express a longing to be near God. In Psalm 73, the psalmist, after telling of his struggle to make sense of the injustice of the world, says:

> Whom have I in heaven but you?
>> And there is nothing on earth that I desire other than you.
> But for me it is good to be near God;
>> I have made the Lord GOD my refuge,
>> to tell of all your works. (Ps 73:25, 28)

Seldom does the Old Testament find such equanimity and peace. More often its prayers are full of expectation for something yet to come. In either case, this tradition of prayer is vibrant and insistent, and it can teach us much about how to carry on our relationship with God until we with the psalmist can say: "And there is nothing on earth that I desire other than you" (73:25b).

Further Reading

Catholic Church, "The Universal Call to Prayer. Article 1: In the Old Testament" in the *Catechism of the Catholic Church*, 616–23. Washington, D.C.: United States Catholic Conference, 1994.

Clifford, Richard J. *Psalms 1–72* and *Psalms 73–150*. Collegeville Bible Commentary of the Old Testament. Vols. 22 and 23. Collegeville, MN: Liturgical Press, 1986.

Mays, James Luther. *Psalms: Interpretation, a Bible Commentary for Teaching and Preaching.* Louisville, KY: Westminster John Knox Press, 1994.

Merton, Thomas. *Thomas Merton: Praying the Psalms.* Collegeville, MN: Liturgical Press, 1956.

Stuhmueller, Carroll, ed. *The Collegeville Pastoral Dictionary of Biblical Theology.* Collegeville, MN: Liturgical Press, 1996. See the articles on "Praise," "Prayer," and "Psalms."

Chapter 2

New Testament Boldness

Eugene Hensell, O.S.B.

There is no theory of prayer in the New Testament. What we do find, however, is people praying. This chapter will look at five different manifestations of prayer in the New Testament. First, we will consider some of the oldest forms of prayer found in the New Testament, hymns and canticles. Second, we will look at Jesus himself as one who prays and who teaches others about prayer, followed by an examination of the most important prayer found in the New Testament, the Lord's Prayer. Fourth, we will focus on the Acts of the Apostles and the various experiences of prayer that are found there, and, finally, we will center our attention on St. Paul and the role prayer played in his life and ministry.

Hymns

Hymns in the New Testament provide us with a window through which to glimpse some of the very earliest faith expressions preserved and handed down through Christian tradition. These faith expressions come to us in the form of poetry and they were part of the early Christians' praise and worship. We need to remember that following the early Christians' faith recognition that Jesus had been raised from the dead, their very first response was to pray and worship. A significant part of

This hymn is all about God's faithfulness in keeping promises. The ultimate fulfillment of those promises is to be found in the coming of Jesus. The role of John is described in the second half of the hymn (Luke 1:76-79). He is to be the one who prepares the way for Jesus the Messiah. All of this constitutes God's redemptive purpose for humankind. The fulfillment includes both deliverance and restoration of God's people. The subject matter of this deliverance and restoration is not only political oppression but also sin, that fundamental distortion that prevents humankind from responding faithfully to God's gracious offer of salvation.

In Catholic tradition these New Testament hymns have been kept alive within the very same context from which they arose, the Church's liturgy. Their importance for us today is that they connect us intimately with the faith of the early followers of Jesus. Their hope is our hope, their belief in the faithfulness of God is our belief, their conviction that Jesus the Messiah has delivered us and restored us for the kingdom of God is our conviction. This kind of prayer requires singing because it involves the whole person offering praise to God.

Jesus and Prayer

All the gospels agree that Jesus was a person of prayer. He was a Jew and therefore much of his prayer reflected traditional Jewish practices. Jews traditionally prayed in the synagogue. They also prayed before their meals and engaged in personal prayer upon rising in the morning and before going to bed at night. It is simply assumed that Jesus regularly prayed in this manner. Whenever the gospels mention specifically that Jesus prays, it is usually a special occasion over and above the traditional Jewish prayers. By mentioning this, the gospel wants to draw our attention to something important. An example of this would be Jesus' attraction to solitary prayer. "In the morning, while it was still very dark, he got up and went out to a deserted place, and there he prayed" (Mark 1:35). "After saying farewell to them, he went up on the mountain to pray" (Mark 6:46). An environment of solitude for prayer seems to be connected with Jesus' understanding that for him prayer expresses an intimate relationship with God. This is where he communicates most deeply with the very source of his life and mission.

In Mark's Gospel a crucial moment in Jesus' self-understanding of his fate comes toward the end of his ministry where he enters the Garden of Gethsemane to pray about his future.

They went to a place called Gethsemane; and he said to his disciples, "Sit here while I pray." He took with him Peter and James and John, and began to be distressed and agitated. And he said to them, "I am deeply grieved, even to death; remain here, and keep awake." And going a little farther, he threw himself on the ground and prayed that, if it were possible, the hour might pass from him. He said, "Abba, Father, for you all things are possible; remove this cup from me; yet, not what I want, but what you want." He came and found them sleeping; and he said to Peter, "Simon, are you asleep? Could you not keep awake one hour? Keep awake and pray that you may not come into the time of trial; the spirit indeed is willing, but the flesh is weak." And again he went away and prayed, saying the same words. And once more he came and found them sleeping, for their eyes were very heavy; and they did not know what to say to him. He came a third time and said to them, "Are you still sleeping and taking your rest? Enough! The hour has come; the Son of Man is betrayed into the hands of sinners. Get up, let us be going. See, my betrayer is at hand." (Mark 14:32-42)

This prayer of petition is also a prayer of negotiation. Jesus addresses God as "Abba" which is a term of intimacy not ordinarily used in Jewish prayer. Jesus is portrayed as very worked up and disturbed. His prayer is a request that God intervene and prohibit what he knows is inevitable, his own imminent death. Jesus makes this petition three times. He is willing to do whatever God decides, but his preference is clearly stated. However, Jesus' petition is not granted by God and thus the course for the future is set. Again this prayer is all about communication, even if the response from God was not what Jesus was hoping for. He knows what he must do to fulfill God's mysterious plan of salvation.

A final very significant prayer of Jesus occurs when he is on the cross. "At three o'clock Jesus cried out with a loud voice, 'Eloi, Eloi, lema sabachthani?' which means, 'My God, my God, why have you forsaken me?'" (Mark 15:34). Mark's Gospel portrays Jesus as having a tremendous feeling of having been abandoned by God at this final moment of his life. The words of Jesus are a quote from the opening line of Psalm 22. The irony of this utterance, however, is that at the very moment Jesus feels abandoned by God, still he remains faithful. His final words are words of prayer. We know of course that Jesus was not in fact abandoned by God, but at this final moment of his life that is what he feels and that is what informs his prayer.

There are two prayers of Jesus found in the New Testament that are extremely important and have played a very significant role in forming Christian spirituality from the time the gospels were written right down to our modern era. The first of these is the Lord's Prayer, which is found in both Matthew 6:5-15 and Luke 11:1-4. The second is Jesus' prayer to the Father located in John 17. Any treatment of prayer in the New Testament must give consideration to these two prayers of Jesus.

The Lord's Prayer (Matt 6:9-13; Luke 11:1-4)

A good place to begin a consideration of the Lord's Prayer is not a gospel commentary but rather the lived experience of the Christian community celebrating the Eucharist. The communion rite of the Catholic liturgy begins with the Lord's Prayer. The rite itself suggests four different formulas that can be used to introduce the prayer itself. These formulas capture an understanding of the Lord 's Prayer that extends back very early in the Church's history.

1) "Let us pray with confidence to the Father in the words our Savior gave us."

2) "Jesus taught us to call God our Father, and so we have the courage to say."

3) "Let us ask our Father to forgive our sins and to bring us to forgive those who sin against us."

4) "Let us pray for the coming of the kingdom as Jesus taught us."

These four introductions contain all the major elements needed to interpret the Lord's Prayer. First there is a strong emphasis on the disposition required to pray this prayer. One must be bold, confident, and courageous. Second, we are to call God our Father. This is not about the gender of God. It is about the intimate relationship that exists between a parent and a child no matter how old the child is. This is the relationship that Jesus had with God and by giving us this prayer he also hands on to us that very same relationship with God. Third, we are taught by the Lord's Prayer to ask for God's forgiveness. However, the boldness of this is that we want God to forgive us to the same degree we are willing to forgive others. And fourth, we are to pray for the coming of the kingdom of God as Jesus taught us. In the Lord's Prayer Jesus teaches us to pray for the kingdom to be present here and now and not only in the future at the end of time. In fact the petitions of the prayer are all in the imperative mood, which means they are almost demands.

The Lord's Prayer has been handed down to us in two forms, a longer form (Matthew) and a shorter form (Luke). There is also a form of this prayer found in a writing that is slightly later than these gospels called the *Didache* or the *Teaching of the Twelve Apostles*.

Matthew 6:5-15	Luke 11:1-4
[5] "And whenever you pray, do not be like the hypocrites; for they love to stand and pray in the synagogues and at the street corners, so that they may be seen by others. Truly I tell you, they have received their reward. [6] But whenever you pray, go into your room and shut the door and pray to your Father who is in secret; and your Father who sees in secret will reward you.	He was praying in a certain place, and after he had finished, one of his disciples said to him, "Lord, teach us to pray, as John taught his disciples."
[7] "When you are praying, do not heap up empty phrases as the Gentiles do; for they think that they will be heard because of their many words. [8] Do not be like them, for your Father knows what you need before you ask him.	[2] He said to them, "When you pray, say:
[9] "Pray then in this way: Our Father in heaven, hallowed be your name. [10] Your kingdom come. Your will be done, on earth as it is in heaven. [11] Give us this day our daily bread. [12] And forgive us our debts, as we also have forgiven our debtors.	Father, hallowed be your name. Your kingdom come. [3] Give us each day our daily bread. [4] And forgive us our sins, for we ourselves forgive everyone indebted to us.

¹³ And do not bring us to the time of trial, but rescue us from the evil one.

¹⁴ For if you forgive others their trespasses, your heavenly Father will also forgive you;
¹⁵ but if you do not forgive others, neither will your Father forgive your trespasses.

And do not bring us to the time of trial."

Luke's rendition of the Lord's Prayer is probably closest to what Jesus actually said. Matthew's version has been expanded because of its use in the Church's liturgy. Both authors seem to have had access to the same body of material. Matthew has shaped his material to provide "instructions on how to pray for people who do pray," whereas Luke molds his material to serve as "an encouragement to people who do not pray to do so."[2] Matthew's audience was mostly Jewish and therefore had a long tradition of praying. Luke's audience was mostly Gentile and therefore could not be presupposed to have the rich Jewish prayer background. Still, all the essentials are in both versions of the prayer.

The significance of the Lord's Prayer for us is very similar to what it was for the followers of Jesus who originally received it. It should not be understood merely as a mandate on how to pray. It is better to understand this prayer "as an invitation to share in the prayer-life of Jesus himself."[3] This means that when we pray the Lord's Prayer we are also sharing in that same relationship with God that Jesus had and which is designated by the phrase "Our Father" (*Abba* in the Aramaic language of Jesus). It is this relationship that allows us to be bold in our prayer. It is also this relationship that guides our life and makes us aware of the reality of God's presence here in our midst—the kingdom of God.

[2] Joachim Jeremias, *New Testament Theology: The Proclamation of Jesus* (New York: Scribner's, 1971), 193–95.
[3] N. T. Wright, "The Lord's Prayer as a Paradigm of Christian Prayer," *Into God's Presence: Prayer in the New Testament*, ed. Richard N. Longenecker (Grand Rapids, MI: Eerdmans Publishing Company, 2001), 132.

Jesus' Prayer to the Father (John 17)

The Gospel of John is quite different from the Synoptics.[4] John emphasizes from beginning to end the divinity of Jesus and the intimate union that has always existed between the Son and the Father. This union is experienced while Jesus is on earth, but even here it transcends the categories of time and space. Because of this, many find in the Gospel of John a mystical element not found in the other gospels. In the Synoptic Gospels Jesus' prayer in the Garden of Gethsemane is a central moment in his self-realization and acceptance of God's will. In John, Jesus' prayer to the Father replaces that prayer in the Garden of Gethsemane. John 17 can be read as having three major sections. In the first section (John 17:1-8) Jesus prays for his own glorification. In the second section (John 17:9-19) Jesus prays for the disciples. And in the third section (John 17:20-26) Jesus prays for both present and future believers.

Jesus Prays for His Own Glorification (John 17:1-8)

The biblical understanding of glorification is rich and diverse. In John's Gospel when Jesus speaks of his own glorification he is referring to his exaltation. This is when Jesus will depart from this world and return to the Father from whom he came. The time for this to take place is referred to as Jesus' "hour." Jesus indicates in this prayer that his work has been accomplished successfully here on earth and therefore everything is in place for his return to God.

Jesus Prays for His Disciples (John 17:9-19)

In this section, Jesus speaks as if he has already departed from this world. Therefore, his attention shifts away from himself and focuses clearly on his disciples. The disciples are now in charge of carrying on the work that Jesus began. They have been well prepared, and now it is time for them to assume this very important work. In order that they may carry out their task successfully, Jesus prays first of all that they be

[4] An excellent and very readable commentary on John's Gospel that also has a very good analysis of chapter 17 is Gail O'Day, "John," *New Interpreter's Bible*, vol. 9 (Nashville: Abingdon Press, 1995), 491–865. A very helpful analysis of John 17 can also be found in Andrew T. Lincoln, "God's Name, Jesus' Name, and Prayer in the Fourth Gospel," *Into God's Presence: Prayer in the New Testament*, ed. Richard N. Longenecker (Grand Rapids, MI: Eerdmans Publishing Company, 2001), 155–80.

kept in the divine name. This will be the source for the strength they will need to carry on their work. Jesus also prays that they be protected from the evil one. Jesus himself could do this while on earth, but that is no longer the case. The evil one refers to all the forces of the unredeemed world that work against faith and are hostile to it. Many of these are subtle and therein lies their danger. Finally, Jesus prays that the disciples be sanctified in truth. Here truth is not a philosophical concept. Truth in John's Gospel is the revelation of God in Jesus. Jesus identifies himself as the truth and indicates that the truth will make the disciples free.

Jesus Prays for Present and Future Believers (John 17:20-26)

Jesus' prayer is not meant only for the disciples. It extends beyond the disciples to include all believers present and future. This means that we are included in Jesus' prayer. In praying for believers, Jesus emphasizes two things. First is the essential aspect of unity among all believers. Believers are included in the divine mutuality wherein Father and Son share an intimate unity. By believing in Jesus, the disciples and others also share in that unity which is important for demonstrating the truth of Jesus' mission and ministry. Second, Jesus prays that believers will eventually end up where he already is—with the Father. Thus it is not only for their work in the world that Jesus prays for believers but also for their ultimate destiny which transcends the here and now.

The remarkable thing about the prayer of Jesus in John 17 is the realization that even at this very moment Jesus, who is united to the Father in glory, is praying for believers carrying out his work in the world today. There could be no greater source of strength and encouragement. Another significant aspect of this prayer is that a careful reading of it discloses that its major concerns are very similar to what we found in the Lord's Prayer of Matthew and Luke. The language is different, but below the surface is that same boldness and empowerment which urges believers to carry out the mission of proclaiming the Gospel by word and deed.

The Acts of the Apostles and Prayer

The Acts of the Apostles is St. Luke's follow-up volume to his Gospel. Acts is purposely composed as an idealized portrait of the early Christian community. It shows what a community should be like that lives its life totally committed to the risen Christ. It is obviously based on some real-life experiences but it goes beyond those so as to offer us a vision of authentic Christian living.

According to Acts, at the heart of all authentic Christian living is prayer. Notice this emphasis at the beginning of the book:

> Then they returned to Jerusalem from the mount called Olivet, which is near Jerusalem, a sabbath day's journey away. When they had entered the city, they went to the room upstairs where they were staying, Peter, and John, and James, and Andrew, Philip and Thomas, Bartholomew and Matthew, James son of Alphaeus, and Simon the Zealot, and Judas son of James. All these were constantly devoting themselves to prayer, together with certain women, including Mary the mother of Jesus, as well as his brothers. (Acts 1:12-14)

> So those who welcomed his message were baptized, and that day about three thousand persons were added. They devoted themselves to the apostles' teaching and fellowship, to the breaking of bread and the prayers. (Acts 2:41-42)

In the gospels, Peter and the other disciples were not depicted as particularly strong and confident. In Acts that is all changed. They are transformed by their faith in the risen Lord, and now they witness to that transformation, especially by their commitment to prayer. Prayer becomes a defining characteristic of what it means to be the people of God, and the model for their prayer is none other than Jesus himself. While on earth, Jesus centered his prayer on God and God's revelation. In Acts the people center their prayer on Jesus, God's Son, and his teaching. Just as Jesus prefaced the major moments of his life and ministry with prayer, so the believers in Acts engage in prayer as the fitting preparation for everything, including choosing leadership, facing persecution, or discerning the mission of the Church.

There can be little doubt that the Acts of the Apostles was written to inspire its readers. These readers were the members of the Church which was struggling to find its way in the midst of a world empire that was both attractive and dangerous. In order to survive and grow under such circumstances, it was absolutely essential to be in constant communication with the source of their strength and guidance—the risen Lord and his Spirit. Prayer was the linchpin of that communication. This prayer was not encased in a piety of passive resignation. Quite the contrary. It was characterized by a sense of empowerment and a piety of confidence and boldness as exemplified by Peter and John in the following passage.

> After they were released, they went to their friends and reported what the chief priests and the elders had said to them. When they heard it, they raised their voices together to God and said, "Sovereign Lord, who made the heaven and the earth, the sea, and everything in them, it is you who said by the Holy Spirit through our ancestor David, your servant:
>
> 'Why did the Gentiles rage,
> and the peoples imagine vain things?
> The kings of the earth took their stand,
> and the rulers have gathered together
> against the Lord and against his Messiah.'
>
> For in this city, in fact, both Herod and Pontius Pilate, with the Gentiles and the peoples of Israel, gathered together against your holy servant Jesus, whom you anointed, to do whatever your hand and your plan had predestined to take place. And now, Lord, look at their threats, and grant to your servants to speak your word with all boldness, while you stretch out your hand to heal, and signs and wonders are performed through the name of your holy servant Jesus." When they had prayed, the place in which they were gathered together was shaken; and they were all filled with the Holy Spirit and spoke the word of God with boldness. (Acts 4:23-31)

The Acts of the Apostles has much to teach contemporary believers about being Church and about the role prayer must play in that Church. The most important lesson is that prayer must be the defining characteristic in any Church identity. It must permeate everything we do both collectively and individually. A corollary to this lesson is that we must always pray with confidence and boldness. The reason for this is that our prayer is always offered in the name of Jesus who we believe lives and reigns with the Father and the Holy Spirit.

The Letters of St. Paul and Prayer

In the Acts of the Apostles St. Luke clearly portrays Paul as a man of prayer. While there is no need to question that assessment, those reports are still secondhand. They are not from Paul himself. Our primary source for obtaining information about this very significant Apostle to the Gentiles is his own letters. Even there we run into a challenge. What we find in the letters of Paul are reports about prayer which are addressed to the letters' recipients. These letters were written to address particular issues in each community. They are not theological treatises, nor are they well-developed narratives. Nevertheless, we can find in this material many examples of the supreme importance prayer played in the life and ministry of St. Paul.

The first point to be made is that St. Paul was a fervent and devoted Jew steeped in the traditions of Judaism. Therefore, prayer was always part of his daily life as it was for every devoted Jew. In his adult life Paul underwent a profound conversion experience which changed his life forever.[5] This experience was a conversion not in the sense that he abandoned his Jewish faith and embraced something altogether different, but in the deeper sense of understanding the reality of the risen Lord as the fulfillment of his Jewish faith. After this experience Paul remained a Jew and a follower of Jesus for the rest of his life. This experience also affected his understanding and practice of prayer. As a Jew, Paul's prayer would have been characterized by both inwardness and spontaneity. His prayer would have also included ritual, and it would have been steeped in the traditions of the Jewish Scriptures. None of this disappears after his conversion. However, now all of his prayer is understood and practiced from the perspective of being in Christ Jesus. We get a glimpse of this in the famous quote from 1 Thessalonians: "Rejoice always, pray without ceasing, give thanks in all circumstances; for this is the will of God in Christ Jesus for you" (1 Thess 5:16-18).

There have been many attempts to categorize and analyze the various forms Paul uses in his prayers.[6] The detail and debate of all that is important but beyond our interest here. A good overall perspective can still be gained by looking at Paul's prayer from the traditional categories of adoration, thanksgiving, and petition.[7]

---

[5] See the accounts in Acts 9:1-19; 22:1-16; 26:9-18. Paul's own account is found in Galatians 1:11-24.

[6] Classic examples are: Paul Shubert, *Form and Function of the Pauline Thanksgivings* (Berlin: Topelmann, 1939) and Gordon P. Wiles, *Paul's Intercessory Prayers: The Significance of the Intercessory Prayer Passages in the Letters of St. Paul* (Cambridge: Cambridge University Press, 1974).

[7] Richard N. Longenecker, "Prayer in the Pauline Letters," *Into God's Presence: Prayer in the New Testament*. (Grand Rapids, MI: Eerdmans Publishing Company, 2001), 212–23.

Adoration

Prayers of adoration typically emphasize blessing and praise. Blessings generally come at the beginning of a prayer form, while praise tends to be more toward the end. The Old Testament is filled with these kinds of prayer where the blessing and praise is always directed toward God. A good example of blessing in the letters of Paul is the following: "Blessed be the God and Father of our Lord Jesus Christ, the Father of mercies and the God of all consolation, who consoles us in all our affliction" (2 Cor 1:3-4a).

A typical expression of praise is the following: "To the only wise God, through Jesus Christ, to whom be the glory forever!" (Rom 16:27).

What is important to notice in any of these prayers of blessing or praise is the central mediating role of Christ Jesus. Be it blessing or praise, it always goes through Christ Jesus.

Thanksgiving

In the Pauline letters it is generally understood that the thanksgiving serves to set forth the occasion as well as the contents of the letter they introduce. There is no doubt that the thanksgiving does function this way, but that is not all it does. For Paul the thanksgiving expresses thanks for God's saving activity that has come about for his readers through Christ and the Holy Spirit. Paul also proclaims thanks for the way the Gospel has been both preached to and received by his readers. And finally he gives thanks for his readers' ongoing spiritual growth. An example of this can be found in the letter to the Philippians.

> I thank my God every time I remember you, constantly praying with joy in every one of my prayers for all of you, because of your sharing in the gospel from the first day until now. I am confident of this, that the one who began a good work among you will bring it to completion by the day of Jesus Christ. It is right for me to think this way about all of you, because you hold me in your heart, for all of you share in God's grace with me, both in my imprisonment and in the defense and confirmation of the gospel. For God is my witness, how I long for all of you with the compassion of Christ Jesus. And this is my prayer, that your love may overflow more and more with knowledge and full insight to help you to determine what is best, so that in the day of Christ you may be pure and blameless, having produced the harvest of righteousness that comes through Jesus Christ for the glory and praise of God. (Phil 1:3-11)

Petition

Paul's prayers of intercession are generally found in his prayer reports. They come within the contexts of both praise and thanksgiving. This is where Paul expresses his deep pastoral concern for the spiritual well-being of his readers. Quite often the form of the intercession is very traditional and standard, but the content is specific and personal. Paul petitions for things he knows his readers need, based on the particular situations in which they find themselves. Not only will he pray for their spiritual needs, but he will also ask that they receive encouragement and guidance in dealing with those needs. The following is an example of a typical Pauline intercession: "May the God of steadfastness and encouragement grant you to live in harmony with one another, in accordance with Christ Jesus, so that together you may with one voice glorify the God and Father of our Lord Jesus Christ" (Rom 15:5-6).

Two major factors are always present in St. Paul's prayers, regardless of the particular form they might assume. The first is that all prayer necessarily goes through Christ Jesus. The second is that since Christ Jesus is the mediator of all prayer, the baptized believer now shares a special intimacy with God by nature of being in Christ Jesus. This allows the believer to have confidence and boldness when engaging in prayer.

From Jesus' ministry through the ministries of Paul and the apostles, prayer was an integral part of the early Church's relationship with God. The early prayers were bold in their requests and built on the Jewish tradition. They were also intimate and reflected a desire for God to draw near and for God's will to be done. The essentials of our worship are found in prayer: thanksgiving, praise, petition, and adoration. In prayer we seek God in all things, and as Jesus and the apostles and earliest participants in the Church did, we walk with God in our daily lives.

Further Reading

Cullman, Oscar. *Prayer in the New Testament*. Minneapolis: Fortress, 1995.

Jeremias, Joachim. *The Prayers of Jesus*. Trans. J. Bowden. London: SCM, 1967.

Koenig, John. *Rediscovering New Testament Prayer: Boldness and Blessing in the Name of Jesus*. San Francisco: Harper, 1992.

Longenecker, Richard N., ed. *Into God's Presence: Prayer in the New Testament*. Grand Rapids, MI: Eerdmans Publishing Company, 2001.

Wright, N. T. *The Lord and His Prayer*. Grand Rapids, MI: Eerdmans Publishing Company, 1996.

Chapter 3

Private Prayer in
the Early Christian Centuries

Matthias Neuman, O.S.B.

From the very beginning the early Christians prayed both communally and individually. These first followers of Jesus saw the very basis of their faith as an acknowledgment of praise and thanksgiving to Almighty God for the marvelous things done in and through Jesus Christ. The New Testament gives ample evidence of such communal gatherings: "All who believed were together and had all things in common. . . . Day by day, as they spent much time together in the temple, they broke bread at home and ate their food with glad and generous hearts, praising God and having the good will of all the people" (Acts 2:44, 46-47). The New Testament also provides a clear attestation of the practice of private individual prayer: "But whenever you pray, go into your room and shut the door and pray to your Father who is in secret; and your Father who sees in secret will reward you" (Matt 6:6). This personal, private prayer continued as the Church grew and spread through the first centuries of its existence.

This chapter will explore some of the ways that early Christians prayed privately; other chapters of this book cover liturgical prayer in common. However, we should note that the two kinds of prayer frequently overlapped; expressions of private prayer in all likelihood became a part of a group's common prayer when it was agreed that the prayer of an individual spoke for all of them. Saint Paul possibly hints at this when he writes: "What should be done then, my friends? When you come together, each one has a hymn, a lesson, a revelation, a tongue, or an interpretation. Let all things be done for building up" (1 Cor 14:26). Similarly, the shape of communal prayer would have had a profound effect on how people prayed privately. They would have echoed in their individual prayers the expressions and moods that touched them deeply in liturgical gatherings much as we hum to ourselves songs we love from eucharistic services.

This chapter begins with the first generations of Christians, evident through the New Testament writings, expanding richly in the following two centuries, and concluding in the middle of the third century. Over the course of those almost three hundred years we find that Christian private prayer grew organically out of traditions of private prayer that people were familiar with before becoming Christian. Thus, we will first need to explore something of the Jewish and Roman backgrounds in ways of praying privately. These earlier traditions were grafted onto and transformed by the newly founded Christian faith.

Jewish and Roman Backgrounds

The structure and mood of traditional Jewish prayer can be seen most clearly in the biblical book of Psalms. Each psalm is a prayer and song to God. Psalms were sung liturgically (in common) and devotionally (by individuals alone). They express a uniquely human response to God's presence in particular situations of life. The psalms served as private prayers, used by individuals, as well as a part of the common religious tradition of the people of Israel. The book of Psalms became a prayer book of the Church, used both in the liturgy and private individual prayer by Christians.

The psalms are treated in depth elsewhere in this book. However, one particular point for our purposes should not be forgotten. The psalms as written are only the first step of a larger process. Most Jewish prayer erupted in spontaneity; it flowed from the person's creative, praying heart and was spoken immediately to God. This direct, personal, prayerful address to the divine was considered the very core and heart of true prayer. The use of a written psalm might serve as a beginning or a conclusion to this spontaneous prayer, but it did not replace it. Since obviously one does not write down the spontaneous utterances, it's easy for later generations to forget about them. But they are an integral part of the whole prayer process.

This same style of spontaneous, creative prayer will carry over into the praying style of the first followers of Jesus. Saint Paul reflects this kind of spontaneous prayer in several passages in his letters. It is important to remember that Paul dictated his letters to a scribe, and in the course of dictation he would frequently break into such spontaneous prayer while narrating his message. His letters provide solid examples of this style of praying: "O the depth of the riches and wisdom and knowledge of God! How unsearchable are his judgments and how inscrutable his ways!" (Rom 11:33). Or again: "The Messiah, who is over all, God blessed forever. Amen" (Rom 9:5). And again: "The will of our God and Father, to whom be the glory forever and ever. Amen" (Gal 1:4-5).

Another background to the style of early Christian prayer that should not be overlooked can be found in the dominant Greco-Roman culture of the Roman Empire. As the Christian faith moved primarily into this arena and began to attract more and more people from the Greco-Roman cultural background, those "converts" brought with them a rich legacy of prayer and religious activity. Many of these practices will get grafted onto the Christian vine. The ancient Roman culture was a deeply religious culture. A biblical historian describes it thus:

> Early Christian worship did not take place in a religious vacuum. The Roman world was chock-full of religiosity, with a dizzying array of religious groups, movements, customs, activities and related paraphernalia. Earliest Christian faith did not represent religiousness over against irreligious culture, but had to enter the "traffic" as a new movement on a very crowded and well-traveled highway of religious activity. This vibrant and diverse religious environment of the Roman world is very significant for understanding that world and for any accurate appreciation of earliest Christian worship.[1]

Traditional Roman religion was very expressive both publicly and privately. In public they loved carrying statues of their gods and goddesses in procession and singing canticles and acclamations to them. The

---

[1] Larry Hurtado, *At the Origins of Christian Worship* (Grand Rapids, MI: Eerdmans Publishing Company, 1999), 7.

practice of shouting acclamations to the emperor when he appeared in public or when a victorious general returned in a procession through the city contributed to the spontaneity of their prayer to the gods. "As Vespasian entered Rome for the first time as emperor in A.D. 70 after returning from the East, he was greeted by a vast and enthusiastic crowd lining the road into the city, who shouted many of the same acclamations he had received in Alexandria, including 'Benefactor,' 'Savior,' and 'Only worthy emperor of Rome,' and decorated his route with flowers and garlands."[2] These practices would later be adapted and become part of public Christian worship in the fourth century as sung litanies.

Their private expressions to their gods were likewise rich, spontaneous, and personally involving. A Roman man or woman who visited one of the temples of the gods would usually bring some offering (an item symbolizing the gift of self) and an epigram as a prayer. The offering would be given, the epigram prayed and left in the temple as a memento of the person. In addition many Roman homes had house shrines and people prayed often before their "household gods." These were also later shaped into Christian practices.

Perhaps one of the most powerful legacies of Roman religion in Christian practice was the attitude of friendship that the Roman sensed between his god and himself, a friendship that issued in an easy familiarity. This showed itself particularly in the many gifts that Romans would bring to the shrines of their gods:

> Naturally, these offerings and prayers continued into adult life; women offered the work of their hands, men that of their industry or the products of their hunting. But the most touching gifts are the most humble ones: cakes, a cup of wine, olives, a bunch of grapes, a biscuit. . . . It is clear that what counts is not the value of the gift itself but the gesture, and this gesture can be understood only if the giver is confident that the gesture is valuable in the eyes of god. This presupposes a feeling of friendship.[3]

---

[2] Gregory Aldrete, *Gestures and Acclamations in Ancient Rome* (Baltimore: Johns Hopkins University Press, 1999), 112.

[3] H. D. Saffrey, "The Piety and Prayers of Ordinary Men and Women in Late Antiquity," in *Classical Mediterranean Spirituality*, ed. A. H. Armstrong (New York: Crossroads, 1986), 204–5.

That also would carry over into a feeling of closeness between the Christian and the person of Jesus Christ!

Early Christian Writings

One of the earliest Christian writings that we possess outside the New Testament books is called the *Didache* or the *Teaching of the Twelve Apostles*. It dates from somewhere toward the end of the first or beginning of the second century. What makes this document so important is that a part of it constitutes the oldest "Christian church order" that we possess. A church order was a how-to manual of standard Christian practices: how to baptize, how to celebrate the Eucharist, how to fast, and how to pray. Here are the directives the *Didache* gives:

> Your prayers, too, should be different from theirs. Pray as the Lord enjoined in His Gospel, thus: our Father, who art in heaven, Hallowed be thy Name, Thy kingdom come, Thy will be done, as in heaven, so on earth; Give us this day our daily bread, And forgive us our debt as we forgive our debtors, And lead us not into temptation, But deliver us from the Evil One, For thine is the power and the glory for ever and ever. Say this prayer three times every day.[4]

This instruction is possibly one of the reasons that the Lord's Prayer became so prominent in early Christian treatises on prayer which we will explore later. Even though not explicitly mentioned, it would be a good assumption that the individual praying the Lord's Prayer would immediately follow it with his or her own spontaneous expressions, as many of the later writings on prayer emphasize.

Another privileged place to see the developing practice of Christian private prayer lies in the accounts of the early Christian martyrs. Here men and women praying in situations of great danger had much need of God's help. One of the most precious of early Christian writings was *The Martyrdom of St. Polycarp*. Polycarp served as bishop to the Christian community in the city of Smyrna in Asia Minor (modern-day Turkey) in the middle of the second century. In the course of a local persecution of Christians he was hunted down and captured by Roman officials,

---

[4] Maxwell Staniforth, trans., *Didache*, in *Early Christian Writings* (New York: Penguin Books, 1982), 231.

tried, found guilty, and executed by being burned alive. A member of his congregation soon afterward composed an account of his capture and subsequent execution as a testimonial sent to other Christian communities. This marvelous document supplies precious insights into the early Christian practice of prayer.

As Polycarp was being sought by officials as the leader of the Christians, his congregation urged him to go into hiding in the country. "And so he did, to a little farm, not far from the city, and passed the time with a few companions, doing naught else but pray night and day for all and for the churches throughout the world, as was his custom. And while praying he fell into a trance three days before he was taken and saw his pillow being consumed by fire. And he turned and said to those with him, 'I must be burned alive.'"[5] Later when the Roman police arrived at the farmhouse, they were amazed at Polycarp's behavior: "He bade food and drink to be set before them at that hour, as much as they wanted; and besought them to give him an hour to pray undisturbed. On being given leave, he stood and prayed, being so full of the grace of God that for two hours he could not once be silent, and the hearers were astonished, and many repented for having assailed an old man so godlike."[6] Polycarp was eighty-six years old at the time.

This passage shows that he prayed standing and aloud, the normal position and expression of prayer that had been inherited from the early Jewish tradition. But what were his words like? We have a clue. Later in the narration, after he has been condemned to death by burning, he prayed again aloud as the pyre was prepared. These words, now given as an integral prayer, would have been passages that members of his congregation (standing anonymously in the crowd) later remembered, put together, and wrote down:

> Lord God Almighty, Father of Thy well-beloved and blessed Son, Jesus Christ, through whom we have received the knowledge of You, God of Angels and Powers and of the whole creation and of all the race of the righteous who live before You, I bless You that You did deem me worthy of this day and hour, that I should take a part among the number of martyrs in the cup of Christ to the resurrection of life eternal of soul and

---

[5] Anne Fremantle, ed., "The Martyrdom of St. Polycarp," in *A Treasury of Early Christianity* (New York: Viking Press, 1953), 186–87.

[6] Ibid., 187.

body in incorruption of the Holy Spirit: among whom may I be accepted before You today, a rich and acceptable sacrifice, as You did foreordain and foreshow and fulfill, God faithful and true. For this above all I praise You, I bless You, I glorify You through the eternal and heavenly High Priest Jesus Christ, Your well-beloved Son, through whom to You with Him and the Holy Spirit be glory now and forever. Amen.[7]

A similar type of expressive prayer is found at the conclusion of the martyrdom account of Saints Felicity and Perpetua:

O valiant and blessed martyrs! O truly called and chosen to the glory of Jesus Christ our Lord! He who magnifies, honours, and adores that glory should recite to the edification of the church these examples also, not less precious at least than those of old; that so new instances of virtue may testify that one and the selfsame Spirit is working to this day with Father, God-Almighty, and with His Son Jesus Christ our Lord, to whom belong splendor and power immeasurable for ever and ever. Amen.[8]

Sometimes these direct, personal prayers were addressed to Jesus, the Lord. "The Abitena martyrs prayed as follows: 'O Christ, the Lord, let us not be confounded. Son of God, come to our aid; help us, O Christ, have pity, Lord Christ, give us courage to suffer.'"[9] Notice the direct, familial expression of these prayers. They are spontaneous addresses to a divine presence all around them; they remain precious glimpses of how those early Christians prayed both privately and publicly.

Personal Prayer in Tertullian and Clement of Alexandria

By the year A.D. 200 Christian writers had begun to compose specific treatises on Christian prayer. These writings give us a clear view as to how this practice was developing among the growing Christian communities. One of the finest of these treatises, *On Prayer*, was composed by Tertullian, a priest of the Christian community of Carthage in North Africa around A.D. 198–200. This work was probably given originally as a presentation to catechumens, those preparing to receive Christian

[7] Ibid., 190.

[8] Ibid., 228.

[9] Joseph Jungmann, *Christian Prayer through the Centuries* (New York: Paulist Press, 1978), 16.

baptism. He outlines for them the daily practice of prayer expected of a devout Christian believer. The opening chapter deals with Jesus giving a new form of prayer to his disciples, then follows a series of chapters explaining the deeper significance of the Lord's Prayer (chapters 2–9) and concludes with a lengthy series of instructions about the hows and whys of daily private prayer (chapters 10–28). The whole treatise affords a marvelous insight into the early Christian practice of private prayer.

In his first chapter Tertullian notes that Christ admonished his followers to "pray in secret," in the enclosed rooms of their homes, expressing the Christian belief that God is indeed everywhere and hears prayers uttered everywhere. He then moves into an explanation of the deeper meanings for each of the phrases of the Our Father, noting that in these few expressions "there is contained an abridgement of the entire Gospel."[10]

The chapters commenting on the Lord's Prayer show that each of the phrases in the prayer opens us up to a larger view of God and the world. "Our Father, who art in heaven" encompasses a fundamental act of faith in God; it both honors God and promises to follow his commandments. "Thy will be done in heaven and on earth" becomes a prayer for our salvation and the salvation of the whole world. "Give us this day our daily bread" leads into petitions for all of our earthly needs.

The longer section of instructions on "how to pray" provides a detailed look into the exact manner of Christian private prayer that was encouraged at the beginning of the third century. Tertullian first notes that saying the Lord's Prayer is but a foundation, a launching pad so-to-speak, for the spontaneous prayers which are to well up from the depths of each individual's heart.[11] Every person has prayers to make "according to the circumstances of each individual." Interestingly enough, Tertullian next admonishes his readers that one should never pray when one holds a grudge or is angry: "Since the attention of our prayer is bestowed by and directed to the same Spirit, it should be free not only from anger, but from any and every disturbance of the mind. For the Holy Spirit does not recognize an impure spirit."[12]

---

[10] Tertullian, "On Prayer," in *Tertullian: Disciplinary, Moral and Ascetical Works*, trans. Rudolf Arbesmann, Sister Emily Joseph Daly, and Edwin Quain, vol. 40 of *The Fathers of the Church* (New York: Fathers of the Church, 1959), 159.

[11] Ibid., 168.

[12] Ibid., 169.

The proper posture for prayer is standing, with hands uplifted, arms spread out in imitation of Christ's passion, eyes cast down, and speaking one's prayers softly.[13] This custom of praying aloud, but softly, was widely practiced in the early church, but not everywhere. The prayer posture that Tertullian describes was depicted exactly in wall frescos in the Catacombs of Priscilla in Rome, which date from the same time period.

Tertullian observes that there are no set regulations for times of daily private prayer, but some times are becoming customary among Christians: as the first light of day is breaking, at the third, sixth, and ninth hours (our 9:00 A.M., noon, and 3:00 P.M., respectively), before meals, and before bathing. Morning and evening prayers should be the major prayer times of the day; people may fill in other times as they wish. It is recommended, however, that everyone have set times for personal prayers.[14]

This marvelous treatise ends with confessing prayer to be the "spiritual sacrifice" which each believer offers to God. "We are the true worshippers and the true priests who, offering our prayer in the spirit, offer sacrifice in the spirit—that is, prayer—as a victim that is appropriate and acceptable to God."[15] "What need, then, is there of further discussion of the duty of prayer? Even our Lord Himself prayed, to whom be honor and power forever and ever."[16]

At about the same time as Tertullian, but in another part of the Roman Empire, another Christian writer, Clement of Alexandria (in Egypt), was also emphasizing the importance of regular prayer for a Christian believer. Clement was trying to show the uniqueness of Christian prayer by comparing it with the different ways that believers in the Roman and Greek gods implored their deities. His large work, the *Stromata* (*Miscellaneous Topics*), deals with many aspects of Christian life in the midst of a pagan world. In chapters 6 and 7 of book 7 he describes in detail the Christian practice of daily personal private prayer.

Clement first notes that the Christian believes in a God who is beyond the limitations of this world and who has no need of anything. However, this God does delight in being honored by human beings.

---

[13] Ibid., 170–72.
[14] Ibid., 182–84.
[15] Ibid., 185.
[16] Ibid., 188.

Prayer is then, first and foremost, an act of honoring God. Indeed the prayers of Christians constitute the very sacrifices that the Christians offer. In a beautiful passage Clement notes: "The altar, then, that is with us here, the terrestrial one, is the congregation who devote themselves to prayers, having as it were one common voice and one mind. For the sacrifice of the Church is the word breathing as incense from holy souls, the sacrifice and the whole mind being at the same time unveiled to God."[17]

The Christian believer prays also alone, in every time and every place, believing that the presence of God "is ever beside him." The content of Christian prayer first looks to thanksgiving for all good gifts that have been received in life. After thanksgiving, our desires and hopes come next as topics for prayer. The Christian justly prays for what is needed in life, and that list is headed by a request to be able to live a good and just life. Never should prayer request that evil things happen to anyone. Indeed Christian prayer should include a request that faith, salvation, and knowledge be given to all people, so that God might be even more glorified.

Clement too describes the proper posture for prayer. The one praying whispers his or her words with head raised and hands lifted toward heaven. And at the very end he or she rises on tiptoes, "following the eagerness of the spirit directed toward the intellectual essence, and endeavoring to abstract the body from the earth, along with the discourse, raising the soul aloft."[18] Clement notes that sometimes people pray in silence, knowing that God knows the thoughts of the mind and hears the desires of the heart. Praying toward the east is also recommended, "since the dawn is an image of the day of birth."[19]

He writes that some people counsel prayer three times a day, at the third, sixth, and ninth hours. This can be a useful schedule, but really one can pray any time. He himself suggests before meals, before bed, and sometime during the night. As Tertullian does, Clement insists that the Christian always remember that his prayer forms a personal sacrifice to God, and above all else it is an honoring of God.

---

[17] Clement of Alexandria, *Stromata (Miscellanies)*, in *Fathers of the Second Century*, ed. Rev. Alexander Roberts and James Donaldson, The Anti-Nicene Fathers, vol. 2 (Grand Rapids, MI: Eerdmans Publishing Company, 1983), chap. 6, 531.

[18] Ibid., 534.

[19] Ibid.

Origen's Teaching on Prayer

Without doubt the most influential and widely read treatise on prayer in the first three Christian centuries was that written by Origen, a cate-chetical teacher of the church of Alexandria in Egypt. Origen possessed a towering intellect, but he was also concerned with the practical expressions of Christian life and faith. He wrote *On Prayer* around the year A.D. 235 in answer to a request from two friends, Ambrose and Tatiana, to help them better understand prayer.[20] For centuries afterward this work was cherished by Christians in diverse times and places. It represents a high point in early Christian thinking on the practice of private prayer.

Origen begins by clarifying the various words for "prayer" used in the Bible.[21] He finds a diversity of usage and meaning, but all ultimately intend a "conversation with God." Next he addresses the objections of those people who see no sense in prayer at all and moves on to show the many benefits that true prayer brings to the individual's life. He is quick to note, as other Christian writers before him, that anyone wishing to pray must carefully prepare for it by composing the mind and heart and divesting oneself of any angry feelings. "The person praying must stretch out 'holy hands' by thoroughly purging the passion of anger from his soul and harboring no rage against anyone and by forgiving each the sins committed against him."[22]

For Origen there are four different kinds of address that one may make to Almighty God. "I think that *supplication* is a prayer offered with entreaty to get something a person lacks, while *prayer* (in its best sense) is something nobler offered by a person with praise and for greater objects. And I think that *intercession* is a petition for certain things addressed to God by someone who has greater boldness, while *thanksgiving* is a statement of gratitude made with prayer for receiving good things from God."[23] Origen stresses that prayer should only be addressed to God the Father. Not even Jesus himself should be prayed to, because he himself taught us to pray to God the Father.[24]

---

[20] Origen, "On Prayer" in *Origen*, trans. Rowan Greer, The Classics of Western Spirituality (New York: Paulist Press, 1979), II.1, 82.

[21] Ibid., III.1–IV.2, 86–90.

[22] Ibid., IX.1, 98.

[23] Ibid., XIV.2, 109.

[24] Ibid., XV.1, 112.

The second part of Origen's treatise consists of a lengthy commentary on the various phrases of the Lord's Prayer. He tries to expand upon and deepen people's understanding of these simple affirmations. Oftentimes he gets into some very complex philosophical positions in this part of the work.

The third section, titled "Special Directions," most clearly spells out the practical dimensions of private prayer in his day. He addresses first the posture for private prayer: standing ". . . with the hands outstretched and the eyes lifted up is to be preferred before all others, because it bears in prayer the image of characteristics befitting the soul and applies it to the body."[25] Origen does add that any other posture would be suitable, including sitting down (if the person has a foot problem) or lying in bed (if the person is sick). And it might be best to pray kneeling if one is confessing one's sins to God and asking for forgiveness.

Any place is suitable for prayer, but having a special area in one's house helps: "But everyone may have, if I may put it this way, a holy place set aside and chosen in his own house, if possible, for accomplishing his prayers in quiet and without distraction."[26] This directive mirrors the house shrines that were such a part of regular Roman and Greek religion. In addition, Origen suggests that the proper direction to face should be toward the east "since this is a symbolic expression of the soul's looking for the rising of the true Light."[27]

In his conclusion he turns to the proper content of this daily private prayer of Christians. It should always begin with praise of the Father, Son, and Holy Spirit. Here we can recall the kinds of acclamations that so many people of the Roman Empire were accustomed to; these would have been prayed spontaneously now to God and Christ and the Spirit. Following praise comes thanksgiving for "the benefits given many people and those he has himself received from God."[28] Following thanksgiving there comes a confession of personal faults and the asking of forgiveness from God. "And after confession, the fourth topic that seems to me must be added is the request for great and heavenly things, both private and general, and concerning his household and his dearest."[29] The

25 Ibid., XXXI.2, 164.
26 Ibid., XXXI.4, 166.
27 Ibid., XXXII, 168.
28 Ibid., XXXIII.1, 169.
29 Ibid.

prayer session should always end with another praise of Father, Son, and Spirit. "And having begun with praise it is right to conclude the prayer by ending with praise, hymning and glorifying the Father of all through Jesus Christ in the Holy Spirit, to whom be glory forever."[30]

Conclusion

Throughout the first three centuries of the Christian Church we find a consistent and developing practice of private personal prayer. The individual believer was expected to stop several times a day and offer praise, thanksgiving, confession, and requests to God as Father, Son, and Spirit. This prayer was to rise spontaneously in whispered voice from their hearts. In their homes this often occurred in a special prayer place where the one praying stood with arms outstretched and hands upraised. Daily private prayer became a signal characteristic of those early Christians and was a magnificent expression of the faith they sought to live by.

Further Reading

Didache, in *Early Christian Writings*. Trans. by Maxwell Staniforth. New York: Penguin Books, 1982.

Hurtado, Larry. *At the Origins of Christian Worship*. Grand Rapids, MI: Eerdmans Publishing Company, 1999.

Fremantle, Anne, ed. "The Martyrdom of St. Polycarp." In *A Treasury of Early Christianity*. New York: Viking Press, 1953.

Origen. "On Prayer," in *Origen: An Exhortation to Martyrdom, Prayer and Selected Works*. Trans. by Rowan Greer. The Classics of Western Spirituality. New York: Paulist Press, 1979.

Saffrey, H. D. "The Piety and Prayers of Ordinary Men and Women in Late Antiquity." In *Classical Mediterranean Spirituality*. Ed. by A. H. Armstrong. New York: Crossroads, 1986.

[30] Ibid., XXXIII.6, 170.

Chapter 4

Prayer as a Battle: The Monastic Contribution

Cyprian Davis, O.S.B.

In the early Church, to be a hero was to be a martyr. The Christian fight stood in opposition to the persecution of the state. To win was to die. When Constantine made Christianity a legitimate religion of the Roman Empire in A.D. 313, he also made it ordinary. It was no longer heroic just to be a Christian, so people began to look for new ways to live out their faith in a heroic way.

Even before Constantine, Anthony the Great had gone to the Egyptian desert to be a hermit, and he became a celebrated hero drawing many men and women to live as hermits in the desert. In the later tradition monks fled the city to escape the evil world, but the early hermits saw the desert as the place to meet the devil face-to-face and to engage the demonic in single-handed combat. The desert was not a refuge or a tranquil place, but a place of battle.

The monastic battle centered on prayer. The monastic quest sought to fulfill St. Paul's command in 1 Thessalonians 5:17: "Pray without ceasing." According to this understanding of the world, the demons sought to put obstacles in the way of the hermits at every turn so that they would not pray constantly or even at all. Two figures of the fourth century speak to this problem of how to win the battle against the demons and so to pray always: Evagrius of Pontus and John Cassian.

Evagrius of Pontus

The early life of Evagrius reads like a modern-day novel. Born about 345 in Pontus in what is today Turkey, he was ordained a lector by St. Basil and deacon by St. Gregory Nazianzen, whom he accompanied to Constantinople. There he became part of the imperial government. For all intents and purposes, Evagrius was in line for a brilliant career when he fell in love. The woman was married to a very high official in the Byzantine government. Warned of the danger in a dream, so it seems, he fled the Byzantine capital and arrived in the Holy Land broken, ill, and ruined. He was restored physically and emotionally by one of the famous women of the time, Melania the Elder, a woman of fabulous wealth. Originally from Rome, she left her fortune, moved to the Holy Land, and became the superior of a monastery of women on the Mount of Olives. Used to taking things in hand, she sent this would-be monk to the Egyptian desert.

By 383, Evagrius was settled in a community of hermits who studied the writings of Origen, the great theologian from the previous century (d. ca. 251). Origen had dictated some two thousand works during his lifetime in an attempt to join Greek Platonic thought to Christianity. He believed he could use philosophy as a basis for developing a Christian theology and understanding of the Scriptures. Evagrius became an ardent disciple of Origen, but he also developed original ideas that have had a lasting impact. Two works by Evagrius are important for prayer: *The Praktikos* and *The Chapters on Prayer*.[1]

For Evagrius, those seeking a life of prayer must begin by cultivating a certain wholeness in their inner being. Call it an inner calm, call it spiritual maturity, call it emotional equilibrium—one is made ready for a life of prayer by dealing with the various temptations that all of us must face. This inner calm or spiritual maturity is what Evagrius calls *apatheia*, that is, passionlessness. This inner calm is upset by what Evagrius calls *logismoi* which can be translated as "thoughts," that is, those emotional traps, the soft spots where morally we are most vulnerable. Cassian after him would call them passions, and Gregory the Great turns them into the deadly sins, but for Evagrius they are *logismoi*, obsessive thoughts

---

[1] Evagrius Ponticus, *The Praktikos* and *The Chapters on Prayer*, trans. John Eudes Bamberger, O.C.S.O., Cistercian Studies Series, no. 4 (Kalamazoo, MI: Cistercian Publications, 1981).

which plague a person and destroy one's inner calm. Unlike normal thoughts which can be satisfied, these *logismoi* only grow and become more demanding the more they are indulged.

Evagrius lists eight *logismoi:* gluttony, lust, avarice, sadness, anger, acedia, vainglory, and pride. According to his worldview, the demons foster these *logismoi* in a person, and the hermit must undertake the ascetical practices whereby he or she learns how to fight against the demons and undertake the spiritual battle that will rid himself or herself of these obsessive thoughts. With works of mortification, the hermit roots out weaknesses, overcomes vulnerabilities, and strengthens virtues in order to arrive at *apatheia*, passionlessness. It is like border territory. Cross it and you are in the first regions of prayer.[2]

An example of one of these emotional traps was *acedia*. The term, often translated as sloth, is, in fact, much nearer "spiritual restlessness." Evagrius calls it the noonday demon because often toward midday the hermit becomes restless with his lot as a solitary. It seems to the monk that the day has lasted for fifty hours. He gets up to look out the windows to see if anyone is coming to visit. He goes outside to check the position of the sun. He gets annoyed because no one comes to visit, which indicates how uncaring the brethren are. He begins to think about moving elsewhere or starts to think about how bad it would be to spend the rest of his life in this particular place. Then he thinks how much he hates the place he is in. The monk is mightily assailed by this demon urging him to leave his cell and go away, to abandon his monastic commitment. It is a spiritual battle about perseverance. For Evagrius this means remaining in the hermitage, but it translates into a common problem facing all Christians because we are all tempted to abandon our commitments. According to Evagrius, if the hermit perseveres, there comes "a state of deep peace and inexpressible joy that arise[s] out of this struggle."[3] This state of deep peace is *apatheia* and leads to the practice of prayer.

In *The Chapters on Prayer*,[4] Evagrius writes that "prayer is a continual intercourse of the spirit with God" (#3), and "prayer is an ascent of the spirit to God" (#35). Prayer is not a time for introspection or self-pity.

---

[2] Ibid., 30–31; 37.

[3] Ibid. This passage was used later by Cassian in his treatment of the eight capital sins.

[4] Ibid.

Rather, "prayer is the fruit of joy and of thanksgiving." He writes that while praying one may find reason to become angry, but one must turn from anger to pray (#24). He warns against storing up "injuries and resentments" and thinking that one is praying well. On the contrary, this is like getting water from a well and pouring it into a barrel full of holes (#22). Prayer is the exclusion of sadness and despondency (#15 and 16). Prayer should open us to the presence of others and to their needs. If there are those who think that prayer has nothing to do with social justice, Evagrius writes that "in your prayer seek only after justice and the kingdom of God" and adds later that "it is a part of justice that you should pray not only for your own purification but also for that of every man," adding that this is what the angels do (#38–39). All of this is to bring a person to "pure prayer," that is, prayer without words, prayer beyond image and concept (#66, 69, 70, 72).

Evagrius emphasizes the relationship between our thoughts and prayer, between our emotions and prayer. An essential part of the preparation for prayer must be the spiritual battle that allows us to take control of ourselves. What goes on in our heads and our hearts matters.[5] Evagrius insists on this, but he also insists that prayer is not just thinking and feeling. Prayer is the way that we meet the transcendent God whom we are to worship in Spirit and in Truth (# 59).

Evagrius died in 399 in the Egyptian desert, and his teaching would have an extraordinary imprint on later spirituality, though some of his teachings along with those of Origen were later condemned. As a result, many of his writings survived only in other languages and under the name of other teachers. Particularly, his teaching on *apatheia* was sharply criticized for being too disembodied and too cerebral. Still his impact was felt, particularly through his disciple John Cassian.

John Cassian

Though John Cassian was a disciple of Evagrius, he never mentions his name nor in any way reveals him as a source. Shortly after the death of Evagrius in 399, Theophilus, the patriarch of Alexandria, turned against the Greek-speaking hermits in the Egyptian desert. Politically

---

[5] Mary Margaret Funk, O.S.B., has explored the teaching of Evagrius and John Cassian from a modern perspective in *Thoughts Matter: The Practice of the Spiritual Life* (New York: Continuum, 1999).

astute, Theophilus rejected the writings of Origen and the Greek monks whom he had supported in a former period. The Greek monks were driven out of the desert, and among them was John Cassian who went first to Constantinople, then to Rome, and finally to southern France where he founded a monastery.

John Cassian, born about 360 probably in what is now Bulgaria or Romania, became a monk in the Holy Land and then traveled on to the Egyptian desert. In the fourth century, men and women went there from all over the Roman Empire, searching for God and seeking solitude. Theirs was a life thirsting for God and struggling for virtue. With his friend Germanus, Cassian visited these great figures who had grown old in their search for God. He gathered together the spiritual teachings of the desert monks into two famous books: *The Institutes* and *The Conferences*. Through these writings, Cassian transmitted the spiritual teaching and monastic traditions of the Egyptian monks. His writings set the direction of spiritual teaching through the Middle Ages. Among those whom he influenced was St. Benedict (d. ca. 550).

Evagrius's term *apatheia* (passionlessness) had become suspect, so John Cassian replaced it with a biblical term, "purity of heart," as in Matthew 5:8: "Blessed are the pure in heart, for they will see God." Cassian's substitution for *apatheia* does not have quite the same meaning. When Cassian summarizes the monastic way of perfection in *The Institutes*, he places "purity of heart" not last but next to last, for according to Cassian it leads to "the perfection of apostolic love." [6] Like Basil the Great and Augustine, Cassian makes love the goal of the Christian journey. Prayer plays an essential role in bringing the Christian to the love which unites a person to God.

---

[6] All translations from John Cassian's *Institutes* and *Conferences* in this chapter were made by Harry Hagan, O.S.B. John Cassian, *The Institutes*, Book IV, Ch. 41: "'The beginning of our salvation and of wisdom is the fear of the Lord' (Ps 111:10; Prov 1). The fear of the Lord gives birth to the compunction of salvation. Compunction of heart brings forth renunciation, i.e., nakedness and contempt of all riches. Nakedness breeds humility. Humility brings to life the mortification of desires. The mortification of desires uproots all faults and causes them to decay. With faults driven out, virtues bring forth fruit and spread. With the blossoming of virtues you acquire purity of heart. By purity of heart you come to possess the perfection of apostolic love." For a complete edition of this work, cf. John Cassian, *The Institutes*, Ancient Christian Writers, no. 58, trans. and annot. Boniface Ramsey, O.P. (New York: Newman Press, 2000).

Cassian presents his teaching on prayer in Conferences IX and X given by the figure of Abba Isaac. The abba begins by announcing the fundamental task of every monk: "Every monk aims to perfect his heart by moving toward a continual and unbroken perseverance in prayer. As far as human frailty allows, the monk strives for an unmoved tranquility of mind and a perpetual purity. As a result, we tirelessly and constantly seek to practice bodily asceticism and contrition of spirit."[7] In other words, one must seek "purity of heart." Cassian then divides prayer into four types based on 1 Timothy 2:1: "supplications, offerings, petitions, and thanksgivings." Cassian interprets these four terms to show their place in the search for purity of heart.

The Christian life begins with repentance, and Cassian understands the first form of prayer, "supplications," as seeking forgiveness for sins. The second form of prayer, "offering," is bound up with how we live our lives. By it we promise, vow, or pledge ourselves before God. The third type, "petition," turns outward and looks to the concerns of others. It "is made up of the petitions that we regularly offer for others. Fervent in spirit, we make requests for those dear to us for the peace of the whole world."[8] Finally, "thanksgivings" is an intense movement of prayer of gratitude for all that God has given. As Cassian says:

> We give thanks when, carried beyond words, we recall God's good deeds of the past or contemplate his present ways or look forward to the great deeds of the future which God has prepared for those who love him.[9]

Cassian ties all of these prayer types to the Christian life:

[7] John Cassian, "Conference IX. The First Conference of Abba Isaac on Prayer," trans. Harry Hagan, O.S.B., IX,2,1. For a complete edition of the *Conferences* of John Cassian, cf. *The Conferences*, Ancient Christian Writers, no. 57, trans. and annot. Boniface Ramsey, O.P. (New York: Newman Press, 1997). Abba Isaac's two conferences on prayer can also be found in *John Cassian: Conferences*, trans. Colm Luibheid (Mahwah, NJ: Paulist Press, 1985). Ramsey's translation is based on the Latinate translation in the post-Nicene Fathers which can be found online. Luibheid's translation reflects a more modern English style.
[8] Cassian, *Conf.* IX.13.
[9] Cassian, *Conf.* IX.14.

The richness of prayer arises from these four types of prayer: Supplication is born from sorrow for sins. The prayer of offering flows from faithfulness to giving ourselves and to the keeping of our vows for the sake of a pure conscience. Petitions for others comes from fervent love. And thanksgiving is produced by considering God's blessing and greatness and goodness. From them, we know, there often comes forth the most fervent and fiery prayers.[10]

This last sentence identified a further type of prayer—the wordless prayer of fire:

Sometimes the mind, advancing toward that true state of purity and already taking root in it, holds all these prayers together at one and the same time. Then the mind becomes accustomed to pouring out to God prayers of the purest energy that are beyond word—as if the prayer were a fire, uncontainable and all-devouring, rushing through everything.[11]

This description of a form of ecstatic prayer is clearly an allusion to St. Paul's description of prayer when he writes, "Likewise the Spirit helps us in our weakness; for we do not know how to pray as we ought, but that very Spirit intercedes with sighs too deep for words" (Rom 8:26).

Even though the four types of prayer are presented as a progression and may fit a certain stage of spiritual development, Cassian does not present a lock-step hierarchy, and he argues that even a beginner concerned with supplication may experience moments of intense contemplative prayer. "Even though you are in the first stage and are thinking about future judgment . . . you may be filled with an eagerness of spirit from the richness of your prayer that is as great as the prayers of those who gaze with purity of heart and consider the blessing of God while overcome with that joy and happiness beyond words."[12]

Conference X, the second presentation on prayer by Abba Isaac, deals specifically with how we should pray. Germanus, the ever-present companion of Cassian, asks Abba Isaac about forms of meditation leading one to higher prayer. The old man replies:

[10] Cassian, *Conf.* IX.15.1.
[11] Cassian, *Conf.* IX.13, IX.15.2.
[12] Cassian, *Conf.* IX.13, IX.15.3.

> There is a Scripture verse that every monk intent on the continual remembrance of God regularly ponders. He ceaselessly turns it over in his heart after ridding himself of every other thought because he cannot possibly hold on to this remembrance unless he has freed himself from all bodily care and anxieties. This Scripture verse was handed over to us by a few of those who were left from the oldest abbas, and we do not let just anyone know about it—just those rare people who truly thirst for it.[13]

The special formula is taken from Psalm 70:1: "O God, come to my assistance; O Lord, make haste to help me."[14]

Abba Isaac teaches Germanus and Cassian to repeat this verse over and over. In the tradition this type of prayer is called monological which means "only one word." Abba Isaac directs them to limit themselves to repeating just this one verse because "it embraces all the feelings that human nature can bear, and it can be adapted easily and correctly to every situation and attack."[15] The repetitive nature of the short prayer used in all circumstances and conditions enabled one to walk in God's presence. The brief repetition of prayer was to become a habit of prayer, an automatic rhythm of the prayer that was a means to recall God's presence in the depths of one's being. Although Abba Isaac recommends the exclusive use of Psalm 70:1, the early tradition would choose various biblical verses to repeat over and over. Evagrius even had a collection of verses, called the *Antirrheticos*, for dealing with the *logismoi*. By repeating continually these short prayers, one is led to an inner calm and a deeper sense of prayer, that is, continuous prayer. Earlier in *Conference* X, Cassian states the goal:

> When all love,
> all desire,
> all zeal,
> all impulse,
> our every thought,
> all that we live,
> that we speak,

---

[13] Cassian, *Conf.* X.10.2.

[14] Ibid. During the following centuries down to our own day, this verse has served to open the Liturgy of the Hours for morning, daytime, and evening prayer.

[15] Cassian, *Conf.* X.10.3.

that we breathe
will be God,
then that unity the Father now has with the Son
and the Son with the Father
will fill our feelings and our understanding.
Just as God has loved us
with a sincere and pure and unbreakable love,
so may we also be joined to him
with an unending and inseparable love.
Then we shall be united to this same God in such a way
that whatever we breathe,
whatever we think,
whatever we speak
may be God.[16]

This statement gathers all of life, all our activities both conscious and unconscious, and focuses them on the command to pray always.[17] Again the goal of love is clearly and emphatically stated. Love of neighbor is found elsewhere in the *Conferences*, but here Cassian is focused wholly on God.

The *Conferences* ends with three important principles on prayer. The first warns against limiting the place and time of prayer: "If you only pray when you are on your knees, then you pray too little." The second warns against putting too much emphasis on the external forms of prayer; it is the heart that counts: "If your heart wanders off distracted while you are on your knees, then you never pray." The third insists that we are the same person before and during prayer, and we must seek purity of heart so that we will be ready to pray. "So whatever you want to be while praying, you should be before you begin to pray."[18]

St. John Climacus

Some among the desert monks gathered along the crags and sandy outreaches at the base of Mt. Sinai. In this rugged terrain a monastery, eventually called St. Catherine, was formed with Greek-speaking monks

---

[16] Cassian, *Conf.* X.7.2-3.

[17] Cf. Columba Stewart, O.S.B., *Cassian the Monk.* (Oxford: Oxford University Press, 1996), 95–99.

[18] Cassian, *Conf.* X.14.2.

under the protection of the Byzantine emperor Justinian (ca. 483–565) around 557. St. John Climacus (ca. 570–ca. 649), a seventh-century abbot of this monastery, updated the tradition of Evagrius and Cassian by writing *The Ladder of Divine Ascent*. In time, this book became the most important nonscriptural spiritual text in the Eastern Orthodox Church.

In a series of thirty rungs or steps, St. John Climacus instructs readers on how one progresses toward the climax of perfect prayer. These thirty rungs represent the thirty years of Jesus' life before he began the three years of public life described in the four Gospels. The major portion of the *Ladder*, steps 1–26, deals with ascetical practices, which St. John believed were preliminary to spiritual advancement.

Climacus, a critic of both Origen and Evagrius,[19] is nevertheless influenced by both men. He follows Evagrius's list of passions and adds others.

He observes that the passions are often connected. He concludes that through indulging one of them, another may be increased. For example, he sees gluttony, which he colorfully calls the "hypocrisy of the stomach," as being the "father of fornication." According to Climacus, gluttony leads to impurity, so he says, "let us prune the stomach by thoughts of the future fire."[20]

Showing Evagrian influence, Climacus states that the goal of defeating the passions is to reach a state of "dispassion." One who reaches dispassion reaches the "interior heaven of the mind" and "the resurrection of the soul."[21] But, like Cassian, Climacus understands that dispassion is not an end in itself. Achieving dispassion should give birth to love and virtue. Climacus writes, "The firmament has the stars for its beauty, and dispassion has the virtues for its adornments."[22]

For Climacus, prayer plays an essential role in the war against the passions. Like Cassian, he sees monological prayer as the most effective weapon for combat. He says, "Flog your enemies with the name of Jesus."[23] By praying the name of Jesus, the combatant squashes his

---

[19] Cf. Kallistos Ware's "Introduction" to John Climacus, *The Ladder of Divine Ascent*, trans. Colm Luibheid and Norman Russell with an introduction by Kallistos Ware (New York: Paulist Press, 1982), 1–70, esp. 62–66.

[20] John Climacus, *Ladder*, 140–42.

[21] Ibid., 258–59.

[22] Ibid., 282.

[23] Ibid., 200.

demons. He encourages, "[L]et the Remembrance of Jesus be present with your every breath."[24] In another place, he suggests using the words of the publican in Luke's Gospel, "God, be merciful to me, a sinner," as a monological prayer (Luke 18:13). In later years, Christians would put the name of Jesus together with the words of the publican to form the Jesus Prayer, "Lord Jesus Christ, Son of the living God, have mercy on me a sinner." This is the most popular form of the monological prayer in the Eastern Church and is also practiced by many Westerners.

Finally, Climacus, like so many in the ancient desert tradition, exhorts his followers to pray continuously. The ultimate purpose of all this spiritual combat is continuous intimacy with God. Climacus says, "What have I longed for on earth besides you? Nothing except simply clinging always to you in undistracted prayer."[25] As Harvey Egan, S.J., notes, "Hatred of the body and the world seems to set the tone for the [*Ladder*],"[26] but "the real war is that against self-love and the demons. The monk has promised to master his mysterious nature and to conquer the demons *for a life of unceasing communion with God in Christ*."[27] The ultimate point of asceticism is deeper communion with God. It is the aim to pray always.

Climacus believes it is important for each Christian to have his own experience of God. He writes, "You cannot learn to see just because someone tells you to do so. For that, you require your own natural power of sight. In the same way, you cannot discover from the teachings of others the beauty of prayer."[28] Also, he says, "a body changes in its activity as a result of contact with another body."[29] In other words, for prayer to have its desired effect—the conversion of the person and union with God—then that person must come into his own contact with God. He himself must come to continuous prayer. He cannot simply rely on the faith experience of others.

Climacus's work became an important influence on those who followed in his tradition, such as St. Symeon the New Theologian, Hesychius, St.

---

[24] Ibid., 269–70.

[25] Ibid., 277.

[26] Harvey Egan, *Anthology of Christian Mysticism* (Collegeville, MN: Liturgical Press, 1996), 114.

[27] Egan, *Anthology of Christian Mysticism*, 114 (emphasis added).

[28] Climacus, *Ladder*, 281.

[29] Ibid., 280.

Gregory of Sinai, and St. Gregory of Palamas.[30] When SS. Nikodimos and Makarios compiled the *Philokolia,* an eighteenth-century synthesis of Eastern Christian spirituality, they cited St. John Climacus more than any other thinker.[31] *The Ladder of Divine Ascent* remains one of the most significant texts in Orthodox spirituality. It is still read during every Lent in Orthodox monasteries[32] and has been as popular for Orthodox laity as Thomas a Kempis's *Imitation of Christ* has been for Roman Catholics.[33] The Jesus prayer received popular attention in the West through the distribution of the nineteenth-century spiritual classic *The Way of the Pilgrim,* and as a major theme in J. D. Salinger's twentieth-century masterpiece, *Franny and Zooey,* in which one of the characters is dedicated to reciting the prayer.

The Apophatic Way

Out of the spiritual battle engaged in by the desert monks grew a mystical tradition called the apophatic way. Related as it was to the battle for dispassion and the use of monological prayer, the apophatic way refers specifically to a way of praying that explicitly rejects the use of all or most images. The three most important works of this tradition are Gregory of Nyssa's *Life of Moses, The Mystical Theology* of Pseudo-Dionysus, and the medieval text *The Cloud of Unknowing.*

St. Gregory of Nyssa

Gregory of Nyssa (ca. 330–ca. 395) came from a famous monastic family in Cappadocia, modern-day Turkey. He wrote a biography of his sister St. Macrina, an ascetic who pushed their older brother St. Basil the Great to become a monk. Saint Gregory himself was not a monk but married, and later became a bishop. However, he is best known as an ascetical and mystical writer. In the *Life of Moses,* St. Gregory presents Moses as a great image of contemplative prayer, for Moses climbed the mountain of Sinai and made his way into the dark cloud. There Moses

---

[30] Ware, "Introduction" to *Ladder,* 67.

[31] St. Nikodimos of the Holy Mountain and St. Makarios of Corinth, *The Philokolia vol. 1–4,* trans. G. E. H. Palmer, Philip Sherrard, and Kallistos Ware (London: Faber and Faber, 1979), Index.

[32] Ware, "Introduction" to *Ladder,* 67.

[33] Ware, "Introduction" to *Ladder,* 1.

came face-to-face with God though he could not see him, for no one can see God and live. Being a friend of God, Moses was allowed to glimpse the back of God and so to catch within the darkness a glimpse of God's glory (Exod 24:15-18; 33:18-23; 34:6-9). For Gregory this story held possibilities for all who seek God.

Gregory understood Moses' climb as a model of change and progress. The one who prays moves from the darkness of ignorance to the light of understanding. As Gregory says, "The text teaches us that religious knowledge first appears as light for those who receive it. Whatever opposes religion is darkness, but by turning away from darkness you share in the light."[34] For Moses the burning bush becomes the moment of illumination. Gregory interprets Moses' entrance into the cloud and then his climb up Mount Sinai as a further progression beyond understanding into the dark incomprehensibility of mystery.

> The more the mind moves forward, the more you come, by greater and more perfect diligence, to grasp an understanding of things as they are. And so as you draw near to contemplation you see more and more that the divine nature is invisible. Having left behind all appearances, not only of what the sense perceives but also what the intelligence believes it sees, you move more and more inward until you slip past the mind's busyness to the invisible and the unknowable, and there you see God. In this is the true knowledge of what you seek: this is the seeing which is not seeing because what is sought transcends all knowledge and is separated from everything by its incomprehensibility as by darkness.[35]

For Gregory then, there are two ways to grasp the mystery of God. The way of light seeks to know God by using our rational faculties, but the way of darkness, the way of Moses, according to Gregory, is beyond reason. These two ways correspond to two major divisions in the experience of contemplative prayer: kataphatic prayer and apophatic prayer. Kataphatic prayer is the prayer of light, of images, and many words; it is a response to the beauty of creation. Apophatic prayer is imageless

---

[34] Gregory of Nyssa, *The Life of Moses*, section 162, trans. Harry Hagan from *La Vie de Moïse*, Sources Chrétiennes, vol. 1 (Paris: Les Éditions du Cerf, 1968). For a complete English edition, cf. *The Life of Moses*, trans. Abraham J. Malherbe and Everett Ferguson (New York: Paulist Press, 1978).

[35] Gregory of Nyssa, *Life of Moses*, §162–63.

prayer, simple, unadorned, the prayer of darkness and quiet, without words or thought. Along with Gregory of Nyssa, one of the chief proponents of the apophatic tradition was the Pseudo-Dionysius.

Pseudo-Dionysius the Areopagite.

In the book of Acts we have the account of St. Paul's visit to Athens in Greece. On the Areopagus, St. Paul discussed with the philosophers the existence of God. From that encounter, several Greeks were converted. One of them was Dionysius, an official in Athens (Acts 17:34). About the year 532, a meeting was held in Constantinople between certain Monophysite theologians and those theologians who followed the teachings of the Council of Chalcedon (451). The Monophysites made appeal to a body of writing supposedly written by a first-century Church father who bore the name of Denis the Areopagite. One of the leaders of the Chalcedon group, Hypatius, bishop of Ephesus (ca. 540–50), called these into question because they were not known to St. Cyril of Alexandria (d. 444) even though they were attributed to a witness of the time of St. Paul. Nevertheless, some considered the body of writings authentic, while others insisted that they were forgeries. The fact is that despite certain suspicions throughout the centuries, theologians in the West accepted the writings under the name of Denis the Areopagite. Only in the period of the Renaissance did scholars call into question the veracity of Denis. By the twentieth century all reputable scholars had rejected the authenticity of these texts. The question has remained, however, who was the author? The best hypothesis is that he was a Syrian, probably attached to the church of Antioch, writing sometime in the early sixth century. Seemingly he was a moderate Monophysite and a Neoplatonist, and he has come to be known as Pseudo-Dionysius.[36]

At least five works (including an inauthentic collection of letters) by this author have survived. The teaching on prayer is titled *The Mystical Theology*. It is the shortest of his works, yet one of the most important. Because all through the Middle Ages these writings were considered authentic and practically apostolic, they had a tremendous influence

---

[36] Paul Rorem, *Pseudo-Dionysius: A Commentary on the Texts and an Introduction to Their Influence* (New York: Oxford University Press, 1993), 3–29; 183–213. *Pseudo-Dionysius: The Complete Works*, trans. Colm Luibheid and Paul Rorem (New York: Paulist Press, 1987), 11–24.

on medieval theology. Inasmuch as the author of the *Mystical Theology* pretends to be from the first century, it would be considered the source of apophatic prayer. In fact, Pseudo-Dionysius sets before us a highly developed teaching already rooted in the teaching of Gregory of Nyssa, Evagrius, and John Cassian. What is more important is that his writings would be the conduit which transmitted the apophatic tradition of prayer to the medieval writers like the author of *The Cloud of Unknowing*.

The author presents prayer as ascending movement, a movement onward and upward (again taking our inspiration from the movement of Moses climbing Mount Sinai into the darkness as portrayed in the teaching of St. Gregory of Nyssa).

Trinity!! Higher than any being,
any divinity, any goodness!
Guide of Christians
in the wisdom of heaven!
Lead us up beyond unknowing and light,
up to the farthest, highest peak
of mystic scripture,
where the mysteries of God's Word
lie simple, absolute and unchangeable
in the brilliant darkness of a hidden silence.
Amid the deepest shadow
they pour overwhelming light
on what is most manifest.
Amid the wholly unsensed and unseen
they completely fill our sightless minds
with treasures beyond all beauty.[37]

Addressing Timothy, Dionysius advises that to "look for a sight of the mysterious things is to leave behind . . . everything perceived and understood, . . . perceptible and understandable, . . . is not and all that is, and with your understanding laid aside, to strive upward as much as you can toward union with him who is beyond all being and knowledge."[38]

---

[37] Rorem, *Pseudo-Dionysius: The Complete Works*, 135 (997A; 997B).
[38] Ibid. It is the Pseudo-Dionysius who first uses the Greek term *"mustikos"* in the field of theology and spirituality. He is the inventor of "mystical theology," that is, something secret or hidden.

The prayer presented us by the Pseudo-Dionysius involves stripping away our mind, our thinking, and our feeling, both emotional and affective, to arrive at a total transcendence. Here there is only one short hint of the humanity of Jesus,[39] but it does lead to union with him. "[R]enouncing all that the mind may conceive, wrapped entirely in the intangible and the invisible," we will be brought to him "who is beyond everything."[40] The Pseudo-Dionysius tried to lead his readers to union with God, but one can be left with the sense that he stepped into outer space.

The Cloud of Unknowing

In fourteenth-century England, an author wrote a series of treatises addressed to a young man on how to set out on a life of prayer. He called his book *The Cloud of Unknowing*. This book is, in a sense, a medieval English sequel to *The Mystical Theology* of Pseudo-Dionysius and *The Life of Moses* by St. Gregory of Nyssa.

The Cloud teaches a beginner in prayer how to progress further in the spiritual life. He writes, "Your whole life now must be one of loving" and it must begin "in the depths of your will."[41] The author begins teaching how to strip one's mind of images, how to focus by repeating one word, and how to yearn for God with love. This last point is of capital importance. *The Cloud* has what Denis lacked. It has affectivity for Christ. It stresses the importance of love.[42]

The author of *The Cloud* invites his readers to turn toward God in prayer and wait for him. One is invited to lift up one's heart with love and to give one's whole thought and attention to God and let nothing occupy the mind. One is called to forget everything else, even if it is a

---

[39] Ibid., 139 (1033A).

[40] Ibid., 137 (1001A).

[41] *The Cloud of Unknowing*, trans. Clifton Wolters (Hammondsworth, England: Penguin Books, 1961), 52.

[42] The author of the *Cloud* does not get this goal of love from Denis but from Thomas Gallus (+1246), a canon regular of St-Victor Abbey in Paris. He belonged to the group of theologians which formed its own Scholastic tradition and became known as the Victorines. Thomas Gallus is best known for his commentaries on the works of the Pseudo-Dionysius. He spent the last years of his life in England. It is Gallus who entered the yearning of love into the mystical theology of Dionysius. James Walsh, S.J., ed., *The Cloud of Unknowing* (Ramsey, NJ: Paulist Press, 1981), 43–51. William Johnston, *The Cloud of Unknowing and the Book of Privy Counseling* (New York: Doubleday and Col, Inc. Image Books, 1973), 27–28.

question of meditating on devotions and holy things. At first, one finds darkness to be "a sort of cloud of unknowing." One must be prepared to "rest in this darkness as long as [one] can."[43] "You are to smite upon that thick cloud of unknowing with a sharp dart of longing love . . . lift up your heart to God by a humble impulse of love. . . . Have no other thought of God . . . for a simple reaching out directly towards God is sufficient, without any other cause except himself."[44]

The author of *The Cloud* then suggests the use of a short word or phrase to focus the mind, just as Cassian and Climacus did. He instructs us to place the word in our heart like a shield and a spear. The word is to help us put aside other thoughts and distractions; we are to be prepared to drive away any notion of a "breaking apart" of the word and simply use it to bring back our concentration on God alone.[45]

The first seven chapters set forth the author's teaching on imageless prayer. In the remaining sixty-eight chapters, the author develops and describes the practice of this prayer. The author insists that anyone who enters into this form of prayer must seek the help of a spiritual director. One must have made a good confession. He closes with the encouraging words that at times this practice might be given up or lessened. It is when turning back again to this form of prayer that one "has more joy in the finding of it than ever . . . sorrow in the losing of it."[46]

Conclusion

Today there has developed a new interest in that form of contemplative prayer which we call apophatic. Part of this is the renewed interest in Eastern forms of non-Christian prayer but also a resurgence of interest in the forms of prayer of the Eastern churches. New translations, new experiences, new pathways have led us to more ancient models. Today new editions of *The Cloud of Unknowing* have brought about a newly developed interest in Centering Prayer, *Lectio Divina*, and the Jesus Prayer. Old authors have new interpretations, but the road map is the same. The thirst for God is unremitting. The Way is always above and beyond. God alone can satisfy.

---

[43] Walsh, *The Cloud*, 120–21; 129–30.
[44] Ibid., 131; 133.
[45] Walsh, *The Cloud*, 133–34.
[46] Ibid., 265.

Further Reading

Bondi, Roberta. *To Love as God Loves: Conversations with the Early Church.* Philadelphia: Fortress, 1987.

Egan, Harvey, S.J. *An Anthology of Christian Mysticism.* Collegeville, MN: Liturgical Press, 1991.

———. *What Are They Saying about Mysticism?* New York: Paulist Press, 1982.

Johnston, William. *The Wounded Stag: Christian Mysticism Today.* New York: Fordham University Press, 1998.

Keating, Abbot Thomas, O.C.S.O.; M. Basil Pennington, O.C.S.O.; and Thomas E. Clarke, S.J. *Finding Grace at the Center.* Petersham, MA: St. Bede's Publications, 1978.

Stewart, Columba, O.S.B. *Prayer and Community: The Benedictine Tradition.* Maryknoll, NY: Orbis Books, 1998.

Chapter 5

Prayer as a Journey: Medieval Spiritual Paths

Christian Raab, O.S.B.

In 1321, Dante Alighieri published *The Divine Comedy*, a poetic masterpiece detailing one man's pilgrimage through hell, purgatory, and heaven. Dante's colorful epic was typical of the medieval belief that one's earthly life was a great quest for God with important consequences. Medieval Christians understood their spiritual lives as a journey toward heaven, a journey that would one day end in success or failure.

Every journey has a starting point, a goal, and a way to get there. Christians have usually imagined the starting point in the spiritual life as sin. It is the life without Christ, the life one was living before setting down the pathway with Jesus. Dante began his poem by expressing that he was in this very situation.

> Midway through this journey of our life,
> I found myself in woods as dark as night,
> for the right way had vanished from my sight.[1]

---

[1] Dante Alighieri, *Divina Commedia*, *Inferno*, Canto I, 1–3, trans. by Harry Hagan, O.S.B.

When we find ourselves with the "right way . . . vanished from our sight," then we have a journey to make. Jesus says to us, "The kingdom of God has come near; repent, and believe in the good news" (Mark 1:15). Then he says, "Follow me . . ." (Matt 4:19). Invited by Christ, we leave behind our former worlds and go down the narrow path with him. We become part of a new adventure.

Every journey also is characterized by a destination. As Christians, our longed-for destination is eternal life, as Jesus calls it: "the kingdom of God" (Mark 1:15), "my Father's house" (John 14:2), and "Paradise" (Luke 23:43). When Dante reaches his destination in heaven, he utters the famous lines:

> My mind, completely caught and lifted up,
> transfixed in wonder, could not move or turn
> but gazed in wonder and with wonder burned.
>
> And all who see this light become so changed
> that they could never turn and be content
> to let some shadow claim their full assent.
>
> For every good, the will's sole quest and goal,
> is gathered here, no longer lost or flawed,
> the journey's quest made perfect—all in all.[2]

We also are looking for that place of light and wonder, where our "quest" will be "made perfect." We aspire towards union with our Creator, whom we will meet in heaven.

Yet, while we believe our journey will only meet its final destination in the next life, we understand that something of eternal life is knowable to us now, in this world. Jesus tells us, "The kingdom of God is among you" (Luke 17:21). Our relationship with God need not and should not wait. Medieval Christians knew this, and they sought and found intimacy with God in this life. As the fifteenth-century English hermit Julian of Norwich described, "We are all enclosed in him, and he is enclosed in us . . . he sits in our soul . . . it is his delight to reign blessedly in our understanding, and sit restfully in our soul, and to dwell endlessly in our soul, working us all

---

[2] Dante, *Paradiso*, Canto XXXIII, 97–105, trans. by Harry Hagan, O.S.B.

into him."[3] While heaven is our ultimate destination, God is already within and among us.

Finally, there must be a means of making the journey. Dante's companion and guide into heaven was Beatrice, a beautiful woman who was a symbol of God's grace. We too have a guide and friend who leads us back to heaven. This is Jesus. Christ lets us know that he is the "way" (John 14:6), the "gate" (John 10:7), and the "light" (John 12:35). And he tells us, "I am with you always, to the end of the age" (Matt 28:20). Saint Augustine (d. 430),[4] who is in some ways the first medieval theologian, aptly puts it:

> As we had no way to go to the truth, the Son of God, who is in the Father and ever the truth and the life, became the way for us by assuming man's nature. Walk by Him the man, and you will come to God. You go *by* Him, and you go *to* Him. Do not look for any way to come to Him except by Himself. For if He had not deigned to be the way, we would have always gone astray. Therefore, He became the way by which you could come to Him. I do not tell you, look for the way. The way itself has come to you. Arise and walk.[5]

Christ brings us to God. He is the bridge for humanity to reach eternity. We travel, but we do not make our way alone.

In this chapter, we will explore how medieval Christians prayed, how they encountered and moved closer to this Jesus who was their bridge into heaven.[6] In doing so, perhaps we will discover ways of praying that can still attract us today, so that Jesus can be our companion too along our spiritual journey.

---

[3] Harvey Egan, S.J., *Anthology of Christian Mysticism* (Collegeville, MN: Liturgical Press, 1991), 394.

[4] Jordan Aumann, O.P., *Christian Spirituality in the Catholic Tradition* (San Francisco: Ignatius, 1985), 61.

[5] St. Augustine of Hippo, "Sermon 141" in *The Works of St. Augustine: A Translation for the 21st Century* 3/4, ed., John Rotelle, O.S.A., trans. Edmund Hill, O.P. (Brooklyn, NY: New City Press, 1992), 411.

[6] Historians are not always sure how to mark off the beginning and ending of the Middle Ages. Some historians claim that the Middle Ages begin as early as 410 with the sack of Rome, and end as late as 1517 with the beginning of the Protestant Reformation. This essay will focus mainly on the period between 900 and 1350, with greatest emphasis on the twelfth and thirteenth centuries.

Pilgrimage

Few activities better captured the spirit of the Middle Ages than did pilgrimage. "Every year, thousands of Christians took to the road as pilgrims, motivated by the desire to pray at an especially holy place, to fulfill a vow, to perform a penance, or to engage in pious tourism."[7] Pilgrims ventured to nearby shrines in order to visit the relics of a local saint. Sometimes they traveled long distances, perhaps to Rome or Jerusalem, where they could see the relics of the apostles or experience the places where biblical deeds had been carried out. Pilgrimage was so important during the Middle Ages that one modern scholar has considered it the "key to literary, artistic, and cultural understanding of the Middle Ages."[8] For example, pilgrimage inspired popular poems such as the *Canterbury Tales* of Geoffrey Chaucer (d. 1400)[9] and Dante's *Divine Comedy*. Church practices such as walking the Stations of the Cross were developed as a substitute for those who couldn't make a long pilgrimage. Even the most devastating wars of the Middle Ages, the Crusades, were fought, in part, so that European pilgrims could have certain access to pilgrimage routes and sites in the Holy Land.

The prayer of Christian pilgrimage was not so much a prayer of words or thought as a prayer of action. Pilgrimage was a prayer of the body. In walking (sometimes enormously long distances), pilgrims expressed some of the same sentiments we would expect people to express in verbal prayer: repentance, praise, and longing.

For many, pilgrimage was a penitential act. In it, pilgrims expressed their sorrow and a desire to make up for their sins. Pilgrimage signified a turning away from sin and a choice to focus on the spiritual. The *Veneranda Dies*, a twelfth-century sermon read every year on the feast of St. James to the many throngs of pilgrims who set out on that day to the relics of the apostle in Compostela, Spain, reads:

> The way of St. James is fine but narrow, as narrow as the path of salvation itself. The path is the shunning of vice, the mortification of the

[7] Joseph H. Lynch, *The Medieval Church: A Brief History* (London: Longman, 1972), 270.

[8] Emile Male, quoted in Alan Kendall, *Medieval Pilgrims* (London: Wayland Publishers, 1970), 35. (Compostela, in particular).

[9] C. Warren Hollister, *Medieval Europe: A Short History* (New York: McGraw-Hill, 1994), 361.

flesh, and the increasing of virtue. . . . If [the pilgrim] was previously
a spoliator, he must become an almsgiver; if he was boastful he must be
forever modest; if greedy, generous; if a fornicator or adulterer, chaste;
if drunk, sober. That is to say that from every sin which he committed
before his pilgrimage, he must afterwards abstain completely.[10]

This popular sermon, heard by thousands on this most popular of all
medieval pilgrimages, drove home to its audience the penitential goal
of their journey.

Before a pilgrim embarked on his journey, he symbolically expressed
his choice to turn away from sin and turn toward God. The pilgrim gave
all, or a large part, of his possessions to the poor or to the Church. He
settled personal conflicts. He confessed his sins. He could even receive
a special blessing from a bishop. And like a young man or woman entering a monastery, he could don a religious habit.[11] Once on the road,
the hardships of medieval travel served as penance as well. Voyaging
with little or no money, often begging along the way, pilgrims suffered
from sickness, hunger, and cold, as well as dangers like bad weather and
bandits. For the medieval Christian, however, this very difficulty of the
pilgrim road was tied up with its redemptive value. Walking became a
kind of prayer. By enduring the sufferings of pilgrimage, the Christian
was expressing repentance for his former sinful life, doing just penance,
and purifying his body and spirit in anticipation of the future.

The institutional Church encouraged this focus on pilgrimage by prom-
ising Christians indulgences for the practice. Officially, indulgences were
"authoritative grants from the church's treasury for the remission or payment, in whole or in part, valid before God, of the debt of temporal pun-
ishment after the guilt of sin has been forgiven."[12] This means indulgences
were like special "indulgent" gifts given to the sinner through the mercy of
God, which freed him from some temporal suffering he deserved because
of his sin. They could also be awarded vicariously to the souls of the dead
in purgatory for good actions carried out by the living.

Pilgrimage was also seen as a way to praise God through imitating
Christ. An important draw for pilgrims to the Holy Land (then as now)

[10] Jonathan Sumption, *Pilgrimage: An Image of Mediaeval Religion* (Totowa, NJ:
Rowman and Littlefield, 1975), 124–25.

[11] Kendall, *Medieval Pilgrims*, 35.

[12] Ibid., 29.

was the opportunity to do the things Jesus did in the place where he did them. Many pilgrims to the Holy Land, for example, fasted for forty days. Some were baptized in the Jordan River. Some washed the feet of other pilgrims. A few pilgrims to Jerusalem even went so far as to be scourged at a pillar as Jesus was.[13] But perhaps the best imitation of Christ was just traveling the pilgrim road itself. By joining other pilgrims as a band of poor wanderers on their way to a destination, the pilgrim's life mirrored that of Christ traveling with his disciples on the road to Jerusalem. The pilgrim gave praise by imitating the lifestyle of Jesus Christ and his companions.

Finally, pilgrimage expressed a longing to encounter God. Medieval pilgrims believed that something of God could be experienced in the here and now. The faithful understood that God had become an embodied, physical, human person. They longed to experience God by coming close to the physical relics of Christ, such as his cross or the places he lived, or to the physical remains of the saints who the faithful believed were united to Christ.

There were many popular pilgrimage sites where medieval pilgrims sought such concrete experiences of connection to God. The most popular destinations were the seven churches of Rome; the tomb of St. Thomas à Becket in Canterbury, England; and the tomb of St. James in Santiago, Spain. Most desired of all was a pilgrimage to the many sites known from Scripture in the Holy Land. Here, these pilgrims looked for an experience of union with Jesus.

A medieval description of the pilgrimage of Richard of St. Vannes to Jerusalem in 1026 describes for us the sense of encountering God that some pilgrims sought and experienced:

> After many sorts of peril, he reached the longed-for places of Jerusalem . . . He faithfully toured all the places of the Nativity, Passion, and Resurrection, and when he was not feasting upon them with his eyes, he browsed upon them in his mind, for at the most delectable sight of the wonders of God, which he had so longed and prepared for in his desirous mind, he was filled with an unspeakable joy and gladness . . . Oh, what was his love towards God! What the exultation of his contrite and humbled spirit! What the jubilation of his heart, when he saw himself present where Christ was born, where he suffered,

---

[13] Sumption, *Pilgrimage*, 93.

where he was buried, where his feet last stood when he ascended into heaven. Everywhere that he prayed, he soaked the ground with tears, the cry of his heart rose up to the Lord, his body sank down, his spirit rose aloft. He spent the night continually in vigils, he wore down his body with fasts, never without tears, never without prayers; his whole being exulted in the Lord, but he cloaked the gladness of his mind with serenity and countenance.[14]

The enthusiasm of this medieval pilgrim reaching his destination in Jerusalem is terrific. He rejoices in his encounter with the very places known to Jesus during his life. We are told that "his whole being exults in the Lord." This description of Richard of St. Vannes illustrates for us what many pilgrims, finally reaching Jerusalem or the relics of a saint in Rome or Spain, must have felt upon completing their long journey and seeing themselves in connection to God.

Toward the end of the Middle Ages, many Christians criticized the practice of pilgrimage. Critics challenged that pilgrimage was superstitious, hinting that God was more real in one place than in another. Others lamented that indulgences created the scandalous illusion that somehow people were paying for their salvation. In the fourteenth century, a movement called *Devotio Moderna*, the new devotion, became popular among the lay faithful as an alternative to pilgrimage. Proponents of *Devotio Moderna* encouraged believers to read the Scriptures and receive the sacraments, do private penance and work on one's personal morality. Followers of the *Devotio Moderna* were similar to pilgrims in their great attention to, and affection for, the humanity of Christ; yet their main emphasis was on inner piety and morality, not outward religious acts such as pilgrimage.[15] Thomas à Kempis (d. 1471),[16] a Dutch monk who authored *The Imitation of Christ*, the most important book to come out of the *Devotio Moderna*, explained his belief that God was better sought in the sacraments of the Church than on adventurous trips across the world. He wrote:

> Many make pilgrimages to various places to visit the relics of the Saints, wondering at the story of their lives and the splendor of their shrines;

[14] Diana Webb, *Pilgrims and Pilgrimage in the Medieval West* (New York: Tauris, 2001), 40.

[15] Lynch, *The Medieval Church*, 340.

[16] Aumann, *Christian Spirituality in the Catholic Tradition*, 164.

they view and venerate their bones, covered with silks and gold. But here on the Altar are You yourself, my God the Holy of Holies, Creator of Men and Lord of Angels! When visiting such places, men are often moved by curiosity and the urge for sight seeing, and one seldom hears that any amendment of life results, especially as their conversion is trivial and lacks true contrition. But here, in the Sacrament of the Altar, You are wholly present, my God, the man Jesus Christ; here we freely partake the fruit of eternal salvation, as often as we receive you worthily and devoutly.[17]

Despite such critics as Thomas à Kempis, pilgrimage was a central element in medieval prayer and piety. Its practitioners found in it a way to repent of their sins, praise God, and seek and encounter him on their spiritual journeys.

The practice lives on today in the annual pilgrimage of youth from Paris to Chartres, at the many Marian pilgrimage sites around the world, such as the Swiss Abbey of Einsiedeln (see fig. 2, pg. 251) and in the pilgrimage route to Santiago in Compostela, which thousands of pilgrims continue to travel each year.

Monasticism

Many medieval Christians looked to encounter God in a more quiet way through the monastic life. Either by entering a monastery where they lived a common life of prayer and work with fellow Christians or, as was more rarely the case, traveling the spiritual path alone as solitary hermits, these monks and nuns sought God in silence on a different kind of spiritual quest.

During the Middle Ages, monasticism reached its historical peak. Becoming a monk or nun was widely accepted as the ideal path to Christian sanctity. It may be hard for us to believe today, but monasticism was so popular during the Middle Ages that during the twelfth and thirteenth centuries the Benedictine Abbey of Cluny, for example, boasted a network of 20,000 monks spread out over 1,000 monasteries.[18] New monastic movements, such as the Cistercians in the thirteenth century, were able to grow from five small houses to five hundred

---

[17] Thomas à Kempis, *The Imitation of Christ*, trans. Leo Shirley Price (London: Penguin, 1952), 186.

[18] Lynch, *The Medieval Church*, 197.

sizable monasteries within the span of a century.[19] Monasticism was so esteemed among medieval Christians that the word "conversion" itself actually came to *mean* "joining a monastery"![20] And while there are famous stories of those who ended up in monasteries against their will, it is probably safe to say that most Christians traveled this path out of longing for God and salvation.

Saint Bernard of Clairvaux (d. 1153),[21] who was probably the most famous of all medieval monks, helped popularize monasticism through his message that the monastery was a way to get to heaven. "The soul . . . is a pilgrim and an exile on the earth,"[22] said St. Bernard, but in the monastery one could "find rest, according to the promise of the Lord."[23] For St. Bernard and the many other medieval monks, the key to this rest was prayer.

Most monks and nuns followed the structures of life found in the Rule of St. Benedict (d. 547).[24] According to this rule, monks and nuns practiced various ways of praying. The two most important were the private prayer of *lectio divina* and the public prayer of the liturgy.

Lectio divina, meaning "holy reading," the practice of slowly reading the Scriptures, selecting words or small phrases for one's personal meditation, and privately discussing them with God. As contemporary monk Michael Casey describes it: "Monastic reading was less like study, as we know it, and more like prayer. It was a full and voluntary immersion of the monk in the word of God, allowing it to touch his awareness, to enflame his desire, to direct his understanding, and eventually to serve as a guide and incentive to Gospel living."[25]

For these monks, reading Scripture was contact with the Word of God. It was an opportunity for intimacy with Christ.

---

[19] Hollister, *Medieval Europe*, 203.

[20] Translator's notes, *Bernard of Clairvaux: The Selected Works*, trans. G. R. Evans (Mahwah, NJ: Paulist Press, 1987), 65.

[21] Aumann, *Christian Spirituality in the Catholic Tradition*, 93.

[22] *St. Bernard's Sermons for the Seasons and Principle Festivities of the Year*, trans. A Priest of Mount Melleray (Dublin: Browne and Nolan Ltd., 1921), 46.

[23] Jean LeClerq, *The Love of Learning and the Desire for God*, trans. Catherine Misrahi (New York: Fordham University Press, 1961), 69.

[24] Aumann, *Christian Spirituality in the Catholic Tradition*, 68.

[25] Michael Casey, *The Undivided Heart: The Western Monastic Approach to Contemplation* (Petersham, MA: St. Bede's Publications, 1994), 26.

Saint Benedict, for his part, showed the importance he placed on reading Scripture by prescribing that monks engage in *lectio divina* "between two or three hours each day!"[26] This was especially remarkable considering the fact that so few medieval people could read and given the fact that books were very expensive. It would take the invention of the printing press and the Protestant Reformation to bring this way of prayer to most ordinary people. If a medieval Christian desired to read Scripture for himself or herself, he or she would need to enter a monastery where both books and an education could be obtained.

Liturgy was the aspect of monastic prayer done in common. The lives of monks and nuns were lives of public worship, with monasteries being the great liturgical centers of the Middle Ages. The monks who strictly followed St. Benedict's rule came together eight times a day to recite, chant, or sing the Divine Office, a set of prayers taken mainly from the book of Psalms. Depending on the time of day or time of year, different prayers would be intoned. And, of course, central to their liturgical experience was their daily gathering for Mass. Just as monks encountered the word of God through *lectio* and liturgy, they met God's sacramental presence in the Eucharist.

Monastic prayer, whether as part of *lectio divina* or the liturgy, included the element of conversing with God. It was important to hear the words of Scripture. It was also important to speak personally to God and to listen for his voice. Saint Bernard advised, "Approach the Word with confidence, cling to Him with constancy, speak to Him as a familiar friend."[27] Some monastic figures, such as St. Gertrude the Great (d. 1302),[28] wrote out their conversations with God, just as one might do today in a journal or diary. She described one of her conversations with God at Mass:

> On a certain feast day—as I saw several people who had asked for my prayers approaching Holy communion while I, for my part, was prevented by bodily infirmity from partaking of the sacrament—or rather, as I fear, repulsed by God as unworthy of it—I passed over in my mind all your many benefits, Lord God, and I began to fear that the wind of vainglory would dry up the stream of divine grace, and I desired to

[26] Ibid., 25.

[27] Egan, *Anthology of Christian Mysticism*, 176.

[28] Aumann, *Christian Spirituality in the Catholic Tradition*, 146.

understand how to guard myself against this in the future. In your fa-
therly love you told me that I should regard your affection for me like
that of a father who takes pleasure in hearing his large family of children
complimented by retainers for their elegance and grace. This father has
a small child also, who has not yet attained to the elegance and perfection of the others, but for whom he feels a compassionate tenderness,
pressing him more often to his breast, fondling and caressing him with
more endearing words and little gifts than he gives to the others.[29]

While St. Gertrude approached God as a loving father, some from
the monastic tradition used the language of romantic love and marriage in their conversations with God. Saint Bernard's commentaries
on the Song of Songs, a book which itself employed this bridal imagery,
were among the most popular sermons of the Middle Ages. Saint Bernard described the relationship between the soul and Christ as being
marital. "He [Christ] and the soul are bridegroom and Bride."[30] The
soul "sweetly sleeps within the arms of the bridegroom, in ecstasy of
spirit."[31] Mechtild of Magdeburg (d. 1282 or 1297),[32] another nun in St.
Gertrude's monastery, wrote love poems for God like this one:

> Lord, now I am a naked soul;
> And thou a God most glorious!
> Our two-fold intercourse is Love eternal
> Which can never die.
> Now becomes a blessed stillness
> Welcome to both. He gives Himself to her
> And she to Him.[33]

This bold language of love was a favorite way of talking about prayer
among medieval monks and nuns. Writings such as those of Bernard
and Mechtild became popular far beyond the monastic confines and
influenced the spiritual lives of many medieval Christians.

---

[29] St. Gertrude the Great, *Herald of Divine Love,* trans. Margaret Winkworth
(Mahwah, NJ: Paulist Press, 1992), 119.
[30] Egan, *Anthology of Christian Mysticism,* 176.
[31] Ibid., 173.
[32] Aumann, *Christian Spirituality in the Catholic Tradition,* 145.
[33] Egan, *Anthology of Christian Mysticism,* 256.

Today, many ordinary Christians use methods of prayer found among the medieval monks and nuns. The Divine Office, also called the Liturgy of the Hours, is prayed by many Christians. It can be prayed alone or with a group. *Lectio divina* remains a very popular method of prayer for both Catholics and Protestants, and many Christians find it helpful to pray *lectio* with a journal, writing out their conversations with God.

Mendicants

During the twelfth and thirteenth centuries, Christians who wanted to follow the way of Jesus began to innovate a new lifestyle that was different from either pilgrimage or monasticism. Followers of this new way committed themselves to entire lives of wandering preaching and gospel poverty. At first, they called their way the *Vita Apostolica*, meaning "Apostolic Life," because they were trying to re-create the life of the early Church. In time, they came to be known as *mendicants*, meaning "beggars." Some of them, such as the followers of St. Francis (d. 1226) and St. Dominic (d. 1221),[34] were organized into groups that were officially recognized by the Church. These two traditions have had an enormous impact on the history of Christian prayer.

Franciscan Prayer

Saint Francis of Assisi deserves first mention among the mendicants. A one-time playboy and the son of an Italian merchant, St. Francis had a great religious conversion while still a young man.

He was inspired by the biblical text, "As you go, proclaim the good news, 'The kingdom of heaven has come near.' Cure the sick, raise the dead, cleanse the lepers, cast out demons. You received without payment, give without payment. Take no gold, or silver, or copper in your belts, no bag for your journey, or two tunics, or sandals, or a staff; for laborers deserve their food" (Matt 10:7-10).[35] Saint Francis abandoned his material existence and took up a life of prayer and ministry to lepers. He went to work rebuilding a small church in the Italian countryside. Others soon joined him (including St. Clare who would found a woman's version of the movement). Saint Francis's community, which he called "the friars minor," or "little brothers,"

---

[34] Aumann, *Christian Spirituality in the Catholic Tradition*, 137 and 128.

[35] The account of St. Francis's conversion can be found in Hollister, *Medieval Europe*, 209–12.

were men dedicated to lives of radical poverty in imitation of Christ. By the time St. Francis died, his community numbered in the thousands and had spread throughout Europe and the Middle East. The humble imitation of Jesus that was practiced by the friars won many over to Christ.

Saint Francis was not a traditional teacher of the spiritual life. Rather, he was a poet and a singer whose way of praying is best understood by looking at the texts of the prayers he authored. These pieces, like Francis himself, were romantic, emotional, spontaneous, and free.

Inspired by French troubadours and bards who had crossed over into Italy at the close of the twelfth century, Francis, like St. Bernard before him, applied the language of romance and courtly love to the spiritual life. Always imaginative, Francis wrote as if he were himself a royal fool or chivalrous knight in service to Jesus Christ the King and Mary, "Our Lady." Saint Francis was known for wandering through the countryside, singing songs of praise like this one, which he authored for Mary:

> Hail, O Lady,
> Holy Queen,
> Mary, holy Mother of God,
> Who are the Virgin made Church,
> chosen by the most Holy Father in heaven
> whom he consecrated with His most holy beloved Son
> and with the Holy Spirit the Paraclete,
> in whom there was and is
> all fullness of grace and every good.
>
> Hail His Palace!
> Hail His Tabernacle!
> Hail His Dwelling!
> Hail His Robe!
> Hail His Servant!
> Hail His Mother![36]

An important dimension of St. Francis's prayer was its emphasis on nature and the created world. For St. Francis, the world, and all that we see in it, is an expression of God. Nowhere does this aspect of Francis's spirituality come across more beautifully than in his famous *Canticle of the Sun:*

---

[36] Regis Armstrong, O.F.M. Cap., J. A. Wayne Hellmann, O.F.M. Conv., and William J. Short, eds., *Francis of Assisi: Early Documents*, vol. 1, *The Saint* (New York: New City Press, 1999), 163.

Most High, all powerful, good Lord
    Yours are the praises, the glory, and the honor, and all blessing.
To you alone, Most High, do they belong,
    and no human is worthy to mention Your name.
Praised be You, my Lord, with all Your creatures,
    especially Sir Brother Sun,
    Who is the day and through whom You give us light.
And he is beautiful and radiant with great splendor;
    and bears a likeness of You, Most High One.
Praised be You, my Lord, through Sister Moon and the stars,
    in heaven You formed them clear and precious and beautiful.
Praised be You, my Lord, through Brother Wind,
    and through the air, cloudy and serene, and every kind of weather
    through whom You give sustenance to Your creatures.
Praised be You, my Lord, through Sister Water,
    who is very useful and humble and precious and chaste.
Praised be You, my Lord, through Brother Fire,
    through whom You light the night
    and he is beautiful and playful and robust and strong.
Praised be You, my Lord, through our sister Mother Earth,
    who sustains and governs us,
    and who produces varied fruit with colored flowers and herbs.

Praised be You, my Lord, through those who give pardon for Your love,
    and bear infirmity and tribulation.
    Blessed are those who endure in peace
        for by You, Most High, they shall be crowned.
Praised be You, my Lord, through our Sister Bodily Death,
    from whom no one living can escape.
    Woe to those who die in mortal sin.
Blessed are those whom death will find in Your most holy will,
    for the second death shall do them no harm.

Praise and bless my Lord and give Him thanks
    and serve him with great humility.[37]

This prayer typifies St. Francis's spirit. It is a song of praise, sung by one journeying through the world with Christ, offering thanks to the Father for all the works of creation.

More important, while St. Francis became well known for his loving embrace of the created world, his spirituality was also marked by a deep

---

[37] Ibid., 113–14.

asceticism. Saint Francis was attracted to the poor, suffering Christ, and he wished to imitate Jesus, not only in his love and joy but also in his poverty and humility.

Asceticism is self-denial, usually of something physical, such as food, warmth, sexual activity, or sleep. It is, in fact, like the walk of pilgrimage, a bodily prayer, through which one expresses sorrow and repentance for sins, as one also bears witness to the ultimate insufficiency of the created world. Saint Francis, while being a true lover of the world, was also a great ascetic. He adored Christ in his poverty and wished to join Jesus in humility and suffering. Franciscan spirituality must be seen as both an embrace as well as a denial of the material world.

Saint Bonaventure (d. 1274), one of the members of St. Francis's order, was a notable spiritual teacher who made a great contribution to the history of spirituality. He authored *The Soul's Journey into God*, which some scholars believe was the most important text about prayer to come out of the Middle Ages. In this work, St. Bonaventure developed the tradition of the purgative, illuminative, and unitive ways, a way of understanding the spiritual life that dates back to Origen and Evagrius. According to this view, the spiritual path of each individual progresses in three stages. The first, called "purgation," occurs when a soul repents from sin. During this stage, a person disciplines his passions and senses and achieves a clean conscience. The second stage is called "illumination." During this stage, the person "sees rightly." He comes to a truer knowledge, love, and appreciation of himself, others, and God. This stage is marked by gratitude. In the third stage, called the "unitive way," the soul reaches mystical union with God.

Saint Bonaventure taught that affective emotion played an important role in the soul's journey. A soul needed to love Christ and know Christ's love in order to make much spiritual progress. He wrote:

> Ask grace not instruction
> Desire not understanding
> The groaning of prayer not diligent reading
> The Spouse not the teacher.[38]

---

[38] Ibid.

The human person could really only progress through the three stages of the spiritual life by falling in love with Christ, whom St. Bonaventure calls the "way and the door," the "ladder and the vehicle."[39] Inspired by love, the Christian would follow Christ into repentance, loving activity, and finally union with the Father.

Following the lead of St. Francis, St. Bonaventure and his Dominican contemporary St. Thomas Aquinas led Catholic spirituality in the thirteenth century to an emphasis on the goodness of the created world. For centuries, Catholic theology had been dominated by the philosophy of Plato, who emphasized the importance of abstract ideal forms. Platonic philosophy was compatible with the monastic ideal of leaving behind the world and entering into a cloister to seek God. Bonaventure and Aquinas participated in the reintroduction of the philosophy of Aristotle to Catholic thought. Aristotle emphasized the importance of the concrete world and material experience. By making the turn from Plato to Aristotle, Christian spirituality returned to its Jewish roots, where the natural world had always been seen, together with the revealed Scripture and moral law, as a way of knowing God. Saint Bonaventure wrote, "All creatures of the sense world lead the mind . . . of the wise man to the eternal God."[40] Experience of creation would lead the heart of the Christian to wonder, awe, thanksgiving, and praise of God the Creator. God could be known and loved in one's friends and family, in natural beauty, in listening to a fine piece of music or reading poetry, or in many other encounters with his creation. Opening eyes and ears to the world became a way of praying, a way of encountering God!

Dominican Prayer

Like St. Francis, St. Dominic started a religious order dedicated to the imitation of Christ, poverty, and preaching. Officially called the "Order of Preachers," the Dominicans influenced the spiritual life of the medieval Church in important ways.

Though St. Dominic did not leave us with many writings, the *Nine Ways of Prayer,* is a document of anonymous authorship dating to the late-thirteenth century that describes the example of St. Dominic's prayer.

[39] Ibid., 111.
[40] Ibid.

Interestingly, St. Dominic's *Nine Ways* were not nine types or means of prayer, per se (i.e., mental, vocal, apophatic), but nine positions of the body. The ways include kneeling, standing upright with outstretched arms, bowing, lying prostrate, and walking. The characteristically Dominican devotion to the Incarnation and the Passion is reflected in these nine ways. The body was not an evil thing to be escaped, but Christ, by becoming man, had sanctified the body and used the body to pray.

Saint Thomas Aquinas (d. 1274), as we have already seen, helped lead the turn toward a more concrete spirituality rooted in creation. In conjunction with this contribution, he developed the Church's understanding of the sacraments, particularly the Eucharist. In his *Summa Theologica*, St. Thomas authored what would become the Church's gold standard for the theology of the Eucharist, an understanding that would be codified at the Council of Trent and remains paramount to this day. Saint Thomas defended the real presence of Christ in the Eucharist, and he brilliantly articulated the Church's understanding of the sacrifice of the Mass as the most perfect prayer of the Church. He also contributed to the devotion to the Blessed Sacrament by campaigning for the institution of the feast of Corpus Christi, and he composed many eucharistic hymns and prayers, including the well-known verse "Devoutly I Adore Thee."

Saint Catherine of Siena (d. 1380), a third-order Dominican, typifies another dimension of Dominican prayer, namely, the emphasis on integrating contemplation and action. The motto of the Dominicans is "to contemplate, and to give to others the fruits of our contemplation." Saint Catherine thereby taught the idea of the "cell of the heart." She believed that we must always be in prayer with God, always in contemplation, yet we must also, for example, perform the corporal works of mercy. This can be done if one is always in the cell, which can only be accomplished by always being in the cell of the heart. She believed that contemplation and action were one: i.e., contemplation did not lead to or fuel action but was all the same. Since all was done in the cell, all was done in prayer and as prayer. Saint Catherine also played an important role in promoting devotion to the Eucharist. She sought and received papal approval to have a priest go with her wherever she went so that she could receive Communion daily. Back then, daily Eucharist was unknown. She loved the Eucharist so much that she was given this unique privilege for her day.

Dominicans were also important in popularizing Marian devotion during the Middle Ages. Medieval tales credit St. Dominic with receiving the first rosary from the hands of the Blessed Virgin. The prayer of the rosary involved reciting sets of "Hail Marys" and other prayers while recalling mentally the mysteries of Christ's incarnation, death, and resurrection. Consequently, the Dominicans encouraged lay people to pray the rosary as an alternative to the Divine Office, which required more time and education than were available to most lay people.

A number of medieval Dominicans, such as Meister Eckhart (d. 1327), Henry Suso (d. 1366), and John Tauler (d. 1361), continued to develop the tradition of apophatic prayer. When one prayed this way, he or she generally sat in silence, trying to achieve an inner sense of quiet where the soul could meet God. As Dominican teacher Meister Eckhart put it, "A man must collect all his powers as if into a corner of his soul where, hiding away from all images and forms, he can get to work. Here he must come to a forgetting and an unknowing. There must be a stillness and a silence."[41] Interestingly, the rosary, which on the one hand served as a way of meditating on Christ's humanity, could also be a springboard for apophatic prayer. One could simply recite the repetitive words of the rosary as a monological prayer. In this way it served as a backdrop to a more imageless, contemplative experience. As such, the rosary became the most popular way for ordinary Christians to engage in apophatic, imageless prayer.

The Impact of the Medieval Mendicants

Together, the Dominicans and Franciscans have been credited with solidifying the faith during the darkest hours of the late Middle Ages. The preaching of the mendicants and the scholastic works of thinkers like St. Bonaventure and St. Thomas Aquinas were instrumental in defending the Church against medieval heresies. The personal holiness of the friars, sensed by the faithful, restored confidence in the Church at a time when it was plagued by scandal, wealth, corruption, and a weakened papacy.[42]

---

[41] Richard Woods, *Mysticism and Prophesy: The Dominican Tradition* (Maryknoll, NY: Orbis, 1998), 84.

[42] Already weak from conflicts with political authorities, the Holy See was further challenged when Pope Clement V had to flee Rome in order to avoid civil discontent and settle the papacy in France, as he did in 1308. After Pope Gregory XI returned in 1378,

Perhaps most important, the mendicant orders helped the faithful to cope spiritually with the tragedies wrought by the Black Death.[43] They reminded the faithful of Christ's compassion by spreading devotions to the Incarnation and Passion. The Franciscans generated the nativity scene and the Stations of the Cross, while the Dominicans were essential in spreading devotions to the Blessed Mother and the Eucharist. Suffering Christians were comforted by the knowledge that their God had become a human person. He had suffered and died. He had proved his solidarity with them. It isn't surprising that in the thirteenth and fourteenth centuries, under the influence of Franciscans and Dominicans, images of Christ as tremendous king and stern judge above altars and over doorways of medieval churches began to be replaced by more humble images of Jesus' suffering and death. The image of God was now an image of Christ, the God-man who had entered the depths of human misery and suffered alongside human beings. The mendicant orders played an important role in spreading this consciousness. Indeed, many of the faithful saw the friars themselves as "other Christs," for they had left behind their possessions to live voluntarily among the poor and suffering.

Conclusion

Medieval Christians were close to the metaphorical understanding of spiritual journey. They journeyed as pilgrims acting out their prayer of repentance, praise of imitation, and thirst for encounter. Monks and nuns sought an inner experience of God whom they encountered through Scripture and sacrament. Finally, mendicants sought a radical imitation of Christ in lives of poverty and preaching. A medieval Christian traveling any of these paths was living a journey toward heaven, with Christ as his companion and guide.

---

only shortly thereafter to die, a crisis enveloped the papacy as cardinals failed to come to an agreement on his legitimate successor and a schism occurred in the Church's highest office that lasted for thirty-six years (Lynch, *The Medieval Church*, 323–35).

[43] The Black Death, a contagious disease affecting the lungs or lymph nodes and leaving the sick or dead with a purple coloring (hence the name "black"), was a danger throughout the Middle Ages, making its worst strike between the years 1348–1351, when it killed between one-quarter and one-third of Europe's population (Lynch, *The Medieval Church*, 308).

Further Reading

Alighieri, Dante. *The Divine Comedy* Vols. 1–3. Trans. Dorothy Sayers. New York: Basic Books, 1962.

Armstrong, Regis, O.F.M. Cap., and Ignatius Brady, O.F.M. Cap., ed. and trans. *Francis and Clare: The Complete Works.* Mahwah, NJ: Paulist Press, 1982.

LeClerq, Jean, O.S.B. *The Love of Learning and the Desire for God.* Trans. by Catherine Misrahi. New York: Fordham University Press, 1961.

Sumption, Jonathan. *Pilgrimage: An Image of Mediaeval Religion.* Totowa, NJ: Rowman and Littlefield, 1975.

Woods, Richard, O.P. *Mysticism and Prophesy: The Dominican Tradition.* Maryknoll, NY: Orbis Books, 1998.

Chapter 6

The Counter-Reformation: The Age of Imagination

Denis Robinson, O.S.B.

Introduction: The Aftermath of the Reformations

It is difficult to overestimate the effects of the various reform movements of the sixteenth century on Church life and spirituality. When Martin Luther nailed his theses of protest on the door of the college church at Wittenberg on October 31, 1517, he can scarce have imagined that the hammer strokes would reverberate across the continent of Europe, and even into the New World. Of course, Luther's impulse to reform certain aspects of Church life were not new. For almost two hundred years, various Church leaders had come forward to protest what they saw as the problems of the Church. Such issues as corruption among the clergy, the lack of independent spirituality in the laity, the continued use of Latin as the official language in Church life, and the growing distance between the concerns of theologians and those of average Christians were at the center of many local movements. The Lollards, for example, gained a great deal of notoriety in England under the leadership of John Wyclif (ca. 1324–84). Wyclif had stressed the importance of cultivating a personal spirituality. Another important idea was the availability of the Bible in English in order that those who were able could read it in their own language.

The difference between earlier, local efforts to reform the Church and the virtual revolution instigated by Luther in 1517 was Luther's more universal appeal. The time was right for reform, and reform was certainly needed in many aspects of Church life. Political structures in various nations were growing stronger and were able to assert more independence of thought and action. There was widespread dissatisfaction with Church authorities, particularly over questions of taxation and a lack of education and morality among the clergy. The idea of "personal" spirituality apart from the formal structures of the Church had been taking hold at least since the fourteenth century, when the catastrophic event of the Black Death had introduced a kind of "lifeboat ethic" to European culture. During this time the spiritual movement known as *Devotio Moderna* developed and became widespread. *Devotio Moderna* stressed the importance of private prayer and developing a relationship with God. The ideas of *Devotio Moderna* were disseminated through popular literature in local languages that emphasized private devotions and personal piety. The classic of this period was *The Imitation of Christ* by Thomas à Kempis.

An important contributor to the success of the Reformation and the spread of its ideas was the invention of the movable-type printing press by Johann Gutenberg in the middle of the fifteenth century. With books and pamphlets more readily available and in the language of the people (rather than ecclesiastical Latin), new ideas were able to spread faster than ever. The new printing technology also gave more people access to the Bible and other devotional literature in unprecedented ways.

Other reformations followed in the wake of Luther. John Calvin (1509–64) led a reformation of the Church in Geneva. Calvin's principles of Bible study, personal piety, hard work, and sober living caught the imagination of many who were searching for a more intense, focused, and serious expression of Christianity. Calvin's close associate John Knox (1513–72) brought the reforms instituted in Geneva to Scotland. Ulrich Zwingli (1484–1531) led a more radical branch of the reformation in Zurich. Both Calvin and Zwingli preached a simplified Church with congregational governance, a dramatically reduced sacramental life, and a strong emphasis on personal spirituality, modesty, and morals.

In England, the crisis of the proposed divorce of King Henry VIII set off a religious upheaval that would not be settled for over a century. Through four Tudor monarchs, the English Church vacillated between Protestant and Catholic identities before finally settling on a middle way, a *via media* which satisfied no one completely. The result was a civil war between the Crown and the Calvinist Puritans which changed the complexion of English Church life forever. In France, civil strife, likewise, dictated the course of religious developments, with France finally settling on a primarily Roman Catholic identity and becoming the center of a great religious revival in the seventeenth century.

The response of the Catholic Church to these reforming movements was at first somewhat tepid. The Council of Trent (1545–63) in many ways solidified the theological and spiritual traditions held by the Catholic Church since the period of the early Church. Protestant theology was responded to in doctrinal formulae. In the area of spirituality, however, the Catholic Church experienced its own radical renewal, inspired by the proximity of the devout and serious Protestants.

From the standpoint of spirituality, the Protestant reformations had a number of common characteristics. First, they promoted the spirituality of the individual. According to Protestant thought, the individual was perfectly capable of cultivating and maintaining a relationship with God on his or her own. Second, the Church existed to promote the spiritual development of the person, not as a necessary conduit of God's grace, as Catholics held. Third, this spiritual development came through reading, by living an upright and sober life, and through intense private prayer. Finally, these developments were the results of the newly emphasized role of imagination, which was able to visualize religious realities in individual lives rather than understand those realities solely through doctrinal teachings that demanded assent. Religious truth was now open to all *in the very context of their everyday lives.* Monastic spiritualities began to fade in favor of spirituality in the midst of the world, one that had an impact not only on the religious "professional" but on the average Christian as well.

Spanish Fervor

The first center of Catholic spiritual renewal was solidly Catholic Spain. The sixteenth century was a remarkable period for Spain, both culturally and politically. A strong, highly centralized government whose authority spread throughout much of Western Europe kept Spain resolutely Catholic while many of its neighbors struggled with religious controversies. The wealth of Spain was also greatly increased during this period by the voyages of conquest to the New World. American gold fueled the engine of the Spanish economy, allowing for a resurgence of art, music, and literature that had been without precedence in the Iberian peninsula. Power, militarism, and a fierce sense of Catholic identity became the hallmarks of the renewal of Catholic spirituality in Spain.

Soldiers for Christ: St. Ignatius of Loyola and the Jesuits

The central figure in the flowering of Spanish spirituality in the post-Reformation period was a man whose influence would become of paramount importance in the history of the modern Church. Saint Ignatius of Loyola (ca. 1491–1556) was a Basque nobleman whose early career as a soldier was cut short by a wound he received at the Siege of Pamplona in 1521. During the period of his recovery, he encountered a collection of the lives of the saints and a *Life of Christ* by Ludolf of Saxony, a popular work of imaginative piety in which the gospel stories were embellished with commentaries. Through reading these works, St. Ignatius was converted and decided to do penance for his sins by making a pilgrimage to Jerusalem. He began his quixotic spiritual odyssey at the Benedictine monastery of Montserrat where he hung up his weapons and put on the sackcloth of a penitent. He lived as a beggar for a year. At Manresa he began writing the spiritual classic that would change Catholic spirituality from that point forward, *The Spiritual Exercises*. In 1523, St. Ignatius arrived in Jerusalem, where he remained for two weeks before returning to Spain. He then began a period of study in philosophy and theology that took him finally to Paris. There in 1534, with six friends and fellow students, he formed the Society of Jesus with the goal of returning to Jerusalem to do charitable work. In the end they only made it as far as Rome. In 1540, the Society received papal approval and St. Ignatius spent his last years as superior of the rapidly expanding movement.

The Society of Jesus, or Jesuits as they are popularly known, constituted a new way of living the religious life. They were well-educated priests who did not reside in monasteries, but worked in the world, providing spiritual enrichment, pastoral service, and education wherever they happened to be. They quickly also became missionaries, spreading the Gospel through the Society to every corner of the known world. The fervor of the group was in large part due to the military zeal of the founder. They envisioned themselves as soldiers for Christ and missionaries, not only to the parts of the world where the Gospel had yet to be preached, but also to those parts of Europe where Protestant movements had taken hold. In these endeavors they brought what they perceived as the basic tool for Christian renewal in every place, *The Spiritual Exercises.*

The Spiritual Exercises constitute one of the most influential works in modern Christian spirituality. Their immense popularity is attested to by the thousands today who still avail themselves of the program presented therein to deepen their spiritual lives. The exercises are methods of prayer that can be done in private by individuals or in the context of a retreat and spiritual direction at a Jesuit center. The work is built around the practice of imaginative contemplation. Four weeks of exercises focus on specific themes found in the gospels. Week One considers the purpose of life. Week Two presents the life of Christ. Week Three asks the individual to meditate on the Passion and death of Christ. The fourth week considers the resurrection of Christ. In all of these exercises, the use of the imagination is central. The one praying is required to place himself or herself in the presence of Jesus, to imagine what it would be like to have been at Cana, or on the road to Emmaus, for example. In these exercises of the imagination, the goal is for the individual to learn to live more fully the Christian life by discerning what God wants him or her to do. By physically imagining oneself in the presence of God, the voice of God and God's call become clearer. The outcome of the exercises is not merely to have a better relationship with God, but also to *do* something. It is contemplation in action. In a highly imaginative age, the exercises represented the spiritual expression of a cultural ideal.

An important point to consider, however, is that for St. Ignatius, while the exercises were highly personal and significant to the development of a deeper relationship with God, they were never accomplished in isolation from the broader community of the Church or outside of the formal relationship that one had with a spiritual director. The task of the spiritual director was to reinforce positive development and check any errors of thinking or wrong turns on the spiritual journey. This intimate connection with the Church, the sacraments, and the community would become the hallmark of Jesuit spirituality.

Mystical Union with God:
St. Teresa of Avila and St. John of the Cross

The Jesuits were very influential in the development of the spiritual life of one of the other great figures of the Spanish spiritual renewal,

St. Teresa of Avila (1515–82). Like St. Ignatius, her initial conversion experience came as a result of an illness she suffered and the reading of a book. In St. Teresa's case the book was *The Spiritual Alphabet* by Francisco Osuna, a guide to contemplative prayer. In 1554, she began to experience a series of mystical visions that were extremely corporeal and, indeed, graphic in nature. During these visions she heard the voice of God and experienced God's presence in very physical ways. Initially her confessors believed that she might be possessed by the devil. Eventually she came under the influence of spiritual directors who encouraged her to write down the visions in the form of a spiritual autobiography. Several times she came under the scrutiny of Church authorities. In 1565, she founded a monastery of Carmelite nuns in Avila. While the Carmelites had existed since the twelfth century, it was the reforms of St. Teresa that made the order more prominent. Her more ascetical ideals about religious life, symbolized in the barefoot or "discalced" condition of her sisters, seized the imagination of an age looking for more fervor in living the Christian life. She later founded over a dozen monasteries across Spain. For the nuns she wrote *The Interior Castle*, a significant work in the history of Christian thought. She died in 1582 and was declared a saint in 1622 and Doctor of the Church in 1970.

The Interior Castle is a highly creative work in which the soul is presented in the image of seven rooms of a mansion. The journey of the soul consists in moving from room to room where one encounters various aspects of Christian life: penance, apostolic service, contemplation, love of neighbor, desolation and pain, and finally union with God. This union is central to St. Teresa's thought and she described it as a kind of "spiritual marriage." The work is very complex and St. Teresa acknowledges that the passage of each person will be different and specific to his or her personality and life experiences. With this emphasis on a personal relationship with God and its very intimate, even physical nature, St. Teresa made a lasting contribution to the development of Spanish spirituality. While no less fervent than that of St. Ignatius, she shied away from the more public, militant spirituality of the Jesuits in favor of interiority and familiarity with God.

Unlike St. Ignatius and St. Teresa, St. John of the Cross (1542–91) came from an impoverished family. Under St. Teresa's influence he became a reformer of the men's branch of the Carmelites, which he had joined in 1563. For a time, St. John was spiritual director in St.

Teresa's monastery at Avila. In 1577, he was imprisoned by members of his order who opposed his reforms. In prison St. John wrote his classic poem *The Spiritual Canticle*, using imagery from the Song of Songs. He later composed another pivotal work, *The Dark Night*, in which he described, again in highly imaginative terms, the seasons of the spiritual life, its inevitable ups and downs, and the way to determine or discern the presence of God. His beautiful writings place him among the greatest Spanish poets, and his insights into the soul among the greatest spiritual guides. He died in 1591 and was proclaimed a saint in 1627. Like his friend St. Teresa, he was also named a Doctor of the Church.

The enthusiastic renewal of Catholic spirituality in Spain in the sixteenth century was energized by the presence of these dynamic personalities. The importance of a personal appropriation of the mysteries of faith and an intense relationship with God were common to their thought. The use of written works to spread their ideas was crucial so that they became great literary figures as well. Their mark on the development of Catholic spirituality continues to be felt into the twenty-first century.

The Golden Age of Catholic Spirituality

The seventeenth century in France has been called the "Golden Age of Catholic Spirituality." By the beginning of the century, the revival of Catholic enthusiasm in Spain was beginning to wane. Saint Ignatius himself had actually founded his community in Paris. During this period, France experienced a resurgence in the Catholic imagination, largely fueled by the examples of several important women and men whose ideas and spiritual principles would change Catholic spirituality forever.

One reason for the growing interest on the part of Catholics in spiritual matters was the proximity of their serious and sincere Protestant neighbors. In the late sixteenth century, civil wars over religion plagued France. Families were divided against one another. Members of the nobility, too, were divided between the ruling Catholic party (represented by the king and his immediate courtiers) and those who identified with the Calvinist Huguenots. An iconic event of this period was the so-called St. Bartholomew's Day Massacre which took place in Paris on August 24, 1572. Several thousand Protestants were killed in one night on the orders of King Charles IX and the Queen Mother, Catherine de Medici. In the following weeks of insurrection, thousands more Protestants lost their lives in regional conflicts set off by the events in Paris. This internecine strife continued until 1598 when King Henry IV ratified the Edict of Nantes, which provided for religious tolerance in France. Catholics and Protestants, at last, could live together in peace.

The example of patience, suffering, and often the sacrifice of life exemplified by the Huguenots had a lasting effect on French Catholics. Many Catholics in France began to take their faith more seriously because of the examples of their Protestant compatriots. Some began to wonder if a more purposeful spiritual life were not only desirable but also possible. Their Protestant compatriots read the Bible and other religious literature. They prayed with fervor. They lived lives of ascetical simplicity, fasting, abstaining from drink and many of the worldly pleasures that Catholics took for granted. They dressed with modesty and raised their families to be good Christians, parents often taking in hand their children's education. They also seemed to thrive socially and economically, working diligently and forging important alliances with their coreligionists.

Catholics were soon seeking to follow their example and renewal movements began to emerge in France in copious measure. Many monasteries and religious communities were reformed. Many new orders, often focusing on the importance of personal prayer and the performance of works of charity, began to spring up. Everywhere members of the laity began to flock to Catholic preachers and spiritual directors who represented this new emphasis on the importance of prayer, reading, and an ascetical life. The Catholic Church was entering a new phase in France, one that would continue more or less until the cataclysmic events of the French Revolution at the end of the eighteenth century.

St. Francis de Sales

The figure who overshadowed this century of illustrious spiritual leaders was St. Francis de Sales (1567–1622). Saint Francis was born to a noble family and was educated in Paris and Padua. He studied law in Italy before being ordained a priest in 1593. Just nine years later he was named bishop of Geneva. Because Geneva was the epicenter of the Calvinist movement, St. Francis was never to serve in his diocese but lived instead at Annecy, near the border of France and Switzerland. As bishop-in-exile, St. Francis devoted a great deal of his energy to spiritual direction, reading, and writing. He became increasingly interested in the reform of religious life and promoting the spirituality of lay people in the Church. He read extensively the works of the Spanish reformers, St. Teresa of Avila and St. John of the Cross. Becoming intrigued by their programs of spiritual renewal, he composed his most famous work, *An Introduction to the Devout Life*, in 1609. The work was written for lay people, particularly St. Jeanne de Chantal, a prominent widow he had met five years earlier in Dijon. Their spiritual friendship would bear great fruit in the ensuing years. In 1610, the two founded the Visitation Sisters at Annecy. The order quickly spread and took firm root in Paris. In 1616, St. Francis wrote his second great spiritual work, *Treatise on the Love of God*, for the Visitation Sisters. After a long and energetic ministry, St. Francis de Sales died in 1622.

The spiritual ideas of St. Francis were contained in what became one of the most popular works of the seventeenth century, *An Introduction to the Devout Life*. The book begins with the injunction that became his spiritual motto: "Live Jesus!" The work explored the possibility of a profound spiritual life for every Catholic and the way in which lay people could experience the fullness of that life in the midst of daily cares and concerns. For St. Francis, the spiritual life was a response to the call of God received in baptism. The book stressed the very practical things that people should do in order to cultivate God's presence within them. These included daily prayers and recollections, meditation following a particular method, regular reception of the Eucharist, and seeking the advice of a competent spiritual director.

Saint Francis promoted in his writings a method of prayer now called the "Salesian Method" that stressed the importance of the human imagination in a relationship with God. The method was very practical and consisted of four steps. First, the individual should prepare himself or herself by reading a passage from the Bible or recalling a biblical story while asking for God's assistance. The second step involves reflection on the story or scene by which the imagination of the individual helps make an application to his or her life or situation. Third, the meditating person makes specific resolutions on ways to live a more Christlike life. Finally, a prayer of thanksgiving is offered. The importance of this method is that it is not restricted to specific times of prayer. Rather, St. Francis encouraged practitioners to reflect on the resolutions and the blessings received throughout the day. In that way, prayer became a part of the rituals of daily life, rather than isolated instances of communication with God.

In the course of his ministry, St. Francis influenced thousands of men and women. His practical approach to prayer and the spiritual enrichment of lay people continues to have an impact on spirituality today.

Pierre de Bérulle

Another important figure in the development of the French school of spirituality was Pierre de Bérulle (1575–1629). Bérulle came from an aristocratic family and received a first-class education, establishing himself as both a competent scholar and a man of intense personal spirituality. In 1604, only five years after his ordination to the priesthood, he founded, along with his spiritual friend and companion, Madame Acarie, a group of Carmelite monasteries for women inspired by the reforms of St. Teresa of Avila. Nine years later, Bérulle founded his own order of men, which became known as the Oratory of Jesus Christ. He used as his model for this new community the Oratories founded in Italy by St. Philip Neri. Like St. Francis de Sales, Bérulle was an important and influential figure, particularly in the French court. His writings and spiritual programs centered on a profound identification between the individual and the incarnate Christ, or Christ as he lived in the world. For Bérulle, the goal of the Christian was to follow the example set by Christ when he was active in his ministry. In Bérulle's mind, this involved the complete negation of the importance attached to self. Worldly influence and authority counted for nothing. All that mattered was living a humble, Christlike life. The first step was to engage in a rigorous program of ascetical practices. Fasting, abstinence, long vigils of prayer, and even physical depravations helped turn the heart of the person to a total dependence on Christ. In these endeavors, the mother of Jesus, Mary, was central because of her example. Mary gave birth to the Incarnate Word. She could also aid the follower of Jesus to spiritually "give birth" to Christ's presence in the contemporary world. This spiritual project involved the individual Christian imaginatively picturing the way in which Jesus and his mother lived in order to emulate their actions.

Bérulle's ideas were very influential and his reputation was widespread. Aside from his activities as a spiritual director and writer, he was actively involved in the reform of the training of priests in French seminaries. When Bérulle founded the Oratory, his idea was that the renewal of holiness in the priesthood would have an effect on the lives of lay people. Priests were urged to consider the quality of their interior lives and to deepen their relationship with Christ by way of prayer, devotion to the liturgical worship of the Church, and daily spiritual exercises. Three times a day the priest was to undergo a rigorous self-examination, comparing his life to that of Jesus. Again, the use of the imagination was paramount, calling on the priest to place himself in the presence of Jesus as Jesus went about his earthly life. Renewal of the clergy became a priority in this golden age. Continuing the example established by Bérulle, many of his followers, such as Jean-Jacques Olier, St. Jean Eudes, and St. Vincent de Paul, sought a renewal of Church life at every level, beginning with priests. Prominent among seminary reformers was Jean-Jacques Olier (1608–57), a popular preacher who conducted missions throughout France before becoming pastor of the church of St. Sulpice in Paris. There Olier founded a seminary for the preparation of priests and wrote spiritual works for the edification of his parishioners. The most important of these was *An Introduction to Christian Life and Virtues*. Olier believed that the renewal of Church life was to be accomplished on two fronts, the preparation of spiritually enriched priests and the development of the personal spirituality of lay people. Like St. Francis de Sales, Olier promoted a highly imaginative spiritual program that stressed the importance of *seeing* Jesus with a spiritual eye and acting in ways that he would have acted. When Olier died in 1657, he left a dramatically renewed Church in the lives of both priests and parishioners.

St. Vincent de Paul

One of the most popular and inspiring figures from this period of Church renewal in France was St. Vincent de Paul (1581–1660). Saint Vincent was born in southern France to poor parents in 1581. After his ordination, he went to Paris where he was influenced by Bérulle, Olier, and most significantly, St. Francis de Sales. Saint Vincent always viewed his ministry as involving service to the poor. For seven years he worked among prisoners who were responsible for rowing navy ships. He preached extensively in rural areas among the agricultural workers. His simple manner and peasant-like appearance endeared him to the populations of both country and city. In Paris he founded the Congregation for the Mission, popularly known today as the Vincentians. This group of priests was dedicated to popular preaching, teaching, assisting the poor, and preparing priests. Service to the poor became a hallmark of St. Vincent's spiritual program. Seeing Christ in the suffering and the needy aided people in understanding the meaning of spirituality in their lives. To this end, St. Vincent founded a series of confraternities for work among the urban and rural poor. Members of these groups, who were lay people, united their lives of prayer and meditation with practical endeavors such as feeding the hungry and finding proper shelter for the homeless.

This emphasis on practical Christianity also prompted St. Vincent to found, with his spiritual companion, St. Louise de Marillac, the Daughters of Charity, a group of women religious who devoted themselves to practical labors such as charity work and nursing. This new religious order proved something of a revolution in that most groups of religious women until that time were cloistered, or enclosed within the confines of a monastery or convent, devoting themselves exclusively to contemplative prayer and removed from the cares of the world. The Daughters of Charity, however, were concerned with serving those in need in a very public ministry, providing a blueprint for many groups that would follow.

The Sacred Heart

Under the influence of these various individuals and the groups they founded, French spirituality thrived. Among the laity it became enshrined in an increasingly devotional expression. The most important and long-lasting of these observances was the development of devotion to the Sacred Heart of Jesus. Saint Jean Eudes (1601–80), like St. Vincent de Paul who strongly influenced him, was convinced that the best way to be a Christian was to both pray and work for the betterment of society. In the various men's and women's groups that he founded, he encouraged members to unite their hearts with the hearts of Jesus and Mary. This image of the heart of Jesus grew out of the experience of imaginative prayer encouraged by all the spiritual leaders of the golden age. This prayer involved placing oneself at the heart of biblical stories and identifying with the characters, particularly their feelings at crucial moments in the gospels. Uniting oneself to the heart of Jesus allowed the person to love and experience compassion as Jesus did. The heart of Jesus, like the heart of the person, was the center of experience, devotion, and the power to love. In 1673, a sister of the Visitation Order began having a series of visions. Saint Margaret Mary Alacoque (1647–90) experienced intense visions of Jesus' Passion and heart over a period of several years.

In these visions, St. Margaret Mary was invited by Jesus to unite her heart to his in a single act of love, and she saw Jesus opening his heart (surrounded by a crown of thorns) as a gesture of love to the world. Devotion to the Sacred Heart of Jesus spread and was honored with a special celebration in the Church beginning in 1685. The Sacred Heart was a particular manifestation of the highly corporeal and imaginative spirituality that thrived in France during this golden age.

The Golden Age of Catholic Spirituality was a particularly fertile period in which the spiritual lives of lay people were promoted and sustained by the example and writings of some of the greatest figures in the history of the Church. The centrality of personal prayer, devotion, spiritual direction, and apostolic work in cultivating the Christian life led many to a deeper experience of religion. The emphasis given to the importance of the imagination in making the realities of faith more vivid in the life of Christians was stressed, even in a very physical way. The effects of this revolution in spiritual life are still being experienced in the Church today.

Breakdowns in Imagination

The fervor of Catholics in seventeenth-century France, in the long run, proved to be a two-edged sword. While the rising awareness of ordinary Christians to the practice of faith and a more intense experience of religious life was pronounced, this period also saw some Catholics going to extremes in expressing their Christian identity. Two movements that emerged during this period have had a lasting effect on the Church: Jansenism and Quietism. In both instances, the leaders and members of these groups were seeking the same goals and ideals as their contemporaries. However, in the long term, they were led to extremes of devotion and ascetic and penitential practices that strayed from the mainstream. In the end they amounted to a breakdown in the power of the imagination so rightly stressed among many of the golden age figures, resulting in isolation from the life of the Church and a spiritual elitism that the institutional Church had to finally attempt to suppress.

Jansenism

Jansenism was a complex phenomenon having theological, spiritual, and political implications. As a popular spiritual movement it became widespread during the seventeenth and eighteenth centuries. Theologically,

Jansenism began with the posthumous publication of a work on the theology of St. Augustine by a bishop of the Low Countries named Cornelius Jansen (1585–1638). Jansen's book, published by his admirers and some former students, was called simply *Augustinus*, or *Augustine*. It appeared in 1640 and caused an immediate stir because of its teachings on questions of grace and penance. Condemned in many quarters, including Rome, the work was championed by a group of Cistercian nuns from France who favored Jansen's rather austere (some would say Calvinist) ideas about the difficulty of salvation and the need for extreme asceticism and penance in Christian life. The reform of the Abbey of Port Royal, located just outside of Paris, began in earnest under the influence of its sixteen-year-old abbess, Angelique Arnauld (1591–1661). Mere Angelique, as she was known, wished to return her monastery and its sisters to a more "primitive" observance of the Rule of Saint Benedict which they followed. The principles of this reform included an extremely ascetical way of life, fasting, corporal acts of penance, an intense focus on prayer, infrequent communion, and an attitude of contempt for the world. They also placed a great deal of emphasis on the primacy of the individual conscience in following moral decisions. The centrality of conscience led them into difficulties with both Church and civil authorities when they refused to accept the official condemnations of the book of Bishop Jansen, *Augustinus*.

Making the situation more tense was the reality that the nuns of Port Royal, because of their particular attitude toward an intensified Christian spirituality, had attracted a great deal of attention. Noblewomen went to the monastery for spiritual renewal. Many men, including most members of the prominent Arnauld family, attached themselves to the monastery as *solitaires* or hermits who likewise devoted themselves to a penitential way of life. The men founded a prominent school for boys and the sisters operated a very successful school for girls. In short, their influence on society at the time was pronounced. The authorities considered it to be a dangerous influence. Both Church and state went to great lengths to suppress the spiritual practices of the so-called Jansenists. The nuns were frequently deprived of the sacraments of the Church for extended periods of time because they would not agree to the condemnation of Jansen's teachings. At one point many of the sisters were imprisoned, and finally the monastery was suppressed and its buildings torn down on the authority of King

Louis XIV. However, even these extreme measures failed to suppress the movement completely. Aspects of Jansenist spirituality reemerged in the Low Country as many of its adherents were exiled from France. Its central ideas were popularized in the writings of the philosopher Blaise Pascal (1623–62) whose sister was a member of the Port Royal community and whose important works, *Pensees* (Thoughts) and *The Provincial Letters*, supported the Jansenist ideals of retreat from the world and even from the Church in pursuit of an intense private vision of God through a life of self-denial.

The problem with the spirituality of Jansenism was not in its intensity, but in many ways with its lack of imagination. For the Jansenists, there was no room for opinions on the spiritual life other than their own. The Church was considered superfluous and indeed could be very mistaken in its public opinions and attitudes. The seclusion of the individual in a kind of penitential or ascetical cocoon had the effect of secluding him or her from the imaginative richness of what the Church could teach in relationship to the spiritual life, precisely because it was not cut off from the world but, rather, immersed in it.

Quietism

Another movement that emerged in France during this period of intense development in the spiritual life was Quietism. Like Jansenism, Quietism came to thrive in the same environment that more mainstream spiritual ideas were developed. The origins of Quietism are found in the writings of the Spanish priest, Miguel de Molinos (1640–96). Molinos's *Spiritual Guide*, published in 1675, caused a great deal of controversy among the Roman authorities for its assertion that the heights of spiritual accomplishment and union with God could be obtained completely outside the structures of the Church. The full development of the interior life even allowed the individual to remove himself or herself from the moral law of the Church, allowing illicit acts to be practiced because, as Molinos held, the soul was so far above the body as to not be aware of the body's actions. This strange assertion seemed to have caught the imagination of a number of Molinos's spiritual charges, including a French woman, Marie Jeanne de Guyon (1648–1717). Madame de Guyon was responsible for the import of Molinos's rather odd principles into France, particularly through her publication of *Short and Easy Method of Prayer*, a work she introduced to the French Court and its leading spiritual light, François Fénelon (1651–1715), a bishop and tutor of the heir to the throne of France. Guyon and Fenelon spread the teachings of Quietism throughout the court. Madame de Guyon's book and Fenelon's *Maxims of the Saints* became wildfire best sellers. The basic teachings of these works were: 1) an emphasis on the primacy of a personal and intense relationship with God; 2) that God's will could be known through ascetical practices, prayer, and discernment; and 3) that Church teachings and the sacraments are only "stepping stones" to an authentic spiritual relationship with God. This led the individual to a "quiet" or indifferent attitude to the institutional Church. For its part, the institution, reaffirming the necessity of community and sacramental participation for a full Christian life, condemned Quietism in 1687 and 1699. Like Jansenism, however, its influence continued to be felt in the Church for many years afterward.

Conclusions

This brief look at the development of Catholic spiritual thought and practice after the Reformation has focused on the important personalities who helped to shape that thought and whose influence continues to be felt today. The common theme that these writers and reformers shared was the importance of the imagination in the development of the spiritual life. Like their Protestant counterparts, Catholics hoped that through the imagination individuals could develop more intense, personal relationships with the Divine. Reading and spiritual direction played an important role in this project. Unlike Protestants, however, these thinkers also asserted the importance of living this project of personal enhancement within the context of the Church, community life, teaching, and sacramental worship.

Further Reading

Bilinkoff, Jodi. *The Avila of Saint Teresa: Religious Reform in a Sixteenth-Century City*. Ithaca, NY: Cornell University Press, 1989.

Bireley, Robert. *The Refashioning of Catholicism, 1450–1700: A Reassessment of the Counter-Reformation*. Washington, DC: Catholic University of America Press, 1999.

Dupré, Louis, and Don E. Saliers, eds. *Christian Spirituality III: Post-Reformation and Modern*. World Spirituality Series 18. New York: Crossroad, 1991.

Evennett, Outram. *The Spirit of the Counter-Reformation.* Ed. by John Bossy. Notre Dame, IN: University of Notre Dame Press, 1968.

Hsia, R. Po-Chia. *World of Catholic Renewal, 1540–1770.* New Approaches to European History 30. 2d ed. Cambridge: Cambridge University Press, 2005.

Jones, Martin D. W. *The Counter-Reformation: Religion and Society in Early Modern Europe.* Cambridge Topics in History. New York: Cambridge University Press, 1995.

Chapter 7

Ordinary Life and Contemplation: Prayer in the Modern Period

Harry Hagan, O.S.B., Christian Raab, O.S.B., and Thomas Gricoski, O.S.B.

In the eighteenth century, the philosophical and scientific movements of the Enlightenment exalted reason as the sole criterion for knowledge. In the early nineteenth century, Romanticism made feeling the touchstone of reality. The Enlightenment valued its understanding of fact and order, objectivity and natural law. Romanticism prized individual experience, spontaneity, and nature. While seemingly standing in contrast to each other, both movements, in fact, drew on the ideas of René Descartes, who made the individual self into the primary arbiter of reality. As a result, the concerns of the individual person have become a hallmark of the Modern Age.

The French Revolution is the first great moment of the Modern Age. Born of the Enlightenment, it celebrated *"liberté, égalité, et fraternité"* but quickly became a "reign of terror." Nevertheless, the emerging democratic themes of the Modern Age, typified by the American and French revolutions, were not lost in the life of the Church. Although not a democracy, the Church set these egalitarian themes into the more ancient and authentic Christian context of Christian freedom, the equality that all have in Christ as children of God, and the true community of the Church, the Body of Christ. If in an earlier age, sanctity seemed reserved for the specialist or elite, the Church of the Modern Age has sought to make plain the dignity and ministry of all the baptized. The Second Vatican Council has given these ideas a definitive statement in *Lumen Gentium,* which calls the Church "the People of God" and insists on "the universal call to holiness." The remainder of this chapter explores the development of this call in various contexts.

The Celebration of the Mass: The Personal and the Communal

During the nineteenth century, the Church continued to live off the achievement of the Counter-Reformation with its emphasis on the interior life nourished by the Romantic spirit that rose up in the early 1800s. Romanticism emphasized strong emotion and private religious experience that could create, feed, and sustain the feeling self. The Middle Ages, so despised by the Enlightenment, became for Romanticism the ideal age because of its chivalry and clarity of faith. By the 1850s, Gothic architecture had become the model for both Catholic and Protestant churches alike. The soaring Gothic cathedral seemed to capture the transcendent in the midst of a rational and increasing mechanistic world.

The Mass is the touchstone of Catholic prayer in every age, and in the nineteenth century Catholics focused on the sacrificial offering of the Body and Blood of Christ joined to the saving mystery of Calvary. The Mass was celebrated as either a high Mass with music or a low Mass without music. The high Mass was meant to move people with its grand music and stately gesture, while the low Mass fed the interior spiritual life with its almost silent recitation of the Latin and its action mostly hidden from a congregation that rarely took communion. The Mass was especially a time for personal prayer and adoration. Outside of Mass, many devotions flourished as concrete expressions to move people and feed their personal piety. The devotion to the Blessed Mother, always important in the life of the Church, emphasized her role as mother of us all and so the source of mercy and care.

Early in the twentieth century, Pius X set in motion a liturgical movement that would change the celebration of the Mass. First, he called for frequent communion and lowered the age for First Communion from about fourteen years old to seven. The Blessed Sacrament had been the object of distant devotion, but now people began to receive communion so frequently that it became the ordinary moment of union with God. Second, Pius X reaffirmed Gregorian chant as the music of the Church and, more important, he called for the congregation to participate in the singing. These innovations fed the liturgical movement of the mid-century, which worked for the "full, active participation" of the faithful in the liturgy. With this developed a rich sense of the Church year that celebrates the mysteries of Christ and culminates in the solemn cele-bration of the paschal mystery in the Triduum: Holy Thursday, Good Friday, and Easter. The popular prayer of the Western Church had for so many centuries focused on the crucifixion, and churches filled on Good Friday. The liturgical movement reasserted the importance of the whole paschal mystery, especially as celebrated at the Easter vigil, which draws together the Old Testament themes of creation and the Red Sea with baptism and resurrection. This initiative came to fruition in the vernacular liturgy of the Second Vatican Council.

The hope of Vatican II has not been fulfilled in every instance. At times, a sense of mystery has disappeared in too much familiarity that produced no intimacy. Some people, with little or no sense of the lit-urgy, have made arbitrary changes. Sometimes what should have been sacred has been rendered pedestrian and prosaic. Music is a good ex-ample. Some wonderful new music has appeared to support the English hymn tradition, but not all has been worthy of these sacred celebrations. Some people have sought to return to the past, to the "old Latin Mass," as an antidote. Often they have sought the practice of the recent past and have not recognized that many of the innovations of Vatican II are actually a return to the more ancient practices of the Church. How-ever, nostalgia of any kind is not the reason for the changes of Vatican II. The liturgical reform of the twentieth century has sought to involve the whole praying community in the prayer of Christ and to make each Sunday a celebration of Easter. As such, the liturgical reforms have worked against the modern focus on the individual by emphasizing the Church as community.

Though there have been some shifts in emphasis, Catholics under-stand the Eucharist to be perfect prayer. It is perfect listening and perfect speaking. It is perfect listening because in the Eucharist we receive God perfectly in Christ even if we do not quite understand the mystery, for we receive his body and blood. The Word of God becomes flesh, and we enter into bodily union with him. The Eucharist is also perfect speaking. God speaks to us in the Word proclaimed within the community even though we do not always hear perfectly. In the Eucharist the priest exercises the priesthood of Christ for the priestly people of God by offering the prayer of Christ himself. In this we as Church offer our needs and gifts, our thanks and praise, our laments and sorrows through Jesus Christ who joins them to his perfect sacrifice, for he is the one true mediator to God the Father. The Eucharist then is the perfect prayer joining humanity to God and God to humanity. For this reason, the Eucharist was called, by the Second Vatican Council, "the source and summit of the Christian life." In it we are united to Christ in his offering, and we receive him in his sacrament.

Praying the Scriptures

In the early Church, people like Augustine and Basil made the Scriptures such a part of themselves that they quoted the Bible as part of their thinking process. The practice of prayerfully reading the Scriptures became a hallmark of the monastic tradition under the title of *lectio divina* (literally, divine reading), but with the Scriptures in Latin, only the learned had access to the Word of God. Reading the Scriptures became a pillar of the Reformation. The invention of printing made books common, and the desire to read the Bible served as a major force in the development of literacy. In the modern period, many have learned to read, and Catholics, too, have started to read and pray the Scriptures.

The Enlightenment attacked the Bible as a collection of contradictory fables unworthy of credibility. Modern Christian scholars, often led by German Lutherans, used the methods of modern historical-critical scholarship to examine the Scriptures and uncover both the history behind the text and the history of the way in which the Scriptures were assembled. Today we know more about David and his kingdom, which is the history behind the text. We also know more of the various traditions about David, some of which existed in oral forms before being written down. From a historical point of view, the Old and New Testament is a patchwork quilt of many traditions. They, in turn, were gathered together, not so much by individuals as by the community of faith telling and retelling its stories. The Bible, then, is not a homogenous picture but, rather, a presentation of the many facets of God's relationship with us, not unlike the tradition of the Church. The idea of the Scriptures as a book gathered and held by the community of faith fits well with a Catholic understanding of the Scriptures as a book proclaimed and interpreted by the living community of faith.

History, of course, is important to the Judeo-Christian tradition, which believes and proclaims that God acts in history. A historical perspective also helps us to understand the meaning of words, their historical and social context. It also shows us the difference between our world and theirs so that we can avoid reading the Scriptures as just a confirmation of our own understanding and so make God in our own image and likeness.

The historical-critical method is not without its weaknesses. First, perhaps, is its tendency to emphasize the differences and thus to fragment the text into many small, unrelated passages. Second, in an attempt to avoid the problems of private interpretation, this method gives highest value to what the text meant in its first context (its *Sitz im Leben*). However, this context is difficult to reconstruct, and a text often had more than one context during the biblical period. Moreover, Christians and Jews have used these texts for centuries without giving such primacy to the first context. At times, the historical method becomes more interested in the history than in the text.

This method can also be quite technical and hypothetical because there is much we cannot know. The scholarship has, in some instances, turned the Scriptures into knowledge accessible to only the initiated, leaving both clergy and laity afraid to approach the text. Christians, however, have been reading the Scriptures for centuries without the benefit of these insights. And while they can be helpful, they are not necessary for confronting the Word of God in prayerful reading.

Recently, literary scholarship has underlined the power of the Bible as literature that is able to transcend its historical context as both the inspired and inspiring Word of God. Literary scholarship has returned the emphasis to the text itself. Still, modern literary scholarship has often been marked by a "hermeneutics of suspicion" that suspects the text is hiding the truth rather than revealing it. This approach to interpretation is more interested in doubt than in faith. Many recent theories of interpretation have so underlined the primacy of the individual reader and the subjective nature of interpretation that these theories have become a kind of modern "private interpretation of the Scriptures." For Catholics, however, there is no interpretation of the Scriptures apart from the community and the faith of the Church. The creed provides the essential boundaries for all interpretation, and the magisterium—that is, the teaching authority of the Church as exercised by the Holy Father and the college of bishops—guards this faith. Within these boundaries, the possibilities of interpretation are many and varied.

Literary criticism also shares much in common with the early and medieval Church, who read the Scriptures with the imagination of faith. Patristic exegesis, once denigrated as "allegorical," is newly appreciated as a reading of faith that draws on the literary power of Scriptures to discover the connections to Christ. The liturgy particularly is the essential place where Catholics confront the Word of God, for "when the Scriptures are read in the Church, God himself is speaking to his people, and Christ, present in his own word, is proclaiming the gospel."[1] Therefore, the liturgical reform of Vatican II has put this proclamation in the language of the community and has expanded the biblical readings heard by the Church. In the liturgy, all the Scriptures are in some way about Christ, the Word of God, and the liturgical year becomes the essential context for understanding these readings.

The readings designated for Sundays or for weekdays offer individuals a good place to begin studying and praying the Scriptures. While intending to read the whole Bible, readers often begin with Genesis but get bogged down somewhere in Leviticus; so it is best to begin with a gospel or with the Mass readings of the day. Often, the most difficult part of praying the Scriptures is opening the book. If a person can get the book open, then the Spirit will move.

John Henry Newman: Tradition and Development

The modern period is a time of discovery and innovation, but it is also an age seeking to recover the tradition that went before. In the mid-1800s, Jacques Paul Migne (1800–75), a French priest, published 471 large volumes of the Latin and Greek texts by authors from the early Church. It was a monumental achievement based on work that had been going on at least since the beginning of the Renaissance. Still, Migne was able to accomplish this feat because of the romantic fascination with the genius of past ages. The early Church had become a special focus for scholars, and arguably the most important of these scholars

---

[1] *General Instruction of the Roman Missal*, paragraph 29.

was John Henry Newman (1801–90). His influence on the twentieth century has been considerable.

Newman, raised as an Anglican, was part of the Oxford Movement that sought to return to the sources of Scripture and the writings of the early Church. He carefully studied the church fathers, and his search led him into the Catholic Church. He became a great, universal theologian, familiar with the breadth of Christian teaching and life. Much of his writing was delivered as sermons to ordinary Catholics and offered them a practical and pastoral theology. Pope Leo XIII recognized his contribution by making him a cardinal in 1879.

For Newman, personal prayer is always the prayer of the Church, so private prayer leads into and flows out of public, corporate worship. When believers pray in private, they do so as an extension of the prayer that the whole body of believers carries on as an act of public liturgy. The prayer of the people is possible because of the Incarnation of Christ: because the Son of God became the son of Mary the human person and human nature have been elevated to receive unique access to God. Christ in his priesthood opens the way and becomes himself the way to God the Father. It is Christ's prayer that the Church prays as the body of Christ. Not only do the words of the Lord's Prayer become our own, but Christ prays his prayer to the Father in us and through us now. Early Christians gathered not just on Sunday, the memorial of Christ's resurrection, but daily and at various hours each day to fulfill the psalmist's command to pray seven times a day (Ps 119:164) and St. Paul's admonition to pray always (1 Thess 5:17). Though modern Christians would be bored by the length of these ancient liturgies, Newman encourages people of this age to regard their religious services in the same mind as the early Church: corporate worship is a privilege to be anticipated, not a duty to be dreaded.[2]

Newman is not opposed to personal devotion, but he is opposed to a private, individualistic spirituality that seeks independence from the body of believers. The pitfall of modern prayer is a kind of exaggerated romanticism that elevates the emotions as the true arbiter of religious experience and doctrine. Emotions change, however, and emotions are private, while corporate worship is public and true doctrine is not

---

[2] John Henry Newman, "The Daily Service," in *On Prayer and Contemplation*, ed. Matthew Levering (New York: Rowman and Littlefield Publishers, 2005), 132–33.

subject to whimsy. (At the same time, the Christian who has no emotional attachment to Christ does not truly pray!) For a community to cohere, Newman insists on the importance of right doctrine, which is a matter of faith. When everyone agrees on the basic matters of faith, then everyone can pray together in one spirit. For Newman, prayer is grounded on the faith of the community, rather than on the changing emotions of an individual. However, this faith is not static. Though doctrines are immutable, our understanding of them is not, and it is through a life of faith and prayer that all Christians arrive at a deeper understanding and realization of the mysteries of faith. This is true both for the individual and for the Church.

Newman made another contribution to the modern way of prayer, namely, the popularization of various creative media as aids to prayer and faith. Newman, himself more than a theologian, wrote poetry, hymnody, letters, and even a novel as he endeavored to express in words what goes beyond straightforward telling. Because the Incarnation is such a profound mystery in which all else is to be understood, it takes poetry, metaphors, and an active spiritual imagination to approach it. In this way, Newman seeks to draw people of today, by a rich interior experience, out of the confines of their own selves and into the praying community.

For Newman, prayer itself is poetic, speaking with words and pauses, sound and silence, in a creative interplay that makes room for God to speak and encourages the soul to devotion. The event of the Incarnation made a marriage out of heaven and earth, divinity and humanity, in the person of Christ; thus, the public prayer of Christians somehow heals the rift of mind and body, soul and flesh, individuals and their community. In these ways, the Church as a praying body does not merely call on Christ or remember a historical figure. Rather, in the assembly, Christ becomes present to the world again through the Spirit that dwells wherever two or three are gathered in God's name. All who pray exercise the priestly office of Christ and so feed the body of Christ. They cannot be separated from the college of bishops who exercise the kingly role of Christ by governing the Church, nor from the theologians, teachers, and witnesses of the Gospel who exercise the prophetic role of Christ. Newman understood that no group can exist independently of the other two. He emphasized an essentially communal and corporate vision of the Church, where no member can do without all the rest. In all these ways, Newman helped to bind Christians together in prayer and corporate worship, because in Christ we are already one body. Newman created his vision by immersing himself in the richness of the tradition, and this project has continued in many ways during the twentieth century.

This is part of the genius of Thomas Merton (1914–68). A writer and poet like Newman, Merton's spiritual journey began as a personal search for meaning. Like many in the twentieth century, Merton focused on himself and his own identity and self-understanding. This led him to the ancient monastic search for God at the Trappist Abbey of Gethsemani in Kentucky. He went there to pray, that is, to experience God and to understand himself in relationship to this God. From 1951–65 he served as master of students and then master of novices, and for that work he immersed himself in the writings of the early and medieval Church, particularly the monastic authors. He read not to explain the past but to bring the past to bear on the twentieth century. He saw himself as part of a great, living tradition in search of God. In the course of his journey, his movement inward in prayer brought him the grace and power to let go of the self and turn outward in prayer toward the world and its pain, toward its possibilities and glory.

Father Karl Rahner, S.J., and Father Hans Urs von Balthasar: The Movement Outward and Inward

Our theology shapes the way in which we pray. Since it is not possible to survey all the theologians of the last century, we have chosen two thinkers: Karl Rahner, S.J., and Hans Urs von Balthasar. Although these theologians were important in and of themselves, they also represent two large currents in twentieth-century thought that continue to shape our understanding of prayer.[3]

Karl Rahner, S.J., on Prayer

Karl Rahner, S.J., (1904–84) stands as one of the most influential Catholic theologians of the twentieth century, and his impact on the Second Vatican Council was crucial. His theology opens the Christian to

---

[3] A fuller, more complex treatment of the relationship between these two theologians has been written by Rowan Williams, "Balthasar and Rahner" in *The Analogy of Beauty: The Theology of Hans Urs von Balthasar*, ed. John Riches (Edinburgh: T. & T. Clark, 1986), 11–34. Since the publication of this article the author, an eminent scholar, has become the Archbishop of Canterbury.

the revelation of God, both in the Church and in the world. His is a theology of expectation and openness, and this is reflected in the council's move to engage the world and carry on a dialogue with everyone.

Rahner expands the possibilities of prayer by founding his theology on the principle that God speaks exactly in the human world of history and senses. Everything in the world offers us the possibility of revelation. Like Newman, he takes the Incarnation as his foundation and forges a theology of listening and hearing God's Word, which unites the divine and the human. In his work *Hearers of the Word*, Rahner understands the human person as that mixture of spirit and flesh who stands open to a possible revelation from a free God. God, while still other and beyond human understanding, forms the basis of all human activity. God is the infinite horizon against which everything else is seen and understood.

God speaks to us in a way that we as human beings can understand. We are able to hear precisely because we are an incarnate spirit and are able to know things both physical and spiritual. God has graced humanity with the gift of knowing whatever exists, physical and spiritual. Rahner takes his cue from Thomas Aquinas, in the tradition of Aristotle, who argues that all knowledge, even knowledge of spiritual things, is mediated through the senses, through the flesh. When you perceive a chair, you form an idea of the chair. This idea is not exactly a material thing, but it is itself like a spiritual reality. In other words, knowledge of material things happens through spiritual intuition. Likewise, knowledge of spiritual things (God, angels, the soul) is possible only in and through material means. In this way, human knowledge has the dual nature of the incarnation.

Because we cannot know God except through flesh, the Son of God became a fleshy, sensual person while maintaining his divinity. Christ was not born in a vacuum, or at some ideal time and place. Rather, Christ came into the world of human history and physical space. Everything Christ touches becomes a vehicle of God interacting with the world. Through him, the world becomes a sacrament of God's presence and is no longer opposed to the action and knowledge of God. The ramification for the theology of prayer is significant. The place of prayer now is no longer only church or community or family or solitude. Instead, every human endeavor, because it is human as Christ became human, vibrates with the possibility of God speaking through it. If you want to pray, simply attend to whatever is around you or within you, and there God is.

Rahner's theology is an optimistic stance toward creation and the world and is ready to engage and carry on a dialogue with this world. Some, however, have raised concerns about Rahner's optimistic attitude. They are more wary of this world that crucified the Christ. They see forces in the world that would undermine and seduce a naively optimistic Christian. There is some fear that an uncritical openness to the world will cause Christians to lose their specific sense of Christian identity and vocation as they become like everyone else in the modern world. In part, these are some of von Balthasar's concerns.[4]

Hans Urs von Balthasar on Prayer

Hans Urs von Balthasar (1905–88) received a doctorate in German literature before joining the Society of Jesus in 1928. However, he left the Society in 1950 to found with Adrienne von Speyr a secular institute for laity devoted to contemplation. His writings are numerous, and they reflect his Renaissance grasp of Western culture. Trained as a literary critic but never a university professor, he takes beauty as a starting point and seeks to know the beauty of God revealed in Christ. To grasp this, he turns first inward in contemplation before moving outward to engage the world, as he is anxious to do.

His teaching on prayer is contained in a small, though not easy, book called *Prayer.*[5] While others, like Newman, emphasize the importance of communal and liturgical worship in the life of the Church, von Balthasar emphasizes the importance of solitary prayer in feeding and supporting the active works of the Church. Prayer as contemplation, an intimate union with God, is the vision of prayer that most interests von Balthasar.

According to von Balthasar, mystical practice and experience is not limited to priests and vowed religious, as if they shared an exclusive access to God. Rather, every Christian who is drawn to such a prayer has the privilege of placing himself or herself in contact with God. Prayer is a vocation, part of the universal call to holiness, but especially for

---

[4] John Riches, "Hans Urs von Balthasar," in *The Modern Theologians,* ed. David F. Ford, vol. 1 (Oxford: Basil Blackwell, 1989), 237–54, esp. 239.

[5] Hans Urs von Balthasar, *Prayer,* trans. Graham Harrison (San Francisco: Ignatius Press, 1986). A more accessible introduction to meditation is given by von Balthasar in *Christian Meditation,* trans. Mary Theresilde Skerry, S.Sp.S.A.P. (San Francisco: Ignatius Press, 1989).

those who seek God in solitude. This solitary prayer, however, must not ultimately alienate the contemplative from the whole praying assembly. The contemplative is in an intimate relationship with the Lord, just as the Church is the bride of Christ. What the contemplative experiences, however individual and personal and hidden from the rest of the world, is nothing other than God's action and love toward the whole Church and the world. The community of believers is the means by which every individual and the world at large comes to know and receive Christ. Scripture, especially, which is the safeguard of the community of believers, reveals and mediates the knowledge of God to all.

For von Balthasar, the real starting point of contemplation is an attentive listening or reading of the Word of God in the Scriptures. Not all ways of reading or listening are equal, but each serves its own purpose. Von Balthasar sees legitimate needs for an analytical, critical, scientific reading of Scripture that approaches the Word the way a child looks at pieces of a puzzle.[6] There is also the expectant gaze a child gives its mother when hungry. The contemplative approaches Scripture as a hungry child. This contemplation is a kind of listening that does not judge and analyze. Rather, it places the person in the receptive mode, as the one being addressed by God, as the one at whom God gazes.

Prayer is possible because God has chosen freely to speak to humanity and has created us in such a way that "we must hear the word of God if we are to be ourselves."[7] Since we are historical, fleshly, and also spiritual, God speaks in historical, fleshly, and spiritual terms. In other words, God the Father speaks to humanity in the Word of his Son, who took flesh and dwelt among us. As one like us, Christ speaks the spiritual and eternal Word in temporal, historical terms. Hearing the Word is possible precisely because, in taking on our human nature, Christ has taken us into himself.

Hearing the Word of God entails a response to what is heard. Contemplation must go further than listening. Just as Mary, the model of the contemplative, traveled to her kinswoman Elizabeth and brought the incarnate Word out into the world, so also the contemplative, like

---

[6] For an appreciation of "Balthasar's critique of the historical-critical method in all its nuance and *subtlety*—and subtle it is" (141–52), cf. Edward T. Oakes, S.J., "Balthasar's Critique of the Historical-Critical Method," in *Glory, Grace, and Culture: The Work of Hans Urs von Balthasar*, ed. Ed Block Jr. (New York: Paulist Press 2005), 127–49.

[7] von Balthasar, *Prayer*, 33.

Mary, must become an active missionary sharing Christ with others. In contemplation, the disciple receives Christ and is compelled to share Christ with the world.

This description can make it seem that the Christian need only confront the Word of God to be taken up into that Word, and in a way this is true. Still, it is also true that a Christian must be prepared to receive the Word, and at least part of this means knowing what has been revealed to the Church. At the very least, this means knowing and believing the creed because what a Christian finds must be consonant with this Rule of Faith.

In summary, Father Rahner takes an optimistic view and believes that his going out to the world would bring him a revelation of God consonant with the Rule of Faith. Father von Balthasar is less optimistic in his assessment of the world. He stresses the need first to look to the Word of God revealed in the Scriptures and the tradition of the Church before turning out to the world, lest one be co-opted by a secularism that, at its heart, stands in opposition to religion. For Rahner, the world offers the possibility of revelation. Von Balthasar would not deny this, but he is more suspect and worries that Rahner is being naïve. The divergence represents classic themes in the history of theology. One emphasizes the goodness of creation, and the other finds the world a place of sin and sorrow. Saint Paul and St. Augustine saw the sin and sorrow of the world, and they emphasized the victory in Christ coming to redeem the world. For them, human nature was stricken by sin and radically in need of grace. Saint Thomas Aquinas saw the wonder and majesty of creation pointing to the Creator God. He recognized sin but held that human nature could never be completely alienated from the goodness of creation. These distinctions, though too simple if taken by themselves, help us to see two large theological movements that have shaped the Second Vatican Council (Rahner) and the reaction to it (von Balthasar). This tension, seen from a historical perspective, is a classic theme that should be creative for the life of the Church.

Ordinary Life and Contemplation

While the nineteenth and twentieth centuries have seen thinkers such as Newman, Rahner, and von Balthasar develop the theological understanding of prayer, the same period has also included great practical spiritual wisdom from many corners of the Church. A pivotal emphasis for many Catholics has been the importance of integrating prayer and contemplation with ordinary life. Among the figures who highlight this trend in Catholic spirituality are Therese of Lisieux (d. 1897), Charles de Foucauld (d. 1916), and Dorothy Day (d. 1980).

St. Thérèse of Lisieux

Thérèse Martin was born in 1873 to a middle-class French family of five daughters, all of whom would become nuns (four of them, including Thérèse, at Carmel in Lisieux). Thérèse entered the monastery at the age of fifteen. At twenty-two, she contracted tuberculosis, the disease that would kill her only two years later. In recognition of her already deep spirituality, her sisters encouraged her to write an autobiography, summarizing Thérèse's remarkable insights about the spiritual life. The book was *Story of a Soul*. In it, Thérèse described her approach to prayer.

Thérèse understood her teaching as standing in contrast to a kind of Catholicism that emphasized mortification of the flesh and doing great penances for God. Thérèse believed that she was a "little soul," who was loved by God like a child loved by a parent, and that harsh actions were not necessary for her "little way" to God. She employs the images of a child falling asleep in his or her parent's lap and a patient resting confidently in bed while being worked on by a doctor as ways we should envision what happens in prayer. Asked what she said to God when praying, Thérèse responded, "I don't say anything, I just love him!" Her way of trust in the love of God has become known as "the way of spiritual childhood."

Thérèse's prayer is also catholic, meaning it is universal in its scope. For this reason, it is perhaps especially suited to the modern person. The modern world is small. Mass media allows the modern person to have a global consciousness in a way that it was difficult for persons living in previous centuries. Through telephone and Internet, friends maintain relationships across vast distances. Through television and radio, the sufferings and joys of people in one locale can be known by people everywhere. We understand that wars and famines and natural disasters in one part of the world have an effect on us all. This emerging view of the world is affirmed by the words of the Vatican II document *Gaudium et Spes:* "The world is keenly aware of its unity and of mutual interdependence in essential solidarity. . . . The destiny of the human race is viewed as a complete whole, no longer, as it were, in the particular histories of various peoples: now it merges into a complete whole."[8] The global view can and should affect our prayer, especially our petitions. As the twentieth-century American Bishop Fulton Sheen, a television evangelist, has said: "Embrace the world in prayer."

Thérèse is a model of this kind of praying with a global view. A cloistered Carmelite nun, she understood herself as a missionary. She believed that her prayers worked to evangelize people in faraway places. A startled sister once found Thérèse pacing the floor of her monastic cell late at night. When asked what she was doing, Thérèse said, "I am walking for a missionary." She maintained friendships by mail with priests serving in foreign lands, for whom she served as adviser and spiritual sister, and she united her prayer and quiet life lived in a hidden monastery in the French countryside to their apostolic efforts in mission territories. As a result, Thérèse was named patroness of foreign missions by Pope Pius XII in recognition of the efficacy of her hidden prayers for the conversion of the world.

A third point about Thérèse's prayer is that it is sacrificial. Unfortunately, many people have looked at Thérèse's "little way" and understood it to be promoting passivity in the spiritual life. To the contrary, Thérèse's prayer is active. Rather than going out in search of tremendous penances, Thérèse argues for offering to God, through the sacrifice of the Mass, the little things that cause a person suffering throughout the day. In the same vein, rather than exhorting her followers to great works for God, she characteristically says that they should do little things—sweeping the floor, smiling, bearing an annoyance patiently—with great love.

The lasting import of St. Thérèse's spirituality is immeasurable. While her teaching seems simple enough, it arrived on the Christian scene at the right time and helped play a major role in waking up the Catholic faithful to the fact that the fullness of Christian sanctity could be achieved by any kind of person, no matter how "little" and in any state of life. She was named a Doctor of the Church in 1997, and her spiritual teaching has served as a major influence on such notable modern Catholics as St. Elizabeth of the Trinity, Blessed Mother Teresa of

---

[8] *Gaudium et Spes* (Pastoral Constitution on the Church in the Modern World), December 7, 1965, no. 4–5.

Calcutta, Dorothy Day, Thomas Merton, Hans Urs von Balthasar, and Pope John Paul II.

Charles de Foucauld

While Thérèse was living out her "little way" in the Carmelite monastery of Lisieux, Charles de Foucauld (1858–1916), also of France, was developing his ideas for a new approach to religious life. Charles had been a man of the world, a decorated, though decadent, soldier in the French army serving in Africa. Charles returned to the Christian faith of his youth and, shortly thereafter, entered a Trappist monastery, where he stayed for six years. Eventually, he began to receive inspiration for a new form of religious life. He longed to form a community of men who would join him in a silent Christian witness of living and working among the desert peoples of the Middle East and North Africa. Charles eventually received permission to leave his monastery and begin this new life. Though he failed to attract any followers and died as the only member of the order he hoped to found, his vision bore much fruit after his death. There are now sixteen religious communities that have adopted his spirituality and who consider him their spiritual father. In 2005, he was named Blessed Charles de Foucauld.

The prayer of Charles de Foucauld centers on the three aspects of penance, adoration of the Blessed Sacrament, and "contemplation in the streets."[9] What makes de Foucauld an important spiritual innovator for this period is that he desired to seek and find God in places that were not marked as sacred. He believed he would be most effective as a missionary by living among the people and being a silent witness of God's presence among them in the same way that Christ in the Blessed Sacrament was a silent witness in the world. He intended to imitate Christ in the hidden life at Nazareth, and his mission was to know Christ in the streets, outside the Church and cloister, within the ordinary community in which he lived. As such, de Foucauld was a factor in bridging the gap between sacred and secular. De Foucauld's move to "contemplation in the streets" signaled a shift in the organized spiritual movements of the Church. The twentieth century would see the rise of new ecclesial movements that have sought to incorporate the laity more fully in the

---

[9] This phrase was coined by his follower Carlo Caretto, *Letters from the Desert* (Maryknoll, NY: Orbis, 2002), 64.

contemplative life of the Church. These included Jean Vanier's L'Arche community, Dorothy Day's Catholic Worker, the Focalari movement, Communion and Liberation, Opus Dei, the Charismatic renewal, and the Neo-Catechumenal way. Though these groups differ from each other in many ways, they share the common vision that God can and should be sought in the world by ordinary people among ordinary people in the secular sphere.

Dorothy Day

Dorothy Day (1897–1980) was an important American witness to this "contemplation in the streets." Beginning as a reporter and activist, she joined the Catholic Church in 1927 because she saw it as the Church of the poor and the worker. While this touched her desire for social justice, there was another reason drawing her. Unlike other social activists for whom the humanitarian values were enough, Dorothy Day was searching for a spiritual reality that made sense out of these social issues. In 1922, at the age of twenty-five, she shared a room with a French Canadian in a Catholic household. These ordinary Catholics, praying and struggling with moral problems, "convinced [her] that worship, adoration, thanksgiving, supplication—these were the noblest acts of which men were capable in this life."[10] Ordinary Catholics by their ordinary lives were handing over a great truth of their religion to this seeker. In 1927, Dorothy Day entered the Catholic Church with her daughter, Tamar Teresa. In 1932, she and Peter Maurin founded the Catholic Worker Movement. When a "house of hospitality" was set up in the slums of New York City, she took up residence there and carried on her work for peace and social justice.

Dorothy Day was a good writer and a careful observer of the life and people around her. She remained a good Catholic writer because the things of God kept appearing in her life day-to-day, and, by writing them down, she showed us what we should look for in our daily lives. In her book *House of Hospitality* she records short sketches from the beginning of the Catholic Worker Movement. The first chapter opens with a long quote from Père Gratry's *The Well-Springs*, in which he speaks of Pythagoras, who devoted two-thirds of his day to God in prayer and

[10] Dorothy Day, *The Long Loneliness: The Autobiography of Dorothy Day* (New York: Harper and Brothers, 1952), 107.

study, and of Augustine in his *Confessions* telling of his call to be a writer. Père Gratry then asks: "Now, I ask you, do you think that these things happen only to St. Augustine?" Day begins in mid-sentence:

> But I am a woman, with all the cares and responsibilities of a woman, and though I take these words of Père Gratry and of St. Augustine to heart, I know that what I write will be tinged with all the daily doing, with myself, my work, my study, as well as with God. God enters into them all. He is inseparable from them. I think of him as I wake and as I think of Teresa's daily doings. Perhaps it is that I have a wandering mind. But I do not care. It is a woman's mind, and if my daily written meditations are of the people about me, of what is going on—then it must be so. It is a part of every meditation to apply the virtue, the mystery, to the daily life we lead.[11]

Clearly, Dorothy Day knows herself, her limitations, and the limitations of the life that she feels called to live. Within those limitations, she expects to meet her God. As she continues, note the concreteness of her observation:

> I shall meditate as I have been accustomed, in the little Italian Church on Twelfth Street, by the side of the open window, looking out at the plants growing on the roof, the sweet corn, the boxes of herbs, the geraniums in bright bloom, and I shall rest happy in the presence of Christ on the altar, and then I shall come home and I shall write as Père Gratry advises, and try to catch some of these things that happen to bring me nearer to God, to catch them and put them down on paper.[12]

The relationship between the inside of the church and the outside is striking. She looks at the outside world from inside the church and sees colorful plants growing. Although she had known sorrow and seen much misery, hers is a hopeful vision. In the last section, she talks about her commitment to writing, but it is also a commitment to a life of prayerful reflection in the midst of the day's business.

[11] Dorothy Day, *House of Hospitality* (New York: Sheed and Ward, 1939), 2. This text is not copyrighted and may be found at the website of the Catholic Worker Movement in the Dorothy Day Library: http://www.catholicworker.org/dorothyday/. Charles Healey, S.J., notes the importance of this passage in his essay on her in *Modern Spiritual Writers: Their Legacy of Prayer* (New York: Alba House, 1989), 3–24, esp. 14–18.
[12] Ibid., 2–3.

[This writing] is something I have wanted to do, which I have done sketchily for some years. . . . Now I shall do it as a duty performed joyfully for God. And because I am a woman involved in practical care, I cannot give the first half of the day to these things, but must meditate when I can, early in the morning and on the fly during the day. Not in the privacy of a study—but here, there and everywhere—at the kitchen table, on the train, on the ferry, on my way to and from appointments and even while making supper or putting Teresa to bed.[13]

Although the "little Italian Church on Twelfth Street" served her as a special place for prayer, she found that the whole world offered her the possibility for prayer. As such, she was a clear example of the integration of contemplation and ordinary life.

Dorothy Day's social concern reflected the teaching of Pope Leo XIII at the end of the nineteenth century, which became a hallmark of the Church in the twentieth century. Many others would seek to join a life of prayer to an intense engagement with the plight of the poor and oppressed, the most famous in recent years being Mother Teresa of Calcutta. They have turned their attention to the common people and to the affirmation that "all men are created equal." Some attempts, such as those guided by Marx, have gone badly astray. The American experiment has expanded its understanding of "all men" to be inclusive of both race and gender. While much remains imperfect, the achievement is still impressive. Some of these ideas were first framed as an attack on the Church, which at times was too closely identified with the institutions of power at the expense of the poor. However, these "democratic ideals" that value the individual person and work for the common good have Christian counterparts that place these "democratic ideals" into a larger and richer context. In part, this was the achievement of the Second Vatican Council with its celebration of the "People of God."

The Universal Church

A final and vital point to be made about prayer in the contemporary Church is the inculturation of prayer on a global scale. The "universal call to holiness" is, for the first time, a truly *universal* call! In the modern period, Catholicism has come to include peoples of every continent and

---

[13] Ibid., 3.

race. These believers have, in turn, brought their cultures, languages, and ways of expression to the world of Catholic prayer. While the Church has always yearned to encompass the whole world, it has only been in the modern period that the Church has expanded so far past the Jerusalem Church of the first century, or the European Church of the next two millennia, to embrace persons of every continent and every race. The tradition of Catholic prayer has expanded in the modern era to include a diversity that it had not before known.

Pope John Paul II (d. 2005) recognized the widening breadth of the Catholic tradition as one of the most important happenings in the contemporary Church. Among his great accomplishments was the fact that he traveled far more frequently and more extensively than any pope before him, becoming a symbol of the Church's diversity and unity throughout the world. He named a myriad of non-European saints, including the martyrs of Korea, Vietnam, and China. He beatified Teresa of Calcutta, the Native American Kateri Tekakwitha, and Peter ToRot of the Pacific Islands. He named indigenous bishops and cardinals to key positions in their own countries and at the Holy See.

Each culture has brought its gifts and unique regional traditions to the long tradition of Catholic prayer, and while many aspects of Catholic prayer are consistent throughout the Church, other dimensions reflect the unique character of the culture within which the prayer is expressed. A Catholic who attends Mass in India, for example, will see fire lit and flowers thrown about the altar at the moment of consecration of the Eucharist. The faithful in Zimbabwe use drums in their liturgy, while the Church in Micronesia incorporates beautiful dancing and unaccompanied chant. Every language expresses the prayers of the Church with its own particular beauty, a fact that has been respected through the declaration of the Second Vatican Council that liturgy can be celebrated in the vernacular. Pope John Paul II blessed this richness on his journeys as he used the languages and the customs of the peoples of the world to offer prayer and to celebrate the mystery of the Eucharist.

In conclusion, prayer in the modern era has been marked by a focus on the significance of prayer in the life of ordinary Christians everywhere. The mystery of the Incarnation especially has served as the foundation for so much of the theology and practice in our time. The locus of holiness and sanctity, once understood in some ways as a privilege or responsibility of monks, nuns, and priests, has been recentered in the "people of God" and the life of the Church as a whole as it is manifest throughout the world.

Further Reading

Day, Dorothy. *The Long Loneliness: The Autobiography of Dorothy Day*. San Francisco: HarperSan Francisco, 1993.

Downey, Michael, ed. *The New Dictionary of Catholic Spirituality*. Collegeville, MN: Liturgical Press, 1993.

Healey, Charles J., S.J. *Modern Spiritual Writers: Their Legacies of Prayer*. New York: Alba House, 1989.

Thérèse of Lisieux. *The Story of a Soul*. New York: Doubleday, 1957.

von Balthasar, Hans Urs. *Prayer*. Trans. by Graham Harrison. San Francisco: Ignatius Press, 1986.

Woods, Richard, O.P. *Christian Spirituality: God's Presence through the Ages*, rev. ed. Maryknoll, NY: Orbis Books, 2006.

Part II

Liturgy: Prayer of the Church in Community

Chapter 8

The Liturgical Year:
The Way of Catholic Spirituality

Godfrey Mullen, O.S.B., and Harry Hagan, O.S.B.

Spirituality is much talked about these days, perhaps because it suggests something personal. The word "theology" can sound so abstract or intellectual to many people as opposed to personal immediacy often linked to spirituality and the spiritual life. However, spirituality can be defined simply as personal theology. A theology is simply a way of understanding God: who God is, how God acts, as well as what it means for us to be human and relate to this God. While some theologies have been worked out very carefully, such as the theologies of St. Augustine and St. Thomas Aquinas, everyone has a personal theology whether they know it or not.

Our personal theology informs the way we act, and this means more than doing good or evil. Our moral life is only one dimension of our spiritual life, that is, our relationship to God in Christ. This spiritual life depends on our personal theology, our personal understanding of God. As a result, we must be careful how we nurture our understanding of God but also realize spirituality is more than understanding. It is a lived theology, and certain practices are typically associated with living it out. This personal theology gives definition to our identity and helps us identify what is personally important for us in becoming the Christian that each of us is called to be.

131

The tradition offers various classic spiritualities that have stood the test of time. Franciscan spirituality emphasizes poverty and simplicity. Jesuit spirituality is built around imaginative contemplation as the basis for action. Some spiritualities focus on the Blessed Mother or a saint. Other spiritualities concentrate on an aspect of Christ, such as his Sacred Heart. Sometimes the term "spirituality" refers mainly to a spiritual practice, such as saying the rosary or visiting the Blessed Sacrament. All of these surely have their place and have helped many deepen their relationship with God. The danger of a personal theology, of course, lies in its individual character. If this personal theology becomes too individualistic, people end up isolating themselves from the larger spiritual life of the Church. As a result, the Church offers us the liturgical year as the basic framework for our personal theology and our practice of prayer.

In the course of the liturgical year, the Church leads us in prayer through a celebration of the birth, death, and resurrection of the Lord so that we can conform ourselves more closely to Christ. By celebrating Eucharist within the context of the Church year, we immerse ourselves and share in the saving mysteries of Christ. A mystery, also called a sacrament, is a concrete manifestation of God's grace and love active in this world. The liturgy is itself this manifestation, and the liturgical year is the shape of the official prayer of the Church. As we celebrate these mysteries in the Eucharist and in the Liturgy of the Hours, we pray the official prayer of the Church which should shape our personal prayer. Whatever else we may add must conform to this official prayer which is given to us so that we may be conformed to Christ our Lord.

Sunday

From the beginning, the followers of Jesus gathered on the day of the resurrection—Sunday.[1] The ancient covenant of Israel made the last day of the week, the Sabbath (Saturday), sacred to the Lord, but this tradition shifted in Christianity to the day that began the new order realized in Christ. As the Second Vatican Council taught in its

---

[1] Pierre Jounel provides a thorough but brief treatment of the origins of Sunday's place in Christian gathering and the theology of Sunday: A. G. Martimort, I. H. Dalmais, and P. Jounel, *The Church at Prayer: The Liturgy and Time*, ed. A. G. Martimort, vol. 4 (Collegeville, MN: Liturgical Press, 1985), 11–29.

Constitution on the Sacred Liturgy: "By a tradition handed down from the apostles, which took its origin from the very day of Christ's resurrection, the church celebrates the paschal mystery every eighth day"[2] (because the Church counts the day of the resurrection as the beginning of the week of the new creation). Therefore, the resurrection provides the basis for Christian celebration. And the resurrection is most clearly celebrated on the weekly anniversary of Mary Magdalene running to tell the apostles about the message of the one appearing as a gardener, who was Christ, the risen Lord (John 20). It would be shortsighted, however, if the Church celebrated only the resurrection. To celebrate the resurrection on the Day of the Lord (Sunday) is to celebrate the entire paschal mystery—the life, death, and resurrection of Jesus.

The fathers of the Second Vatican Council go on to say, "The Lord's Day is the original feast day, and it should be presented to the faithful and taught to them so that it may become in fact a day of rejoicing and of freedom from work."[3] The gathering of the faithful on Sunday should shape our thinking of what the whole day is about: giving thanks to God for deeds of love beyond comprehension, celebrating the joy of the resurrection, and generally refraining from work.

The premier element of the liturgical year, then, is Sunday, the weekly celebration of the paschal mystery. The Church's insistence upon Catholics gathering each Sunday for Eucharist merely states the most basic responsibility of an individual to pray with the community.

Seasons of the Year

The liturgical year encompasses five basic seasons: Advent, Christmas, Lent, Easter, and Ordinary Time. Each season has its own character and rhythm. While this is most apparent when the Church gathers for prayer, the spirit of each season should overflow into our individual lives. Sometimes specific practices are associated with a season, but mainly the season should color the way we live. The feasts of saints are celebrated during all five seasons, and this juxtaposition enriches the whole. Let us look at each of the seasons in course and then consider, in conclusion, the celebration of saints.

---

[2] *Sacrosanctum Concilium* (The Constitution on the Sacred Liturgy), December 4, 1963, no. 106.

[3] Ibid.

Advent

The liturgical year begins anew on the first Sunday of Advent at the beginning of December. Advent was first celebrated in the fourth century as a season of preparation for the Christ's manifestation.[4] This four-Sunday season reflects the centuries of waiting for the birth of the Messiah before Jesus was born in history. The Old Testament is a book of desire, and God's chosen people struggled to remain faithful to the covenant even as they awaited the birth of the new king who would set them free from slavery, darkness, and death.

As the earth's natural cycle provides for longer nights and shorter days in the northern hemisphere, as the power of the light seems to dwindle throughout December, the Church awaits the dawning of Eternal Light, the Christ-child. So darker hues of violet-colored vestments are reminders of darkness's threatening gains. The prayers of the liturgy, from the first day of Advent, instruct us in the project of the season:

> Father in heaven, our hearts **desire** the warmth of your love and our minds **are searching** for the **light** of your Word. Increase our **longing** for Christ our Savior and give us the strength to grow in love, that the **dawn** of his coming may find us rejoicing in his presence and welcoming the **light** of his truth.[5]

Stressing the themes of desire and light so characteristic of Advent, this prayer teaches its hearers that the real warming and illumining light comes in Christ's birth—in Bethlehem long ago, in glory at the end of time, and also in the present through the living grace of Christian living.[6] Therefore, it asks Christians to realize that Advent is a time of active and joyful waiting, not merely for the celebration of an ancient event in history, but also for a future event that was foretold when Jesus walked the earth, and in the daily lives of Christ's people.

John the Baptist, dressed in his leather and camel's hair, plays a key role in this celebration as the prophetic voice calling the people

---

[4] See Matias Augé, C.M.F., "The Liturgical Year in the Roman Rite," in *Handbook for Liturgical Studies*, ed. Anscar J. Chupungco, vol. 5, *Liturgical Time and Space* (Collegeville, MN: Liturgical Press, 2000), 201–3.

[5] *The Sacramentary* (New York: Catholic Book Publishing, 1985), 2.

[6] See Pius Parsch, *The Church's Year of Grace: Advent to Candlemas*, vol. 1 (Collegeville, MN: Liturgical Press, 1957), 10–11.

to repentance. He is strident and confrontational in his warning, yet he also points out clearly that Jesus is the Lamb of God and the Messiah foretold of old. Like the season itself, John calls us to look for Christ today so that we may see him when he comes at the end of time in glory.

Perhaps the most famous of all the Magnificat antiphons are found at evening prayer during the week just before Christmas. They are called the "O" Antiphons because each addresses Christ by a specific title:

"O Sapientia"	"O Wisdom"
"O Adonai"	"O Adonai" (Hebrew for "My Lord")
"O Radix Jesse"	"O Root of Jesse"
"O Clavis David"	"O Key of David"
"O Oriens"	"O Rising Sun"
"O Rex Gentium"	"O King of the Nations"
"O Emmanuel"	"O Emmanuel" (Hebrew for "God with us")

These titles capture some of the basic themes of this season, and the antiphons were combined to create the hymn "O Come, O Come, Emmanuel." The first letters of each of the Latin titles, when read backward, yield the Latin sentence: "ero cras," which means "I will be (here) tomorrow." There are many small details like this buried in the liturgy to be discovered by those who follow the liturgy year in and year out.

This season of joyful anticipation is late in arriving to the Western Church, particularly to the Church in Rome. It is first seen in Gaul and Spain in the fourth century, but its four-week cycle of Advent does not appear definitively until the twelfth and thirteenth centuries.[7] Today in the wider culture, the quiet waiting of Advent can get lost in the anticipated celebrations of the coming feast which seems to demand complex decorations and ever-larger gifts. While it is easy to criticize the secular celebration, themes of waiting and preparation, of desire and hope for completeness, are still present amid the glitter. A rich understanding of Advent can set that into a proper perspective. Indeed, many find this season particularly attractive, perhaps because waiting in hope is such

---

[7] Augé, "The Liturgical Year," 201–2.

a part of the human condition. Too often the anticipation is better than the reality. For those who wait for Christ, the expectation is that the reality will be better than the hope, and the Church prays: "Maranatha! Come, Lord Jesus!"[8]

Christmas

At the winter solstice the days begin to grow longer, and the ancient Romans celebrated the birth of the *Sol invictus*, the birth of "the unconquered Sun." By at least the fifth century, Christians identified the *Sol invictus* with the Christ and transformed this pagan celebration into their own feast of the birth of Christ as the true "sun of justice" (see Luke 1:78).[9] The day of Christmas focuses on the birth of the child who is also the Son of God. The feast celebrates the Incarnation, the mystery of the Word made flesh who dwelt among us (John 1:14). In the liturgy, Isaiah becomes a key figure as the prophet of this feast. The Church reads Isaiah 7:14 as a prophecy of the Virgin Mary giving birth to Emmanuel—God with us—and this birth fulfills both Isaiah 9 that announces the birth of the Prince of Peace and Isaiah 11 that describes his peaceable kingdom. Therefore, to the shepherds who represent both Israel and also Luke's people at the edge the angels announce: "Glory to God in the highest heaven, and on earth peace among those whom he favors!" (Luke 2:14).

In the Christmas season, not only does the King appear, but he brings with him martyrs (St. Stephen the Martyr's day is December 26), virgins (St. John's day is December 27), and children (Holy Innocents' day is December 28). These days also reflect the mysteries of Christ: the crucifixion (St. Stephen), the resurrection (St. John), and the Church in the age of the martyrs (Holy Innocents). The Sunday after Christmas has become the feast of the Holy Family, followed on January 1 by the Feast of Mary, Mother of God, celebrating one of her most ancient titles in Greek, the *Theotokos*, given to her at the Council of Ephesus (A.D. 431) to affirm the two natures of Christ (divine and human) in one person.

In the Western Church, the Epiphany commemorates the arrival of the magi at the crib to worship the new king on the twelfth day which

---

[8] Cf. 1 Cor 16:22; Rev 22:20.
[9] Augé, "The Liturgical Year," 195–97.

would be January 6, though the feast in the U.S. and Canada falls on the Sunday after January 1. Here foreign kings, unlike the wicked King Herod, acknowledge Christ as their king. These kings also represent the people of the nations, those who were not originally heirs of the covenant but now have access to God in Christ.

In the Eastern Church, Epiphany has other layers as well. The emphasis is on the epiphany, that is, the manifestation of God in the world. Originally the feast celebrated not just the manifestation to the magi, but also the manifestation of Christ at his baptism by John in the Jordan and at the wedding feast of Cana.[10]

The bridegroom, who is Christ, celebrates the royal wedding (Epiphany), receives his wedding guests (the wise men), and purifies his bride (as he is baptized in the Jordan he purifies the waters of baptism for the church).[11] The celebration of the Holy Family, the Epiphany, and the Baptism of the Lord join the commemoration of St. Stephen, St. John, and the Holy Innocents to fill out the celebration of the Christmas season.

Many Christians respond tenderly to the celebration of the Incarnation of Christ because this feast of light radiates salvation. The preface of the Eucharistic Prayer for Christmas reminds Christians: "In the wonder of the Incarnation your eternal Word has brought to the eyes of faith a new and radiant vision of your glory. In him we see our God made visible and so are caught up in love of the God we cannot see."[12] In this quiet season when light destroys darkness, as the Christ-child is born for the salvation of all, the Church's wisdom would have us bear in mind the sacramental relationship of the visible and the invisible. In Christmas, the invisible covenant of God's love becomes visible once and for all and is manifest most clearly as the season ends with the celebration of Epiphany, when Christ is hailed by the magi, and the Baptism of the Lord, when the voice of the Father is heard and the Spirit is seen descending as a dove on the Father's Beloved Son.

[10] A remnant of this threefold celebration can be seen in the antiphon for the Benedictus on Epiphany; cf. Monks of Solesmes, *Antiphonale Monasticum* (Paris: Desclée, 1934), 293.

[11] Pius Parsch, *The Church's Year of Grace*, vol. 1, 17.

[12] *The Sacramentary*, 379.

Lent

The motif of forty recurs throughout the Old Testament, often as a round number signifying a long time. Israel wandered in the desert for forty years. While there, Moses spent forty days and forty nights on Mount Sinai, where he encountered God (Exod 24:18; 34:28). Elijah, fed by an angel, then made a journey of forty days and forty nights to the same mountain where he also met God (1 Kgs 19:8). The desert and the mountain serve as images of life's journey toward union with God. Before Jesus begins his public ministry, he goes to fast in the desert for forty days and nights. Like Israel, he finds the desert a place of temptation which he conquers.

Lent emerged in the early Church slowly as a season of preparation for Easter.[13] By the fourth century, when a process for welcoming adult members into the Church had become established, Lent became the official preparatory season for those who would celebrate the sacraments of initiation (baptism, confirmation, Eucharist) at Easter.[14] Since there was strong emphasis on Jesus' fast of forty days, there was a desire to provide for forty days of fasting during Lent. Because Sundays (even during Lent) are not days of fasting, the beginning of Lent was moved earlier to what became known as Ash Wednesday.[15]

One of the most vivid symbols of Lent is the ashes given on Ash Wednesday. This practice, dating to the eleventh century, is explained briefly in the prayer of blessing the ashes: "Lord, bless the sinner who asks for your forgiveness and bless all those who receive these ashes. May they keep this Lenten season in preparation for the joy of Easter."[16] Lent becomes the season of repentance for sinners and for those preparing for initiation at Easter. This penitential period urges its participants to long for the new life of resurrection that the entire Church will encounter with the incorporation of its new members at the Easter vigil.

Each year on the Second Sunday of Lent, the gospel tells the story of Jesus' transfiguration with Moses and Elijah at his side. If Lent is a journey through the desert, it's always oriented toward the mountain of

---

[13] Martimort, Dalmais, and Jounel, *The Church at Prayer,* vol. 4, 66.

[14] Ibid., 66.

[15] By the sixth and seventh centuries, its beginning is pushed even earlier as Quinquagesima, Sexagesima, and Septuagesima Sundays are added. This pre-Lenten preparation was removed from the calendar after the Second Vatican Council. Ibid., 68–69.

[16] *The Sacramentary,* 77.

God, toward the paschal mystery celebrated at Easter. Lent is never an end in and of itself. Still, Lent is meant to confront us with the reality of life and death. At the beginning of Holy Week, the Church gathers for Palm Sunday, which celebrates the triumphal entry of Christ into Jerusalem and also proclaims his passion and death so that we might confront reality as it is. On Palm Sunday triumph is followed by tragedy, but at the end of the week the celebration of the cross is followed by resurrection—the true shape of the paschal mystery.

The Triduum: Holy Thursday, Good Friday, and Easter

The holy season of Lent concludes with the beginning of the Mass of the Lord's Supper on Holy Thursday evening. The Easter season begins with the celebration of the Easter Vigil. The time between the two is known as the Paschal Triduum: the three days that mark the culmination of the paschal mystery. These three days also mark the immediate preparation of the catechumens for their initiation with the quiet final rites of the catechumenate. While all the events of these solemn days reflect on the serious nature of the crucifixion, they also look forward to the celebration of the resurrection that Jesus predicted to his disciples. In the same way, the Easter celebrations recall the wounds of Christ that preceded the glory of the resurrection.

Holy Thursday

The Mass of the Lord's Supper on Holy Thursday commemorates the last supper that Jesus took with his disciples before he was betrayed. The three readings for the day capture the central elements. The first reading (Exod 12:1-8, 11-14) retells the story of Israel eating the Passover meal, because this meal becomes for the Church the new Passover feast. In the second reading (1 Cor 11:23-26), Paul recounts the tradition of Christ giving his body and blood to eat "in remembrance." Finally, in the gospel (John 13:1-15), Jesus washes the feet of the disciples, and this is reenacted as part of the liturgy with the celebrant washing the feet of twelve members of the Church while the Church sings: "*Ubi caritas et amor, Deus ibi est.*" "Where charity and love are, there is God." The liturgy reminds the Church of what must be done in order to fulfill the Lord's command of love made manifest in the Lord's gift of himself. At the end of the liturgy, Holy Communion for the next day is reserved in a special place where the faithful may watch and pray as Jesus invited the disciples to do in the garden.

Good Friday

On Good Friday, the Church gathers for a very different liturgy that creates the sense of a day unlike any other. With the church and altar stripped of its adornments, the ministers process in silence and prostrate themselves. Rising, the priest without introduction reads the opening prayer, and the Liturgy of the Word begins. After the readings from Isaiah about the suffering servant (Isa 52:13–53:12) and from the Letter to the Hebrews about Christ as the great high priest (Heb 4:14-16, 5:7-9), the Passion of John is solemnly proclaimed, traditionally by three singers taking the parts of the narrator, the crowd, and Christ. Ten solemn prayers of intercession follow. These prayers gather the concerns of the Church and the whole world into the mystery of Christ's saving death on the cross. Then, removing their shoes, the ministers go and bring the cross in solemn procession into the church; everyone is invited to come forward and reverence the cross with a kiss. Since Good Friday continues the liturgy of Holy Thursday, the Eucharist is not offered, but the faithful are called to share Holy Communion from what has been consecrated the day before. All depart in silence. The stark directness of this celebration testifies to the reality of Christ's death as the suffering servant who dies for all:

> But he was wounded for our transgressions,
>   crushed for our iniquities;
> upon him was the punishment that made us whole,
>   and by his bruises we are healed. (Isa 53:5)

The Easter Vigil

Holy Saturday, too, is a day of silence in immediate preparation for the celebration of the Easter Vigil, which Saint Augustine called "the mother of all holy vigils."[17] In the early Church, great feasts were preceded with all-night vigils taken up largely with the praying of the whole book of Psalms. In the West this vigil had been moved to the morning of Holy Saturday, but in 1951 the first of the liturgical reforms restored the vigil to the night. It is a long liturgy. It stretches the attention of the assembly and stretches them so that in reaching they may conform themselves to the risen Christ.

---

[17] Martimort, Dalmais, and Jounel, *The Church at Prayer*, 39.

The vigil and with it the Easter season begins with the blessing of the Easter fire and the paschal candle. During the blessing of the candle, the priest uses this formula: "Christ, yesterday and today, the beginning and the end, Alpha and Omega, all time belongs to him and all the ages. To him be glory and power through every age for ever. Amen."[18] This formula accompanies the decoration of the candle. Afterwards, the priest inserts five grains of incense into the candle, saying, "By his holy and glorious wounds, may Christ our Lord guard us and keep us. Amen."[19] As if juxtaposing light and darkness time and again, the worship of the Church reminds us of the transition from the darkness of the desert's fast to the brilliant light of the resurrection.

The vigil proper begins with seven readings from the Old Testament to clarify what has happened to the whole world in the resurrection of Christ. The first three readings recount the creation of the world, the sacrifice of Isaac, and the exodus through the Red Sea. As we listen we reflect on the renewal of creation, the perfect sacrifice of Christ, and our passage from death to life in baptism. The next four readings from the prophets reveal the promise of God realized in Christ crucified and risen. The reading from Paul's letter to the Romans (6:3-11) affirms that in baptism we were buried with him so that we might be raised with him. Following the solemn singing of the Alleluia (forbidden through all of Lent), the gospel announces the resurrection of the Lord. The readings, as the proclamation of God's word, tell us what is realized in the liturgy.

The Liturgy of the Word is followed by the Rite of Initiation in which those prepared for reception into the Church are baptized, confirmed, and received into communion. The rite begins with the litany of the saints, asking the intercession of the unseen Church for those to be received. The celebrant then blesses the water by recalling the great biblical motifs: the Spirit breathing on the water at the dawn of creation, Noah's flood which renewed the earth, the waters of the Red Sea through which Israel passed from slavery to freedom, the waters of the Jordan in which Jesus was baptized, and the water that flowed with blood from Jesus' side. The Easter candle is then lowered into the water during the blessing as a sign that those who go down into the water of

---

[18] *The Roman Missal*, 172.
[19] Ibid.

baptism with Christ shall also rise with him. Those to be baptized and confirmed are questioned about their faith and then baptized. Then all present renew their baptismal promises and so profess their faith. Adrian Nocent, O.S.B., in his great work *The Liturgical Year*, warns that we must be careful that we do not give so much attention to what has gone before that we underplay the celebration of the Eucharist on this night. "The Eucharist is the climax of the Vigil service. It is to it that baptism and confirmation are leading, and this Eucharist is, moreover, the most solemn of the year, more solemn even than that of Holy Thursday evening."[20]

The integral link between baptism and the resurrection gives the Easter vigil its essential character, yet it is a complex liturgy with many dimensions suggested by the lighted candle and the water, the complex of readings, its celebration during the night, and even its length. Although the liturgical reform has focused particularly on Easter Vigil and Easter Sunday and the emphasis is shifting that way, the laity of the Western Church remain committed to Good Friday as a high point of the Triduum.

Easter

Recognizing that the magnitude of the resurrection could be celebrated in no single day, from early Christian times, Easter—the Church's fifty-day celebration of Jesus' resurrection—is celebrated as a week of weeks (seven weeks), culminating in Pentecost, the last Sunday of Easter when the Church celebrates the outpouring of the Holy Spirit upon the apostles.[21] So through the Paschal Triduum, the Church moves from fast to feast—a feast that lasts longer than the fast. The battle cry of the season is "Alleluia." At every possible opportunity, the assembly is required once again to sing "Alleluia!" This is only one indication of the demands of the Easter season, but in asking so much, the season provides an opportunity for us to grow in the image of Christ.

The Gospel of John provides some of the most affecting characters of the season: the distraught Mary Magdalene in the garden, the doubting Thomas with his hand in the side of Christ, and the repentant Peter

---

[20] Adrian Nocent, O.S.B., *The Liturgical Year: The Easter Season*, vol. 3 (Collegeville, MN: Liturgical Press, 1977), 144.

[21] Martimort, Dalmais, and Jounel, *The Church at Prayer*, vol. 4, 57.

receiving the Lord's threefold command to feed his sheep (John 20–21). Throughout the Easter season at the Eucharist, we hear the book of Acts of the Apostles proclaimed, the story of the early Church moving out through the ministry of Peter and Paul to evangelize the whole world. Luke sums up the life of the early Church by saying: "They devoted themselves to the apostles' teaching and fellowship [*koinōnia*, i.e. 'the common life'], to the breaking of bread and the prayers" (Acts 2:42). Unlike the first disciples, more and more the members of the Church did not know Christ in the flesh, but like the two disciples at Emmaus, they came to recognize the risen Lord in the breaking of the bread. While there are many solid reasons why Catholics have such an attachment to the celebration of the Eucharist, its power to reveal the risen Lord to us in our own day must be counted as one of the most important.

The fifty days of Easter ends with the feast of Pentecost (which means fifty). The coming of the Holy Spirit pushes the disciples out of the upper room into the whole world in order to fulfill Christ's command: "Go therefore and make disciples of all nations, baptizing them in the name of the Father and of the Son and of the Holy Spirit" (Matt 28:19). So the Church is born and must get on with its ordinary life.

Ordinary Time

If all year was a series of Easters or Christmases, the Church could hardly maintain the level of solemnity in its celebration. Between the Christmas season and the beginning of Lent and again after Pentecost until the beginning of a new liturgical year is the season of Ordinary Time. Before Vatican II, these Sundays were numbered "after Epiphany" or "after Pentecost." Their hallmark in the current configuration of the calendar is the manner in which the readings are chosen. Typically, during Ordinary Time, the majority of one of the three Gospels is read week after week (Matthew one year, Mark and John the next, and Luke the third year). The readings from the Old Testament are chosen to correspond thematically to the gospel. The epistle readings, generally taken from the writings of Paul, James, and the letter to the Hebrews, follow their own cycle and do not typically correspond to the gospel reading and its thematic Old Testament counterpart.[22]

---

[22] Augé, "Liturgical Year," 204–5.

One might rightly conclude that the centrality of Sunday in the liturgical cycle finds its expression in the simplicity of the Sundays of Ordinary Time. And to celebrate the resurrection on a weekly basis is to learn the importance of living the faith that believes in the resurrection. Ordinary Time gives the Christian faithful time to integrate and incorporate the celebration of the birth and resurrection of Christ, prepared for and celebrated in the other seasons of the liturgical year. "This means that one endeavors to hear and follow the Teacher in daily life, that one does not bracket off ordinary life but sees it as a saving moment."[23]

It is also during this season of Ordinary Time that the church celebrates seven feasts of the Lord: the Transfiguration (Matt 17; Mark 9); the Triumph of the Cross; the Dedication of the Lateran Basilica; the Holy Trinity; the Body and Blood of Christ; the Sacred Heart of Jesus; and Christ the King. The origin of each of these feasts has its own peculiar story, sometimes arising from popular piety, at other times counteracting a secular trend in thought or action, and at still other times, as a means of instructing the faithful.[24] Still, these different perspectives add richness to the mysteries of Christ celebrated in the liturgical year.

Veneration of the Saints

While the liturgical year certainly contains no more than five "seasons," interspersed throughout the entire cycle are the days assigned for the veneration of various saints, including most particularly the Blessed Virgin Mary. Finding some of their origins in the anniversary celebrations of the martyrs, these annual commemorations of the birth of the saint into heaven (typically, the date of his or her death) were always festive, based on a strong faith in the resurrection. The practice of celebrating the Mass on days other than Sunday comes partially from the practice of families and disciples of the early Christian martyrs festively gathering in the cemetery to remember the dead on their anniversaries. As devotion to particular martyrs increased, the breadth and solemnity of the celebration increased as well. Eventually, some martyrs, and later virgins, confessors, and holy men and women, be-

---

[23] Ibid., 206.
[24] Martimort, Dalmais, and Jounel, *The Church at Prayer*, vol. 4, 97–107.

come celebrated throughout the universal Church, while others are celebrated more locally, in places where reverence for these particular saints is more concentrated.[25]

The Blessed Mother has been a special case. From the seventh century on, the Church in the West has expanded the number of her feasts, resulting in a vast collection of liturgical texts that appeal to the intercession of Mary under many titles (e.g., Our Lady of Lourdes, Our Lady of the Snows, etc.).[26] In addition to being the Mother of God, she is also the image of the Church. So to celebrate her glory is to celebrate the Church in its many dimensions.

Conclusion

When Pope Paul VI promulgated the Constitution on the Sacred Liturgy in 1963, the reform of the liturgical year was decreed:

> The liturgical year is to be revised so that the traditional customs and discipline of the sacred seasons shall be preserved or restored in line with the conditions of modern times. Their specific character is to be retained so that they duly nourish the piety of the faithful as they celebrate the mysteries of the Christian redemption and, above all, the paschal mystery.[27]

This revision has had a significant impact on the life of parishes, especially the restoration of the catechumenate with its impact on the season of Lent. Furthermore, a renewal of Advent as a season of joyful anticipation instead of "another Lent" seems to be consistent with this desired revision, but these are just a beginning.

The liturgical year is not just for liturgical celebrations. The seasons of the Church year should be present in every aspect of life. They should affect the way we eat, and this means more than just fasting during Lent. A Christmas feast should be different from an Easter feast. Families should have their own practices and prayers that reflect the seasons. Given the noise of our culture, this may seem a tall

---

[25] Ibid., 108–29.

[26] Ibid., 130–50.

[27] *Sacrosanctum Concilium* (The Constitution on the Sacred Liturgy), December 4, 1963, no. 107.

order. Still, the liturgical year forms the basic framework for Catholic spirituality, and by it we conform ourselves to Christ.

Further Reading

Adam, Adolf. *The Liturgical Year: Its History and Its Meaning after the Reform of the Liturgy.* Collegeville, MN: Liturgical Press, 1981.

Martimort, A. G.; I. H. Dalmais, O.P.; P. Jounel. *The Church at Prayer: The Liturgy and Time.* Vol. 4. Collegeville, MN: Liturgical Press, 1985.

Nocent, Adrian, O.S.B. *The Liturgical Year.* Four volumes. Collegeville, MN: Liturgical Press, 1977.

Chapter 9

The Liturgy of the Hours:
The Daily Prayer of the Church

Harry Hagan, O.S.B., and Godfrey Mullen, O.S.B.

Just as throughout the centuries Christian people have used the seasons of the year to structure their celebrations of the life, death, and resurrection of Christ in the liturgical year, so too have God's people from ancient days sought to order each day to bring God's presence to mind and to encourage the building up of holiness. So it is no surprise that we read in the psalms:

> Seven times a day I praise you
> for your righteous ordinances. (Ps 119:164)

The more people realize their need for God's mercy and care, the more they see the need to remember and give thanks. Thus, for the author of this psalm, seven times is the perfect number and means "always."

The gospels tell us that Jesus would go off alone to pray, dedicating parts of the day to conversation with the Father. He was in the habit of praying with others in the synagogue and before meals. Through all this, Jesus gives his disciples, any of his followers, a model of Christian prayer that takes place alone and in the company of fellow believers.

This company of Christian believers is called the Body of Christ. As stated in the *General Instruction of the Liturgy of the Hours:* "There is a special and very close bond between Christ and those whom he makes members of his Body, the Church, through the sacrament of rebirth [baptism]."[1] The prayer of the Church, then, becomes one with the prayer of Christ himself. The prayer of the Body of Christ becomes one with the communication of the Son to the Father. This principle is very important to understand. Any prayer that Christ's followers offer is a joining of that prayer with the endless intercession of Christ before the Father.

From the Christian community's beginning, the Eucharist was celebrated on Sunday, and only later did it become more frequent until it was a daily celebration. The Eucharist holds pride of place in Christian prayer. But the Liturgy of the Hours, or the Church's prayer throughout the day, flows from the intercession, praise, and thanksgiving of the Eucharist.[2] Keeping that in mind, what is the Liturgy of the Hours and what are its sources?

A Closer Look at the History

Robert Taft, S.J., has written a masterful history in his *The Liturgy of the Hours in East and West*, which serves as the foundation and guide of this whole chapter.[3] Like a Jewish community in the synagogue, Christians began to gather at set times and to use the Scriptures as the basis for their prayer.[4] During the first three hundred years, a time of persecution, the practice of prayer was diverse. Still, a theology begins to emerge in the writings on prayer by Origen, Tertullian, and Cyprian.[5] This sets the stage for the development of the Liturgy of the Hours after Constantine makes Christianity a legitimate religion in the Edict of Milan (A.D. 313). This

---

[1] *General Instruction of the Liturgy of the Hours*, no. 7. This document has been printed in various places, including *The Liturgy of the Hours*, trans. International Commission on English in the Liturgy, vol. 1 (New York: Catholic Book Publishing Co., 1975), 21–98. It can also be found in various places on the Internet.

[2] *General Instruction of the Liturgy of the Hours*, no. 12.

[3] Robert Taft, *The Liturgy of the Hours in East and West: The Origins of the Divine Office and Its Meaning for Today*, 2d ed. (Collegeville, MN: Liturgical Press, 1993).

[4] Ibid., 11. In addition to Taft's careful analysis, good summaries of the history can be found in the following: Pierre Salmon, O.S.B., *The Breviary through the Centuries*, trans. David Mary, S.N.J.M. (Collegeville, MN: Liturgical Press, 1962); and J. D. Crichton, *Christian Celebration: The Prayer of the Church* (London: Geoffrey Chapman, 1976), esp. 29–61. Dominic F. Scotto, T.O.R., *Liturgy of the Hours* (Petersham, MA: St. Bede Publications, 1987), 3–42.

[5] Taft, *Liturgy of the Hours*, 13–29.

period is very rich and complex, but this chapter shall focus on two basic traditions represented by two key people: the cathedral office as reported by Egeria and the monastic office as codified by Benedict's Rule.

Egeria

The cathedral liturgy is simply the services celebrated by a bishop with his clergy and the laity at the cathedral church. With the peace of Constantine, the Christian communities emerged from their house churches and began to develop new liturgical services. Constantine supported this by giving the Church a number of large public buildings, called basilicas, which required a new style of celebration. In addition to the Eucharist, the cathedral churches of cities and towns developed celebrations at other times of the day, particularly a daily morning and evening prayer along with a vigil service on Sunday celebrating the paschal mystery.

In 1884, G. F. Gamurrini found a manuscript copied at Monte Casino in the eleventh or twelfth century that describes the liturgy of Jerusalem during ordinary time as well as during Lent and Easter and some other feasts. This manuscript corresponds to information found in a letter from the seventh century by Valerius to his brother monks. In it, he praises the "most blessed nun Egeria" who was "born on the sea shore of the far distant western ocean."[6] Valerius tells how she made a heroic journey to Constantinople, Palestine, Egypt, and Mesopotamia and sent a careful and enthusiastic account to her sisters.[7] Her journey can be dated to 381–84,[8] which puts her in Jerusalem during the episcopacy of the great St. Cyril of Jerusalem.[9] Because of her interest in things Christian and her powers of observation, she was able to give a firsthand account of the cathedral liturgy in one of the great liturgical centers of her time.

---

[6] Valerius, a seventh-century hermit, wrote a letter to his "brothers" in El Vierzo that gives the earliest information about Egeria. For the letter, see *Egeria's Travels to the Holy Land*, trans. John Wilkinson, rev. ed. (Warminster: Aris & Philips, 1981), 174–78, esp. 174, where he calls her a *"moniales,"* and 177. See also Valerius du Bierzo, *Lettre sur la B^se Égérie*, intro. and trans. Manuel C. Díaz y Díaz in Égérie, *Journal de voyage (Itinéraire) et Lettre sur la B^se Égérie*, intro. and trans. Pierre Maraval, Sources Chrétiennes, No. 296 (Paris: Cerf, 1982), 323–49. Large sections of Egeria's journal are now available on the Internet.

[7] The letter is clearly addressed to the "ladies [and] venerable sisters" (*dominae venerabiles sorores*) as in chapter 3.8 *et passim*. Maraval says that this does not prove they were religious (*Journal*, 23); it nonetheless seems to be a reasonable assumption.

[8] Wilkinson, *Egeria's Travels*, 3; Maraval, *Journal*, 38.

[9] Ibid.

Jerusalem at this period was filled with monks and nuns, and Egeria tells us that they gathered before the cathedral office began in the Anastasis, the building surrounding the cave that is the Tomb of the Resurrection.[10] They "join in singing the refrains to the hymns, psalms, and antiphons" with "a prayer between each of the hymns."[11] At dawn, the service of "Morning Hymns" began. According to the *Apostolic Constitutions*, written about the same time, this service began with Psalm 63 (62) which sings of the desire for God. Using this psalm at morning prayer seems to have been the general practice.[12] Egeria recounts how the bishop with his clergy appeared and went immediately into the Tomb of the Resurrection. From inside the screened area, the bishop said the "Prayer for All" in which he could include the name of any he wished. After this he blessed the catechumens, said another prayer, and then blessed the faithful. Coming outside the screen, he then blessed everyone individually, and they kissed his hand.[13] Note that the psalmody was brief, and the service specifically included the laity.

At midday and three o'clock there were again "psalms and antiphons until a message is sent by the bishop."[14] Then at four o'clock, they celebrated the Lucernare, which means the "lighting": "All the people congregate once more in the Anastasis, and the lamps and candles are all lit, which makes it very bright."[15] As a sign of the resurrection, the fire to light the lamps and candles was brought from the Tomb of the Resurrection.[16] "For sometime" there were the psalms and antiphons for this service, including Psalm 141 which is the key psalm for evening prayer in the cathedral office[17] because of Psalm 141:2:

---

[10] See Wilkinson for a complete description of the buildings on Golgotha; ibid., 39–46. Constantine's buildings on Golgotha included the Anastasis, a circle of columns around the tomb of Christ with a screen (a wall with doors) to the west. The court before the cross was to the west of the screen with the shrine of "the Cross" in the southwest corner on Golgotha. Farther west was the Martyrium, a great doubled aisled court with an atrium beyond that.

[11] Wilkinson, *Egeria's Travels*, chap. 24.1, 123.

[12] Taft, *Liturgy of the Hours*, 45. He quotes the *Apostolic Constitutions*, Book 2, 59.

[13] Wilkinson, *Egeria's Travels*, chap. 24.2, 123.

[14] Ibid., chap. 24.3, 123.

[15] Ibid., chap. 24.4, 123.

[16] Taft, *Liturgy of the Hours*, 51.

[17] Ibid., 33, 42–47.

> Let my prayer be counted as incense before you,
> and the lifting up of my hands as an evening sacrifice.

In this psalm, prayer replaces the temple sacrifice, and the offering of incense becomes a great symbolic act of offering thanks and praise at the end of the day. As with the lighting of lamps, the offering of incense became a standard part of the ritual, particularly on Sundays.[18] During the psalmody, they sent for the bishop who came and sat "in the chief seat" with his clergy in their seats. When the designated "hymns and antiphons" were finished, the bishop came out in front of the screen, and a deacon made the intercession, that is, "the normal commemoration of individuals" with "a large group of boys" responding "Kyrie eleison" (Greek for "Lord, have mercy").[19] When the deacon finished, "the bishop [said] a prayer and pray[ed] the 'Prayer for All.'" The deacon called for the catechumens to bow their heads, and the bishop said the blessing over them. Then the deacon called the faithful to bow their heads, and the bishop blessed them. After the dismissal, all went to kiss the bishop's hand. The bishop then processed to "the Cross," that is, the shrine on Calvary, with everyone following for more blessings. "By the end of all this it is dusk."[20] Taft outlines the service as follows:[21]

light service and hymn

vesperal psalms, including Psalm 141

[offering of incense in other texts]

antiphons

entrance of the bishop

hymns and antiphons

intercessions

blessing

dismissal

procession to the Cross (i.e., Calvary) with prayers and blessings

[18] Ibid., 55.
[19] Wilkinson, *Egeria's Travels*, chap. 24.5, 124.
[20] Ibid., chap. 24.7, 124.
[21] Taft, *Liturgy of the Hours*, 51.

The morning and evening services form the hinges for the daily prayer of the Church with the Eucharist celebrated on Sunday.

For Sundays, Egeria also describes the "Resurrection vigil" and says that a great crowd gathered for it before cock-crow "as if it were Easter" itself. They "sit waiting there singing hymns and antiphons, and they have prayers between, since there are always presbyters and deacons there ready for the vigil."[22] "Soon the first cock crows, and at that the bishop goes into the cave in the Anastasis."[23] The people poured into the Anastasis which is ablaze with light. After three psalms with responses, they incensed the cave and then the whole basilica. Then the bishop himself read one of the accounts of the resurrection. The assembly then processed to the Cross for another psalm followed by the intercessions and blessings.[24]

In conclusion, the cathedral liturgy of Jerusalem is striking first because of its liturgical action: the lighting of the lights, the offering of incense, the individual blessings, and the processions. Second, Egeria notes that "the psalms and antiphons they use are always appropriate, whether at night, in the early morning, at the day prayers at midday or three o'clock, or at Lucernare. Everything is suitable, appropriate, and relevant to what is being done."[25] The cathedral liturgy includes only those psalms that are needed; it is not concerned with praying all the psalms as at a monastery. Third, the cathedral office is for the laity as well as the clergy, with the monks and nuns, particularly in Jerusalem, coming early and staying late. The cathedral office is celebrated by all the people of God. The liturgical actions, the selection of psalmody, and its broad membership are even more striking when compared to the monastic office.

The Monastic Office

The monastic office finds its source in the call to pray always (Luke 18:1; 1 Thess 5:17). The early monks pondered how this seemingly impossible command could be fulfilled by a human being. In one story from the Egyptian desert, Abba John the Short decides to go off because

---

[22] Wilkinson, *Egeria's Travels*, chap. 24.8, 124.
[23] Ibid., chap. 24.9, 125.
[24] Ibid., chap. 24.10–12.
[25] Ibid., chap. 25.5.

he "wants to be free of troubles like the angels, who do not work and serve God unceasingly." Within the week he is back, but his brother will not let him in the door despite his continual knocking, until John acknowledges that he is human and therefore must work. Abba John throws himself on the ground and asks for forgiveness.[26] The call to prayer does not absolve the monk from the need to work. In another saying, Abba Lucius says that he spends the whole day working and praying together; as a result, he is able to earn sixteen denarii. He puts two denarii outside his door and lives off the rest. He says that whoever finds the two coins prays for him while he eats and sleeps, and in this way he fulfills the command to pray always.[27] Balancing work and prayer becomes a perennial problem, and not just in the monastic tradition.

St. Jerome (347–419/20) does not feel the need to be so literal and recommends fixed times of prayer in his letter to the monastic virgin Eustochium:

> Although the apostle bids us to "pray without ceasing" (1 Thess 5:17) and although to the saints their very sleep is a supplication, we ought to have fixed hours of prayer, that if we are detained by work, the time may remind us of our duty. Prayers, as every one knows, ought to be said at the third, sixth and ninth hours, at dawn and at evening.[28]

Though the desire to "pray always" remains a monastic ideal, fixed times of formal prayer become the practical solution.

Benedict founded the famous monastery of Monte Casino in 529 and there wrote his famous Rule that would have a large impact on Western Christianity. In his Rule, Benedict gives the definitive shape to the times of prayer developed over several centuries, especially in the monastic liturgies of Rome.[29] He includes a night office to fulfill what Psalm 119:62 says, "At midnight I rise to praise you." However,

---

[26] *The Desert Fathers: Sayings of the Early Christian Monks*, trans. Benedicta Ward (London: Penguin, 2003), 94.

[27] Ibid., 131–32.

[28] St. Jerome, *St. Jerome: Letters and Select Works, A Select Library of Nicene and Post-Nicene Fathers of the Christian Church*, Second Series, vol. 6, trans. Philip Schaff and Henry Wace (Grand Rapids, MI: Eerdmans Publishing Company, 1983), 38. This is widely available on the Internet.

[29] Timothy Fry, O.S.B., *RB 1980: The Rule of St. Benedict in Latin and English with Notes* (Collegeville, MN: Liturgical Press, 1981), 398–400.

being a prudent man, he sets the time a little later in the night so that his monks can get enough deep sleep. Seven services mark the day to fulfill Psalm 119:164, "Seven times a day have I praised you" (RB 16:1, 4). The names of these hours are as follows:

Vigils	about 2:00 A.M. [30]
Lauds	at dawn, also sometimes called Matins
Prime	first morning hour about 7:00 A.M.
Terce	third morning hour about 9:00 A.M.
Sext	sixth hour at noon
None	ninth hour about 3:00 P.M.
Vespers	toward sunset
Compline	at the beginning of the night

Benedict gives specific instructions about which psalms the monks should say, but he does not give any directions about ritual practice such as lighting lamps or offering incense. His emphasis falls squarely on the recitation of the psalms. In the monastic tradition, the words themselves constitute an event. Therefore, unlike the cathedral office which chooses appropriate psalms for each office, Benedict insists on reciting all 150 psalms each week. As he says, "We read, after all, that our holy Fathers, energetic as they were, did all this in a single day. Let us hope that we, lukewarm as we are, can achieve it in a whole week" (RB 18:28).

Benedict calls this prayer the "Work of God" or the "Divine Office." The Latin word *officium*, like the Greek word "liturgy," refers to "a helpful or beneficial act done to someone in fulfillment of an obligation, a service."[31] Benedict conceives of the monastic office as a duty, but it is a wonderful and sacred duty in which the interior

---

[30] RB 8:1-2, 203. Since the Roman day and night always had twelve hours, the Roman daytime "hour" was longer in the summer (about an hour and a half) and shorter in mid-winter (about forty-five minutes).

[31] *Oxford Latin Dictionary*, ed. P.G.W. Glare (Oxford: Clarendon Press, 1982), s.v. *officium*. Henry George Liddell and Robert Scott, *A Greek-English Lexicon*, 8th ed. (Oxford: Clarendon Press, 1897), s.v. *leitourgia*: "1. a burdensome public office or duty . . . 2. any service or work of a public kind . . . 3. the public service of the gods."

and exterior self are joined together in prayer "in such a way that our minds are in harmony with our voices" (RB 19:7). Such integration is not quickly achieved.

The importance of the Divine Office to Benedict cannot be underestimated. In RB 58:6-7, eagerness for the work of God becomes a hallmark of the desire to "seek God" that stands at the very center of this vocation. In RB 43:3, he says that "nothing is to be preferred to the Work of God." Elsewhere, Benedict says that nothing is to be preferred to the love of Christ (RB 4:21) or to Christ himself (RB 72:11). He puts the Divine Office virtually on the same level as Christ himself because it is the prayer of the Body of Christ and therefore of Christ himself.

As in other monastic rules, Benedict makes provision for those who "need to learn some of the psalter or readings" (RB 8:3). Although some of the Office would have been done as responses to a cantor taking the main part of the psalms, as the laity did in the cathedral office, the monks learned large parts of the psalmody and readings by heart. While the idea of learning even the book of Psalms by heart seems monumental today, those who participate daily in the Liturgy of the Hours become so familiar with the psalms that they can repeat them in community often without much prompting from a book. As a result, this familiarity allows a person to rise above the words of the psalms and to ride his or her emotions or even become absorbed in the experience of the prayer in a way that is comparable to praying the rosary. The words and their meaning serve as an anchor for this experience, but there is an experience of repetitive prayer, even as complex as the Divine Office, that allows people to transcend both the text and themselves. However, it is never just an individual experience because this prayer is done together with the community which represents the whole Church.

Music becomes an integral part of the liturgical experience both at the Eucharist and in the Liturgy of the Hours. Clearly a strong music tradition develops in Italy, often associated to Gregory the Great (540–604) who gives his name to Gregorian chant. This music developed in order to serve the words and meaning of the text. It was not music for music's sake, but music for the sake of the word. This music is carried north of the Alps in the eighth and ninth centuries, where it was preserved and transformed in the monasteries, as earlier in Italy, by musical geniuses. This great treasury of the Church became more and more a museum piece as other needs and the lack of talent often reduced the choir to singing everything on a single note at great speed in order to meet the obligation expeditiously. The liturgical movement which began at the Abbey of Solesmes in the nineteenth century brought a resurgence of the Latin chant in the twentieth century, but as the liturgy moved into the vernacular much of that impetus was lost. At the moment, the Church is faced with the challenge of finding a way both to preserve and to transform this great musical heritage for our liturgy today.

The Emergence of the Breviary, Private Recitation, and the Breviary of Pius V

Charlemagne was crowned Roman Emperor of the West in A.D. 800 and was already engaged in bringing order and unity to law, education, and religion throughout his empire, which covered most of western Europe. His father, King Pepin, had adopted the Roman liturgy, and Charlemagne strengthened this commitment by having Pope Hadrian (772–95) send a Gregorian sacramentary to his capital, Aachen, so that the empire could follow the same text and sing the music of the Roman Church as well. He also had a copy of the Rule of Benedict made from the original, and his son Louis imposed this rule on all the monasteries of the empire. As Benedict's rule became dominant, his legislation for the monastic office became the ideal.

Up through this period, the cathedral churches of the empire carried on their various services, with morning prayer marked by the praise Psalms 148–150 and evening prayer with the lighting of lamps and the offering of incense as Psalm 141 was recited.[32] A night office of vigils was celebrated before Easter, Pentecost, and other great feasts. In Rome the vigil was comprised mainly of "Scripture lessons, psalmody [apparently responsorial psalmody between the lessons], prayer, and preaching, as well as the endless kneeling for prayer that characterized vigil services everywhere."[33]

Originally it was the bishop's clergy that had the obligation to see that the cathedral office was duly celebrated, but in the mid-eighth century, Chrodegang, bishop of Metz (d. 766), made what Taft calls "an innovation

[32] Taft, *Liturgy of the Hours,* 163.
[33] Ibid., 176.

with far-reaching effects."[34] Both Basil the Great and Benedict required their monks working away from the monastery or on a journey to pray the Office while away from the monastery.[35] Monks had an individual and not just a corporate responsibility to pray the Office. Chrodegang extended this requirement to his clergy so that they too became responsible for praying the office individually whether they were present in the cathedral or not.[36] Moreover, the cathedral office, under the influence of Benedict's rule, came to look very much like the monastic office with its night vigil and seven daytime offices embracing the full 150 psalms.

As clergy began to live away from the cathedral community for reasons of pastoral care, the need to recite the Office in private grew. The practice expanded with the advent of mendicants who were constantly on the road and also with clerics studying at the universities far from their communities. Out of these practicalities emerged the need for a single volume to serve those obliged to pray the Office. As time went on, the private recitation of the office became the norm for both clergy and many religious communities.[37] The need for breviaries also created a market for these books, and some are masterpieces of design.[38]

By the end of the Middle Ages, the Divine Office had gathered many additions, often connected to the cult of saints. These accretions dominated the liturgical year, often displacing Sunday or even overshadowing the great feasts celebrating the mysteries of Christ. Local churches too added their particular mark to the office, until it became weighed down with local and even personal devotions. In an attempt at reform, Cardinal Quignonez in 1535 simplified the Office, but the reform did not hold. In 1568, reflecting the spirit of the Council of Trent, Pope Pius V revised the breviary mainly by removing its accretions and then ordered its observance everywhere by those bound to say the Roman

---

[34] Ibid., 299.

[35] Basil the Great, "The Long Rules," in *Ascetical Works*, trans. M. Monica Wagner, C.S.C., The Fathers of the Church, vol. 9 (Washington, D.C.: The Catholic University of America Press, 1950), 306–11, esp. 309. RB 50. See also Salmon, *Breviary*, 3.

[36] Salmon, *Breviary*, 9–11. He cites chapter 4 of the *Rule of St. Chrodegang*, P.L. 89 1101.

[37] Ibid., 11–20.

[38] See for instance: Roger S. Wieck, *Painted Prayers: The Book of Hours in Medieval and Renaissance Art* (New York: George Braziller in association with the Pierpont Morgan Library, 1997).

Office.[39] The emphasis on uniformity underlines the universality of the prayer, although it continued to be prayed almost exclusively in private by the clergy.

The spirituality of the "devout life" promoted by Francis de Sales (1567–1622), like the *devotio moderna* before it, nurtured a personal and interior piety, and the private recitation of the Office suited this emphasis. The pastoral need which first created the necessity for private recitation only seemed to grow with the Church in the modern period. Since the recitation of the Divine Office took an hour, those obliged to recite it under pain of mortal sin would pray it when they could, often in one or two sittings without any relation to times of the day. Even in monasteries, the burden of reciting the Office often devolved on the junior members while their seniors, busy with many things, prayed the Office privately. Even so, many prayed this universal prayer with great devotion in private. Still, the Divine Office, whether recited privately or in choir, had become something very different from its early practice in Egeria's Jerusalem or Benedict's monastery.

The Reform of Vatican II

The Second Vatican Council in its Constitution on the Sacred Liturgy,[40] called for a reform "in order that, in present circumstances, the Divine Office may be better and more perfectly carried out, whether by priests or by other members of the church."[41] The council made it clear that "it is the very prayer which Christ Himself, together with His body, addresses to the Father."[42] This prayer then is the work of the *entire* church, not merely those required to pray it.[43] And it is continuous as people in various countries and places take up the prayer appropriate to the daylight's action in their own locale.

---

[39] Salmon, *Breviary*, 19–20; Crichton, *Prayer of the Church*, 52–54.

[40] *Sacrosanctum Concilium* (The Constitution on the Sacred Liturgy), December 4, 1963. This document is typically referred to by the abbreviation SC followed by the paragraph number.

[41] SC, no. 87.

[42] SC, no. 84.

[43] Paul VI, "*Laudis Canticum*" in *The Liturgy of the Hours*, trans. International Commission on English in the Liturgy, vol. 1 (New York: Catholic Book Publishing Co., 1975), 11–20. This document appears in various places on the Internet.

The Constitution on the Sacred Liturgy not only mandates a reform, but it also includes specific directions for that reform, which took place between 1964 and 1971. Stanislaus Campbell has summarized the process in his engaging book *From Breviary to the Liturgy of the Hours.*[44] The reform stipulated by Vatican II can be outlined as follows: Since this liturgy is "to sanctify the day," the hours are reformed so that they reflect the times of day when they are to be prayed but also fit the conditions of modern life, especially as lived by "those engaged in apostolic work."[45] As a result, the Council calls for the following changes:[46]

a) The morning prayer of Lauds and the evening prayer of Vespers should serve as "the two hinges on which the daily office turns."

b) Compline should "be drawn up so as suitably to mark the close of the day."

c) The night office, variously called Vigils or sometimes Matins (a term also used for Lauds), should be "adapted so that it may be recited at any hour of the day" to provide the flexibility needed to shape this prayer to different contexts. Moreover there should be "fewer psalms and longer readings." The reform has produced a two-year cycle of readings from the Scriptures, although in practice only the first year is used. Likewise there is now a large selection of readings from the Doctors of the early Church and others, with many readings coming from St. Augustine.[47]

d) Prime is "suppressed."

e) The little hours of Terce, Sext, and None are to be observed, but "outside of choir it is permissible to select one of the three most suited to the time of the day."

So that those who pray the Divine Office may "attune their minds to their voices, . . . the psalms are no longer to be distributed over one week, but over a longer period of time."[48] The decision to keep the

---

[44] Stanislaus Campbell, F.S.C. *From Breviary to the Liturgy of the Hours: The Structural Reform of the Roman Office, 1964–1971* (Collegeville, MN: Liturgical Press, 1995).

[45] SC, no. 88.

[46] SC, no. 89.

[47] *General Instruction on the Liturgy of the Hours*, no. 145.

[48] SC, 90–91.

whole 150 psalms evolved after much discussion.[49] Some argued for a return to the cathedral usage of only select psalms. Although the reformers recognized that the use of the whole psalter was "monastic in origin," its long usage in the Roman Office prevailed over a return to the cathedral usage. Still, the reform achieved a manageable psalmody (if sacrificing some familiarity) by spreading the whole psalter[50] over four weeks while adding new canticles from the Old and New Testament. The reform, therefore, has lightened the burden of the Divine Office considerably and made it more manageable for those engaged in the modern world of ministry or of work and family.

Pope Paul VI promulgated the reform with the Apostolic Constitution *Laudis Canticum* in 1971. The *General Instruction on the Liturgy of the Hours* followed in 1975. The changes in the structure of Lauds and Vespers are the most significant, because the reform sought to make the morning and evening prayer the foundation stones for the whole.

Lauds and Vespers follow the same pattern. Both open with the traditional verse established by John Cassian as the summary of all prayer: "God, come to my assistance. Lord, make haste to help me" (Ps 70:1). The hymn, originally after the reading, now follows immediately and establishes the theme of the Office. The Latin hymn tradition, with texts by St. Ambrose, Venantius Fortunatus, and others, contains texts of great beauty and great theology. The English hymn tradition, with its translations from the Latin, is also wide and deep. Still, there are possibilities yet to be realized.

The psalmody has been reduced from eight psalms in the morning and five in the evening to two psalms with a canticle. This change evolved after much questioning and discussion. With great reluctance the reform let go of Psalms 148–150, the traditional part of Lauds. Some were anxious to use Psalm 141 daily as in the cathedral tradition. In the end, pastoral concern dominated. The reform reduced the psalmody to make it viable for those who would pray it. Importantly, a New Testament canticle was added to the psalmody of Vespers. This reflects a basic thrust of the reform to bring more of the word of God to the praying community.

---

[49] Campbell, *From Breviary*, 139–69, 187–90, esp. 153.

[50] Three cursing psalms, Psalms 57(58), 82(83), 108(109), along with some verses of other psalms have been omitted "because of certain psychological difficulties." See *General Instructions on the Liturgy of the Hours*, no. 131.

These canticles also bring a clear christological dimension which "could assist in fostering a Christian understanding of the Psalter."[51]

Before and after each psalm there is an antiphon: a short verse giving the psalm some context. On ordinary days of the week, the antiphon may focus attention on a line in the psalm. On Sundays and feasts and during liturgical seasons, the antiphon highlights the imagery and theology of the celebration and so draws the psalm into the mystery of Christ. Since the ancient practice of saying the psalms included silence after each psalm for private prayer, the reform has added a "psalm-prayer" which typically links the psalm to Christ and the Church. Still, silence should continue to play a part in this praying with Christ.[52]

After a short reading and response, Lauds and Vespers reach their climax with the Gospel canticles: at Lauds the Canticle of Zachary, called the *Benedictus* (Luke 1:68-79), and at Vespers the Canticle of Mary, called the *Magnificat* (Luke 1:46-55). During the communal celebration of Lauds and particularly Vespers, the altar, the symbol of Christ, may be incensed during these canticles.[53] Both of these hymns celebrate the ancient covenant that is realized in Christ Jesus. Zachary tells us that he is the Rising Sun who shines on those who sit in darkness and guides our feet in the way of peace. Mary tells of God's remembered promise, the covenant realized in her, for she is the mother of God's mercy to every generation.

The reform has added intercessions to both Lauds and Vespers.[54] The documents suggest a difference between those for Lauds and Vespers, although it is not always easy to distinguish. The intercessions at Lauds "are invocations to commend or consecrate the day to God"[55] while at Vespers they are similar to those at Mass with the last always being for the dead.[56]

---

[51] Campbell, *From Breviary to Liturgy*, 193.

[52] "In order to receive in our hearts the full sound of the voice of the Holy Spirit and to unite our personal prayer more closely with the word of God and the public voice of the Church, it is permissible, as occasion offers and prudence suggests, to have an interval of silence." *General Instruction on the Liturgy of the Hours*, no. 202.

[53] *General Instruction on the Liturgy of the Hours*, no. 261.

[54] Some have criticized the intercessions as "monastic," but Taft says that this shows "a total unawareness of the large place such petitions held in early cathedral usage." *Liturgy of the Hours*, 315.

[55] *General Instruction on the Liturgy of the Hours*, no. 181.

[56] Ibid., no. 180, 186.

The Lord's Prayer follows, and with its recitation at Mass the Church returns "to the ancient Christian custom of reciting this prayer three times each day."[57] The office ends with new prayers and a dismissal.

Lauds	Vespers
opening verse (Ps 70:1)	opening verse (Ps 70:1)
hymn	hymn
psalmody	psalmody
morning psalm	psalm
OT canticle	psalm
praise psalm	NT canticle
short Scripture reading	short Scripture reading
response	response
Gospel Canticle of Zachary	Gospel Canticle of Mary
intercessions	intercessions
Our Father	Our Father
prayer and conclusion	prayer and conclusion

Robert Taft eloquently argues that the image of light plays a central role for both Lauds, the prayer of sunrise, and Vespers, the prayer of sunset. According to 1 John 1:5, "God is light," and this is "a constant New Testament theme, especially in the Johannine literature."[58] Taft attributes to Cyprian (200–58) the honor of drawing the connection between the resurrection and the prayer at morning and evening.[59] The rising sun

[57] Ibid., no. 8. This is first found in the *Didache*, chapter 8:3; cf. "The Didache: An English Translation," trans. Aelred Cody, O.S.B., in *The Didache in Context: Essays on its Text, History, and Transmission*, ed. Clayton N. Jefford, Supplements to Novum Testamentum, vol. 77 (Leiden: E.J. Brill, 1995), 9.

[58] Taft, *Liturgy of the Hours*, 349.

[59] Cyprian, "The Lord's Prayer" in *Treatises*, trans. Roy J. Deferrari, The Fathers of the Church, 36 (New York: Fathers of the Church, Inc., 1958), 157–59. "For we must also pray in the morning, that the resurrection of the Lord may be celebrated by morning prayer. . . . Likewise at the setting of the sun and at the end of the day necessarily there must again be prayer. For since Christ is the true Sun and the true Day, as the sun and the day of the world recede, when we pray and petition that the light come upon us again, we pray for the coming of Christ to provide us with the grace of eternal light."

seems a natural image for Christ rising from the dead, and Cyprian calls him "the true Sun and the true Day." The new day represents the gift of the risen Christ to those who have gathered to pray. At Vespers, those who gather light lamps to remind themselves that Christ is always their light. As the darkness comes, it invites them to pray for the coming of Christ the Light at the end of time. As important as the theme of light may be, it does not exhaust the meaning of these hours. For Basil the Great (330–79), prayer early in the morning consecrates the day and puts us in the presence of God—a realization that should bring us joy. When the work is over, he says that we should offer thanksgiving for what we have received or accomplished and also confess any sin committed during the course of the day "in words, deed, or in the heart itself."[60] Taft sums up his fuller exploration of texts this way:

> The Liturgy of the Hours, then, is a sanctification of life by turning to God at the beginning and end of each of its days to do what all liturgy always does—to celebrate and manifest in ritual moments what is and must be the constant stance of our every minute of the day: our unceasing priestly offering, in Christ, of self, to the praise and glory of the Father in thanks for his saving gift in Christ.[61]

The reform has given the Church a Liturgy of the Hours that draws on the tradition but that also meets the pastoral needs of so many, both those who have undertaken the obligation to pray the Hours and those who desire to participate in the official prayer of the Church. Many religious communities now pray in common the Liturgy of the Hours, or some part of it. Those who pray it privately have a manageable prayer, although pastoral demands can make it difficult to spread this prayer through the day. Many laypeople too have begun to pray the Liturgy of the Hours, especially morning and evening prayer. Though Paul tells us to pray without ceasing (1 Thess 5:17), it is good to have a prayer with a beginning and an end so that we can say that we have prayed today. It is also good to have a prayer with words given by the Church that take us beyond our narrow concerns and our personal understanding of God. By praying this prayer we join ourselves to the Body of Christ, becoming catholic in its many senses.

[60] Basil, Long Rules, 309–10.
[61] Taft, *Liturgy of the Hours*, 359–60.

Conclusion

We human beings, fashioned in God's image, know a built-in desire to turn to God in prayer. As Christians, we rightly desire to respond to what is given, to what has been offered, to what has been made possible by God. The liturgy is the Church's school of prayer,[62] and we learn by the Church's liturgy that we are made to give thanks and praise to God, all the while interceding, as Christ does, for those in need.

In its wisdom, the Church has provided seasons that follow each other to shape us in our sacramental experience of Jesus' birth, life, death, and resurrection. Equally stunning is the wisdom the Church has shown in relying on Jewish habits (and texts) of prayer to remind the Christian people of the need to turn back to God in thanks, praise, and petition. Each day provides the opportunity for the whole Church to join Christ in his ceaseless prayer. And each year reminds Christians of the power of Christ's eternal gift of life over the shadows of death.

Using the music of the soul, at morning and evening and at points in between, the Body of Christ expresses the feelings and hopes, the disappointments and concerns, of the human race to God whose concern is ceaseless. At the same time, the Church situates itself in the annual cycle of death bearing life. This recurring cycle with its seasons that make real the sanctification of time keeps the Church grounded in its work each day and always. Flowing from the power of the Eucharist and shaping private prayer, the Church's official liturgy gathers its people in for prayer.

Further Reading

Brook, John. *The School of Prayer: An Introduction to the Divine Office for All Christians*. Collegeville, MN: Liturgical Press, 1991.

Catholic Church. *Shorter Christian Prayer: The Four-Week Psalter of the Liturgy of the Hours Containing Morning Prayer and Evening Prayer*. New York: Catholic Book Publishing Co., 1999.

Johnson, Maxwell E., ed. *Benedictine Daily Prayer: A Short Breviary*. Collegeville, MN: Liturgical Press, 2005.

---

[62] Taft, *Liturgy of the Hours*, 367–73.

Murray, Seth H. *Lord, Open My Lips: The Liturgy of the Hours As Daily Prayer*. El Sobrante, CA: North Bay Books, 2004. This is a step-by-step introduction for laypeople to help them learn how to pray the Liturgy of the Hours.

Taft, Robert. *The Liturgy of the Hours in East and West: The Origins of the Divine Office and Its Meaning for Today*. Rev. ed. Collegeville, MN: Liturgical Press, 1993.

Chapter 10

The Eucharist:
The Prayer and Work
of the People of God

Kurt Stasiak, O.S.B.

A loaf of bread and a cup of wine. A learned Jewish teacher reclining at table, sharing the Passover meal with his closest friends.

From these humble beginnings comes the celebration of the Eucharist, the "source and summit of the Christian life,"[1] the sacrament in which "is contained the entire spiritual wealth of the church, namely, Christ himself."[2] The *Constitution on the Sacred Liturgy*, the first of the documents promulgated by the Second Vatican Council, describes the liturgy in the most impressive terms: "For the liturgy, through which 'the work of our redemption takes place,' especially in the divine sacrifice of the Eucharist, is supremely effective in enabling the faithful to express in their lives and portray to others the mystery of Christ and the real nature of the true church."[3] These phrases say it all: "source and summit, . . . entire spiritual wealth, . . . supremely effective

---

[1] *Lumen Gentium* (Dogmatic Constitution on the Church), November 21, 1964, no. 11 (can also be found in the *Catechism of the Catholic Church*, 2d ed., 1997, par. 1324).

[2] *Presbyterorum Ordinis* (Decree on the Life and Ministry of Priests), December 7, 1965, no. 5 (can also be found in *Catechism*, par. 1324).

[3] *Sacrosanctum Concilium* (Constitution on the Sacred Liturgy), December 4, 1963, no. 2 (can also be found in *Catechism*, par. 1068).

. . ." Clearly, the Eucharist, the Mass, is of the utmost importance for us Catholics.

Many Catholics, however, understand the Eucharist somewhat differently than in the impressive words found in Church documents. A conversation such as the following surely is familiar to all: "What Mass are you going to this Sunday?" "Oh, I always go to the 9:30. That's Father Michael's Mass." Church documents speak eloquently and elegantly about the significance of the Eucharist, and rightly so. But perhaps our conversational vignette reflects more accurately the attitude toward the Eucharist many Catholics have. Granted, the conversation is a casual one and does not intend to address profound theological truths. But it does illustrate what comes first to the minds of many when talking about the Eucharist. *Whose Mass is it?* "It's the *priest's* Mass. After all, *he's* the one who does everything, says everything. *He's* the one we watch."

The actions and words of the priest at the Eucharist are of the utmost importance. But the Eucharist is not his prayer, nor is it the priest alone who has an active role in the Mass. The celebration of the Eucharist is the prayer of the Catholic community par excellence. It is our prayer as we, united by our baptism and our faith in God, his Son, and the Holy Spirit, offer praise and thanksgiving, ask forgiveness for our sins, and intercede for the needs of others. The Eucharist belongs to the Christian community and it shapes that community, giving it an identity and a mission. The Eucharist, as we have seen, is "supremely effective in enabling the faithful to express in their lives and portray to others the mystery of Christ and the real nature of the true church."

Acknowledging that the Eucharist is the sacrifice of Christ, the *Catechism* speaks of the Eucharist also as the sacrifice of the Church. The community is not only present at the Eucharist, they present themselves through their participation in the Eucharist:

> The Church which is the Body of Christ participates in the offering of her Head. . . . In the Eucharist the sacrifice of Christ becomes also the sacrifice of the members of his Body. The lives of the faithful, their praise, suffering, prayer, and work, are united with those of Christ and with his total offering, and so acquire a new value.[4]

---

[4] *Catechism,* par. 1368.

The celebration of the Eucharist is the prayer *of, by,* and *for* the community.

An Early Description of the Mass

The way the community has celebrated the Eucharist has evolved dramatically from that Passover meal Jesus shared with his disciples. Over many centuries elements were introduced, then modified, and often subsequently eliminated—or restored. How the Mass developed to the form in which we know it today is beyond the scope of this chapter.[5] To illustrate our remarkable continuity with the past, however, we consider briefly one of the earliest accounts we have of the Church celebrating the Eucharist. This description comes from Justin, a Platonist philosopher who converted to Christianity.[6] He writes around the year 150:

> And on the day called Sunday an assembly is held in one place of all who live in town or country, and the records of the apostles or the writings of the prophets are read as time allows. Then, when the reader has finished, the president in a discourse admonishes and exhorts us to imitate these good things. Then we all stand up together and send up prayers; and as we said before, when we have finished praying, bread and wine and water are brought up, and the president likewise sends up prayers and thanksgiving to the best of his ability, and the people assent, saying the Amen; and the [elements over which] thanks have been given are distributed and everyone partakes; and they are sent through the deacons to those who are not present. And the wealthy who so desire give what they wish, as each chooses; and what is collected is deposited with the president . . . [to help] all those who are in need.[7]

---

[5] Among the many works detailing the history and development of the Eucharist, we recommend especially two: Johannes H. Emminghaus, *The Eucharist: essence, form, celebration,* rev. ed. (Collegeville, MN: Liturgical Press, 1997), and Theodor Klauser, *A Short History of the Western Liturgy: An account and some reflections,* 2d ed. (Oxford: Oxford University Press, 1981).

[6] Justin was subsequently martyred for his faith, hence the frequent references to him in our tradition as "Justin Martyr."

[7] *Apologia I,* ch. 67, trans. R. C. D. Jasper and G. J. Cuming, *Prayers of the Eucharist: Early and Reformed,* 3d rev. ed. (Collegeville, MN: Liturgical Press, 1990), as quoted in Emminghaus, 36.

Written almost two thousand years ago, Justin's account remains a basic description of the Mass even as we celebrate it today. The community gathers on Sundays. The Scriptures (the "accounts of the apostles" and the "writings of the prophets" refer, respectively, to the New and Old Testaments) are proclaimed, and then the celebrant explains them with a homily. The people offer prayers for themselves or those who have special needs (the General Intercessions). Bread, wine, and water are brought forward, and the presider offers "prayers and thanksgiving"—a Eucharistic Prayer. Communion is taken to those who cannot be present. There is even a collection. Justin's account is interesting also in that it clearly shows that the Mass is not the work of the priest alone, for different ministries had already begun to develop within the Church. A president prays and gives thanks, deacons take the Eucharist to those absent, and lectors read. Although the ritual details of celebrating the Eucharist will change in many ways as time goes on, the Mass will always reflect the basic structure recorded by Justin.

Development and Standardization

The fourth century is an important milestone for the Church and its liturgy, for it saw not only the end of the persecutions of Christians but also an increasing acceptance of Christianity as the "official religion" of the Western world. As the Church increased in numbers, stature, and influence, liturgy became more elaborate and complex. Masses celebrated by the pope or bishops often involved many ministers, processions, and ceremonies within ceremonies, and required quite a bit of time. But it was a much simpler way of celebrating the Eucharist, the "private Mass," that eventually became the norm for many centuries—a norm which, in some ways, continues to influence our understanding and experience of the Eucharist even today.

The private Mass, so called because ordinarily only the priest and his altar server were present, had become a regular practice in monasteries by the tenth century. Although the sixth century Rule written by St. Benedict had specified that monks ordinarily would not be priests, monasteries began to be centers of missionary activity. This meant that more priests were needed to celebrate Mass and administer the sacraments, so the number of monks ordained to the priesthood steadily increased. Not all were engaged in missionary work all the time, however, and when they were at their monasteries they understandably wanted to preside at the

Eucharist to receive the graces of the sacrament and to honor the prayer requests of the people. Concelebration—several priests celebrating one Eucharist together—was not a usual practice at this time, so each ordained monk would celebrate his own Mass. If there were many ordained monks in a monastery, there could be several Masses being celebrated at the same time at different altars located throughout the church.

Adjustments while celebrating these private Masses had to be made, of course, and these adjustments continued to shape the normative way of celebrating the Eucharist. Since often there were no other people present (other than the assisting altar server), the priest would assume all liturgical ministries. He, rather than a lector or deacon, would read the first reading (the epistle). There was no choir to chant the antiphons so he would recite them. And as there was no congregation present, there was no need for him to deliver a sermon.

How did this influence the manner and the experience of celebrating the Eucharist?[8] Over time what happened was that while people continued to *attend* Mass, they no longer *participated* at the Mass in the same way as they did in the early Church (for example, in Justin's account). They were prayerful and reverent, but the prayers they were saying often were independent of those the priest was praying. While the priest quietly recited the readings and the prayers (including the all-important Eucharistic Prayer), the people said their own prayers. Priest and people prayed at the same time, but they did not pray the same thing. Remember, too, that now there was little for people to look at during the Eucharist, for virtually the entire Mass was celebrated with everyone facing the same way—which meant the priest had his back to the people. The ringing of bells was introduced to catch people's attention when "something special" was happening (at the elevation of the consecrated bread and wine, for example).

The private Mass was the standard of celebration when the Council of Trent met to respond to the attacks made by the Protestant reformers on Church teaching and authority. The council first met in 1545 and, frequently interrupted, concluded its work some eighteen years later. One of the council's contributions was the *Roman Missal*, sometimes called the *Missal of Pius V*, published in 1570. This *Missal* established

---

[8] Again, I offer the necessary caution that for the sake of space we are condensing centuries of history into a few true, but highly generalized, statements.

in great detail how the Mass was to be celebrated. And so it was, with only a few minor changes, for almost the next four hundred years.

Recent Restoration and Renewal

The Second Vatican Council, convoked by Pope John XXIII, began its work in 1962. Its first document, published in December of the following year, was the *Constitution on the Sacred Liturgy*. Its call for a restoration and renewal of the liturgy to make it more accessible and understandable for the people led to the publication in 1969 of a new Roman Missal, often referred to as the *Novus Ordo* (the "New Order") or the *Ordo of Paul VI*. Before we consider the individual elements of the Mass, it is important to note some of the major differences between the Roman Missals of 1570 and 1969, for in doing so we can better understand our emphasis today on the Mass as the prayer *of, by,* and *for* the community.

Language. Since the introduction of the *Novus Ordo* (1969), the Mass has been celebrated in the common language of the people, as it was until the latter part of the fourth century. Prior to the council the Mass was said in Latin, and those present could not understand the prayers or the readings unless they had their own missal.

Ministers. Prior to the Second Vatican Council, the priest said the prayers, read the readings, and distributed communion. He was assisted only by one or two altar servers, whose primary responsibilities were to respond quietly to his prayers, to move the book from one side of the altar to the other, and to bring him the wine and water. For the most part the congregation watched silently or devoted themselves to following the Mass in their own prayer books. Many would say favorite prayers, such as the rosary, or recite various devotions and litanies. Today, in addition to acolytes, the priest is assisted by lectors, extraordinary ministers of the Eucharist, cantors, and, in many places, permanent deacons. Moreover, as all prayers are said aloud and in the people's own language, those attending are better able to "pray the Mass" along with the priest, rather than attending to their private devotions.

Architecture. Church architecture has changed dramatically over the past four decades. Most new churches are constructed so that the community is gathered somewhat *around* the altar rather than in front of it. Just as the structure of the Roman basilica influenced the manner in which the Eucharist was celebrated and experienced, contemporary architects hope the "auditorium style" will encourage greater community participation.

Receiving Communion. Three changes have occurred in the practice of receiving communion. The first actually began almost one hundred years ago when Pope Pius X, wanting to encourage the more frequent reception of communion and therefore a greater degree of participation, lowered the age of First Communion from twelve to about seven. And within the past generation, people have been given the option of receiving communion in the hand and often under both species—both reminiscent of practices in the early church.

Having surveyed the primary differences between the Ordos of Pius V (1570) and Paul VI (1969), we now consider the individual elements of the Mass. How does our celebration of the Eucharist today encourage us to understand the Mass as *our* prayer? How can we truly pray and participate in the Mass that makes us Church, rather than just going to church to watch the Mass being said? We will consider a Sunday Eucharist in Ordinary Time as our reference point.[9]

Introductory Rites

The introductory rites consist of an entrance song; the sign of the cross, the greeting by the priest, and the people's response; the penitential rite; the *Gloria;* and the Opening Prayer. These rites do what their name implies: they introduce the Mass by reminding the community they are about to begin a special time in a special place. As

---

[9] "Ordinary Time" refers to those Sundays falling outside the liturgical seasons of Advent, Christmas, Lent, and Easter. These are the first half-dozen or so Sundays of the calendar year, and most of the Sundays from (usually) late May until the end of November: the Sundays when green vestments are worn. There are thirty-four weeks of Ordinary Time. The last Sunday of Ordinary Time is the Solemnity of Christ the King in late November, after which follows the First Sunday of Advent and the beginning of the Church's liturgical year.

the *Sacramentary*[10] points out, "Their purpose is to ensure that the faithful who come together as one establish communion and dispose themselves to listen properly to God's word and to celebrate the Eucharist worthily."[11]

The *penitential rite* and the *Gloria* reflect two traditional types of prayer, as they reflect also two themes the Eucharist sets before us time and again: our unworthiness to celebrate these mysteries on the one hand and, on the other hand, our thanksgiving to and praise of God who continually offers us his gifts of pardon and peace.[12]

The *Collect* or Opening Prayer concludes the introduction to the liturgy. This is the first of three "presidential prayers," so-called because "[t]hese prayers are addressed to God in the name of the entire holy people and all present, by the priest who presides over the assembly in the person of Christ."[13] This prayer expresses the character or theme of the celebration,[14] and helps the community "collect" its thoughts as it prepares for the Liturgy of the Word. Consider the Collect for the Twenty-Second Sunday in Ordinary Time:

Almighty God,

every good thing comes from you.

Fill our hearts with love for you,

increase our faith,

and by your constant care

protect the good you have given us.

We ask this . . . .

The prayer follows a typical prayer-structure. It addresses God by one of God's attributes (almighty). It praises God and implicitly offers

[10] The *Sacramentary* is the book containing the prayers said by the priest during the celebration of the Eucharist. The references here are from its introduction, the *General Instruction of the Roman Missal* (GIRM), 3d typical edition, (International Committee on English in the Liturgy, Inc., 2002).

[11] Ibid., par. 46.

[12] Because of the penitential nature of the Lenten season and the special nature of the Season of Advent, the *Gloria* is omitted on the Sundays of these seasons.

[13] GIRM, par. 30.

[14] Ibid., par. 54.

thanks for what God has done (every good thing comes from you). And it petitions God for continued care and assistance (fill our hearts, . . . increase our faith, . . . protect the good you have given us). Although called a "presidential prayer," the Collect (and the two other presidential prayers later in the Mass) are *our* prayers: they are said on our behalf and they ask something for our good. As is the case with all the prayers offered by the presider, the people, "uniting themselves to this entreaty, make the prayer their own with the acclamation, *Amen.*"[15]

The Liturgy of the Word

The Liturgy of the Word consists of three readings and a psalm from the Scriptures, a homily, the Profession of Faith, and the Prayer of the Faithful. The *Constitution on the Sacred Liturgy* assures us that "Christ is always present in his Church, especially in her liturgical celebrations," and one of the ways Christ expresses his presence is "in his word since it is he himself who speaks when the holy scriptures are read in church."[16]

The first reading is from the Old Testament (except during the Easter season, when it is from the book of Acts) and is related in some way to the gospel that will soon be proclaimed. In this way it is hoped that the community will better see the unity between the two testaments.

As a response to the first reading, a psalm is recited by the cantor, with the people repeating an antiphon.[17] Then, a second reading is proclaimed. Taken from one of the New Testament letters, this reading has only a coincidental, if any, connection to the gospel (or the first reading). Its selection is based upon the continuous reading of a particular New Testament letter over successive Sundays. The intention is that faithful participants in the Sunday Eucharist will over a period of time hear a rather substantial selection of the New Testament texts.

The priest or deacon then proclaims the gospel. One major contribution of the Second Vatican Council to the liturgy was the establishment of a three-year cycle of gospel readings for Sundays, thus allowing

[15] Ibid.

[16] *Sacrosanctum Concilium* (Constitution on the Sacred Liturgy), December 4, 1963, no. 7 (can also be found in *Catechism*, par. 1088).

[17] "By their silence and singing the people make God's word their own . . ." *GIRM*, par. 55.

Catholics a greater familiarity not only with the gospels but also with the particular style and focus of each individual gospel.[18]

The homily, considered an integral part of the liturgy, follows. The homily ordinarily explains to the community the significance the gospel and the other readings have to their lives. It is meant, then, not so much to impart *information* but, rather, to assist the Catholic community in its ongoing *formation*.[19]

The Liturgy of the Word concludes with the recitation of the Creed and the Prayers of the Faithful. The Creed is the community's further response to the readings and the homily and allows them to express their common identity.[20] Through the Prayer of the Faithful the community, "responds in a certain way to the word of God which they have welcomed in faith and, exercising the office of their baptismal priesthood, offer prayers to God for the salvation of all."[21] These intercessions generally include the needs of the Church, the leaders of our local and national governments, the oppressed, the sick and the suffering, and needs specific to the community. The Prayer of the Faithful is one way the community ministers to others: these prayers draw us out of ourselves so we might open our hearts to others. These prayers *of* and *for* the Christian community are, ultimately, prayers for all the peoples of the world.

The Liturgy of the Eucharist

Just as there are preparatory or introductory rites for the Liturgy of the Word, so are there preparatory rites to the Liturgy of the Eucharist.

---

[18] Prior to the Second Vatican Council, the gospel at the Sunday Eucharist was almost always from the gospel of Saint Matthew—the "first" and longest of the four gospels.

[19] The connection between the readings and the homily is another contribution of the council to the liturgical reform. Prior to the council, for example, it was not uncommon for the priest to begin his homily by saying, "Today we are beginning a series of sermons on the Ten Commandments," or "For the next seven weeks I will be preaching about the seven gifts of the Holy Spirit." Another example of how the sermon was not necessarily derived from or connected with the readings was the common practice of the priest beginning and concluding his sermon by making the sign of the cross, thereby suggesting that the sermon was an isolated, independent part of the Mass.

[20] "[The people] affirm their adherence to [God's word] by means of the Profession of Faith." *GIRM*, par. 55.

[21] Ibid., par. 69.

This was called the "Liturgy of the Faithful" in the early Church, to distinguish it from the preceding "Liturgy of the Catechumens." Only those baptized had the privilege of participating in the entire Eucharist, so the catechumens, those still preparing for baptism, were dismissed at this point.[22]

In most parishes a family brings the bread and wine to the altar and presents it to the priest. In the early Church the people themselves would have made the bread and the wine used in the celebration. "Even though the faithful no longer bring from their own possessions the bread and wine intended for the liturgy as in the past, nevertheless the rite of carrying up the offerings still retains its force and its spiritual significance,"[23] namely, the people offer themselves by offering gifts for the sacrifice. "This is also the time to receive money or other gifts for the church or the poor brought by the faithful or collected at the Mass."[24] As we saw in Justin's description of the Mass, concern for the poor and needy was an important part of celebrating the Eucharist from the beginning.

The preparatory rites for the Liturgy of the Eucharist conclude as the priest prays the second of the three presidential prayers, the Prayer over the Gifts. (It was once called the "Secret Prayer" because it was prayed silently.) This prayer again helps the community "collect" its thoughts for, referring to the gifts that have been prepared, it expresses the community's hope that these offerings will work toward their salvation. Here, for example, is the Prayer over the Gifts from the Twenty-Second Sunday in Ordinary Time:

Lord,

may this holy offering

bring us your blessing

and accomplish within us

its promise of salvation.

Grant this through Christ our Lord. (Amen.)

---

[22] This notion will be familiar to those whose parish conducts the *Rite of Christian Initiation of Adults.*

[23] *GIRM*, par. 73.

[24] Ibid., par. 49.

The Eucharistic Prayer

While the *Dogmatic Constitution on the Church* refers to the Eucharist as the "source and summit of the Christian life,"[25] the *Sacramentary* calls the Eucharistic Prayer the "center and summit of the entire celebration."[26] The Eucharistic Prayer is also referred to as the *Anaphora*, a Greek word meaning "offering." The Prayer begins with the Preface, a prayer of thanks and praise to God. The Preface itself begins with a dialogue between priest and people. At the very beginning of this "center and summit" of the Mass, then, the community is reminded that they are not only present but also are to present themselves in this sacrifice:

> The priest invites the people to lift up their hearts to the Lord in prayer and thanksgiving; he unites the congregation with himself in the prayer that he addresses in the name of the entire community to God the Father through Jesus Christ in the Holy Spirit. Furthermore, the meaning of the Prayer is that the entire congregation of the faithful should join itself with Christ in confessing the great deeds of God and in the offering of Sacrifice.[27]

The Preface concludes with the community proclaiming the "Holy, Holy, Holy," the first of several acclamations they will make during the Eucharistic Prayer.

In addition to the thanksgiving expressed and the acclamation exclaimed in the Preface, each Eucharistic Prayer consists of six distinct elements.[28] The first of these is the *epiclesis*, a Greek word meaning "to call down." The *epiclesis* asks that the Holy Spirit "come upon these

---

[25] See note 1.

[26] *GIRM*, par. 78.

[27] Ibid.

[28] The celebrant has several Eucharistic Prayers from which to choose—this yet another contribution of the Second Vatican Council. Until the Ordo of Paul VI there was only one Eucharistic Prayer said at each Mass: the Roman Canon (which we now call Eucharistic Prayer I). The immediate liturgical reforms of the council and subsequent developments have given us an additional twelve Eucharistic Prayers (EP): II, III, and IV, Eucharistic Prayers for Masses of Reconciliation I and II, Eucharistic Prayers for Masses with Children I, II, and III, and four versions of a Eucharistic Prayer for Masses for Various Needs and Occasions.

gifts to make them holy, so that they may become for us the Body and Blood of our Lord Jesus Christ" (Eucharistic Prayer II).[29]

The *epiclesis* leads directly into the institution narrative and the consecration of the bread and wine. Using the words of the Scriptures, the priest recalls the words and actions of Jesus at the Last Supper. These words not only effect the transformation of the bread and the wine into the Body and Blood of Christ ("This is my Body, . . . this is my Blood"), but they also describe the significance of this wondrous mystery ("given up for you, . . . so that sins may be forgiven"). Prior to the Second Vatican Council, the people would adore the host in silence while the priest elevated first the consecrated host and then the chalice.[30] Now, however, a more communal response is called for, for what has taken place at the altar is for the benefit of all gathered around that altar. The congregation responds with one of the forms of the Memorial Acclamation, in which they affirm Christ's death, his resurrection, and his future coming in glory.

The *Anamnesis* follows; the word is the Greek for "memorial." Once again God's saving work through Jesus Christ is announced to the community. An Offering, in which "the Church here and now gathered . . . offers in the Holy Spirit the spotless Victim to the Father,"[31] concludes with a "second *epiclesis*." Coming immediately after the consecration, this second invoking of the Spirit is sometimes not appreciated, but it is essential to the meaning of the Eucharist. "The Church's intention, . . . is that the faithful not only offer this spotless Victim but also learn to offer themselves, and so day by day to be consummated, through Christ the Mediator, into unity with God and with each other, so that at last God may be all in all."[32] The offering and this "second epiclesis," then, make it clear that the Eucharist is not only about a change in the bread and wine. As the *Catechism* notes: "The *Epiclesis* ('invocation upon') is the intercession in which the priest begs the Father to send the Holy Spirit, the Sanctifier, so that the offerings may become the

---

[29] In the Ordo of Pius V, when the priest stretched out his hands over the bread and wine, the altar server would first ring a bell to call the congregation's attention to the fact that something of great importance was about to happen.

[30] Again, the altar server would ring a bell, calling the people's attention to this important event.

[31] *GIRM*, par. 79-f.

[32] Ibid.

body and blood of Christ and that the faithful by receiving them, may themselves become a living offering to God."[33]

In the prayer tradition of our Church, prayers of praise, thanksgiving, petition for forgiveness, and intercession for the needs of others are closely connected. The Eucharistic Prayer has to this point concentrated on praise of God and thanksgiving for the great gift of God's Son, made present among us now through the sacramental signs of bread and wine. We have also acknowledged that this offering is for the forgiveness of our sins, and we have asked that as the gifts have been made holy, so too may we be made holy. The Eucharistic Prayer now moves into a series of Intercessions, when we pray for the people of our Church and our world. As the Eucharistic Prayer draws to a close, this is yet another opportunity to recall that this great prayer is the prayer *of* the people, *by* the people, and *for* the people. As the *Sacramentary* comments, through the intercessions "expression is given to the fact that the Eucharist is celebrated in communion with the entire Church, of heaven as well as of earth, and that the offering is made for her and for all her members, living and dead, who have been called to participate in the redemption and the salvation purchased by Christ's Body and Blood."[34]

The Eucharistic Prayer concludes with the Final Doxology or the "Great Amen," a final acclamation of praise to God. As is the case throughout the Mass, "Amen" signals the community's affirmation and acceptance of what has been proclaimed.

The Communion Rite

Immediate preparation for receiving Holy Communion includes several prayers and ritual actions. Chief among the prayers is the Our Father. It is significant that when the apostles asked Jesus how to pray, he taught them not as individuals but as a community. There are no singular pronouns in the Our Father. The *Catechism* explains the significance of the Our Father in the Eucharist in this way:

> In the *Eucharistic Liturgy* the Lord's Prayer appears as the prayer of the whole Church and there reveals its full meaning and efficacy. Placed between the *anaphora* (the Eucharistic prayer) and the communion,

[33] *Catechism,* par. 1105.
[34] *GIRM,* par. 79-g.

the Lord's Prayer sums up on the one hand all the petitions and intercessions expressed in the movement of the epiclesis and, on the other,
knocks at the door of the Banquet of the kingdom which sacramental
communion anticipates.[35]

Although the Rite of Peace dates back to the early Church, it had
fallen into disuse for several centuries. Its restoration into the Eucharist
following the Second Vatican Council is yet another indication that the
Eucharist is not the prayer of any one individual but the prayer of the community. In exchanging a sign of peace, "the faithful express to each other
their ecclesial communion and mutual charity before communicating in
the Sacrament."[36] That this rite of peace occurs just prior to receiving
Communion reminds us that the Eucharist calls us to make peace with
one another before we receive the Prince of Peace. We are, in other words,
to continue to strive for unity among ourselves even as we receive him
in whom we are one. The Fraction or the Breaking of the Bread follows,
yet another action of Christ at the Last Supper, and another reminder
that "the many faithful are made one body (1 Cor 10:17) by receiving
Communion from the one Bread of Life which is Christ."[37]

Concluding Rites

The Concluding Rites are concise, particularly when compared with
their pre-Vatican Council II format.[38] Just as an Opening Prayer helped
the community collect its thoughts and focus on the Eucharist about to
be celebrated, a Prayer after Communion brings the eucharistic celebration to a close. The prayer is about much more than taking leave,
however, for the prayer does not ask that the power of the mysteries that
have been celebrated end but, rather, that they bear fruit in the lives of
those who have participated in the celebration. This prayer is yet another
reminder that the Eucharist is about the changing of bread and wine into
the Body and Blood of Christ, but it is also about changing our lives in

[35] *Catechism*, par. 2770.

[36] *GIRM*, par. 82.

[37] Ibid., par. 83.

[38] For example, after the words, "Go, the Mass is ended," the priest would give his
blessing, then recite the "Last Gospel" (the prologue of Saint John's Gospel) and then,
returning to the steps leading up to the altar, would lead the congregation in a series of
"Prayers after Mass."

such a way that we are instruments of Christ's Body the Church here on earth. Here, the Prayer after Communion from the Twenty-Second Sunday in Ordinary Time:

> Lord,
>
> you renew us at your table with the bread of life.
>
> May this food strengthen us in love
>
> and help us to serve you in each other.
>
> We ask this in the name of Jesus the Lord. (Amen.)

The Mass concludes with the final blessing and the dismissal. In fact, the very word "Mass" comes from the two dismissals that took place during the Eucharist in the early Church: the dismissal of the catechumens from the community of the already-baptized prior to the preparation of the gifts and, here, the dismissal of the congregation so that they would, as the rite expresses it, "Go in peace to love and serve the Lord." *Dismissal* and *mission* come from the same root, and to be dismissed from the Eucharist is not to be told to simply "leave." It is to be missioned—to be sent out—to share the gifts one has received.

Concluding Thoughts

While the exact manner of celebrating the Eucharist has varied, the essentials of the celebration have remained. Furthermore, no matter the ritual details, the Eucharist has always been considered the "source and summit" of the Christian life. It is in the Eucharist we receive the greatest sacrament of God's love, the Body and Blood of his Son, truly present under the appearances of bread and wine.

The Eucharist is the sacrament of Christian unity and Christian identity. Christians gather around the table of the word and the table of the Lord as God's adopted children. They receive Christ so that they may become more Christlike.

The Eucharist is also the sacrament of charity, an act of love through which Christ offers himself, an act of love for which we must always give thanks. (The Greek word *eucharistein*, in fact, means "to give thanks.") But the Eucharist is the sacrament of charity also in that the love we receive is a love we must not keep to ourselves. To understand this we turn to the Gospel of John and consider his account of the Last Supper.

John's Gospel, the last of the gospels to be written, offers us a unique perspective on the *consequences* of the Eucharist. As do the other gospel writers, John records Jesus instructing his disciples to "do this in memory of me." In John's Gospel, however, Jesus' instruction concerns not the bread and wine but the lives of those with him at table. In John's words:

> [Jesus] got up from the table, took off his outer robe, and tied a towel around himself. Then he poured water into a basin and began to wash the disciples' feet and to wipe them with the towel that was tied around him. (13:4-5)

What he did no doubt puzzled his disciples at first, but Jesus quickly explained the mystery:

> So if I, your Lord and Teacher, have washed your feet, you also ought to wash one another's feet. For I have set you an example, that you also should do as I have done to you. (13:14-15)

The question is this: if the bread and wine are changed but those who receive them are not, then what, ultimately, do we have? Or, better, what is still missing? For the Eucharist is not something we receive in church and then walk away from, leaving it behind as something done and accomplished. Nor is the Eucharist the prayer and work of the priest alone. It is the prayer and work *of* the community, *by* the community, and *for* the community. In the Eucharist the community finds itself, by finding the One who has called it together to celebrate in his name, and to continue to proclaim his name long after any particular Mass has ended. We celebrate the Eucharist so that we may receive the love Christ offers us and, now walking in a new and better way, may go out and love one another as he has taught us to do in memory of him.

Further Reading

Aquilina, Mike. *The Mass of the Early Christians.* Huntington, IN: Our Sunday Visitor, Inc., 2001.

Champlin, Joseph. *The Mystery and Meaning of the Mass.* New York: Crossroad Publishing Company, 1999.

Hurtado, Larry. *At the Origins of Christian Worship.* Grand Rapids, MI: Wm. B. Eerdmans Publishing Company, 1999.

Irwin, Kevin. *Responses to 101 Questions on the Mass.* Mahwah, NJ: Paulist Press, 1999.

Johnson, Lawrence J. *The Mystery of Faith: A study of the structural elements of the order of the Mass.* Rev. ed. Federation of Diocesan Liturgical Commissions, 1984.

Kodell, Jerome. *The Eucharist in the New Testament.* Collegeville, MN: Liturgical Press, A Michael Glazier Book, 1988.

Wagner, Nick. *Modern Liturgy Answers the 101 Most-Asked Questions about Liturgy.* San Jose, CA: Resource Publications, Inc., 1996.

Part III

Special Topics on Catholic Prayer

Chapter 11

St. Augustine on Prayer

Paul Nord, O.S.B.

Saint Augustine of Hippo (354–430) is a towering figure in the history of Western Christianity. His influence on almost every area of Christian life and thought was unchallenged for centuries and remains strong to this day. His writings guided the development of Western theology and were held in the highest authority by later theologians such as St. Thomas Aquinas (1225–74). His work *The City of God* influenced the development of European political institutions, particularly through the person of the emperor Charlemagne (742–814), who loved to hear it read at his table.[1]

We might be tempted to think that a man so intellectually gifted would be necessarily dispassionate, possessing the reserved aloofness of a professor, avoiding passion and desire with a cool skepticism. If we tried to fit Augustine in such a mold, the mold would break. For Augustine was a man in whom the most brilliant intellect and the most fiery passions burned together brightly, side by side.

To understand how Augustine prayed, we need to understand who Augustine was. He was a man of strong desires, of fervent loves. Augustine's strong desire for physical intimacy with a woman presented perhaps the greatest struggle in his spiritual quest as he considered whether or not he

[1] Einhard, *The Life of Charlemagne*, trans. Samuel Turner (Ann Arbor, MI: University of Michigan Press, 1960), 52.

should marry. His intense desire for honors and social esteem elevated him to the prestigious position of professor of rhetoric in Milan, an extraordinary accomplishment considering his unremarkable family and social background. He knew the agony of conflicting desires, an agony that had led others to take refuge in a dispassionate stoicism, in a rational faith devoid of desire. For Augustine, however, desire was central to the Christian life and therefore it is key to understanding his view of prayer.

The strongest of Augustine's many desires was his intense desire to know the truth; he sought it for years with a restless heart. When he found the truth in Christianity, he realized that his desire for God must supersede all other desires. His desire for truth had led him to the Source of all Truth, the God who would thereafter be the object of the most overwhelming desire he had ever known.

Augustine's desire to know the truth was closely connected to his desire for happiness. He believed that all people desire to be happy, and that happiness requires living according to the truth. People seek happiness in a multitude of things, but true happiness can be elusive. We are not happy unless we possess what we love, the object of our desire. Augustine knew from personal experience, however, that we tend to desire every apparently good and beautiful thing that we see. These desires, even if fulfilled, will not make us truly happy. We will only be truly happy if we possess God, so we must desire God with such intensity that all other desires pale in comparison.

How, then, are we to grow in our desire for God? First, we must recognize that desire for God is itself a gift from God. God reveals himself to us and moves our hearts to desire union with him. Desiring God, our will is stirred and we choose to love him. Our desire for God moves us to prayer, and prayer deepens our desire for God. Still, our every inclination toward union with God is itself a gift. Prayer, love, and desire for God are all gifts from God. Therefore, it is from our desire for God that our prayer springs forth, and the fruit of our prayer is an ever-deepening desire for God. As Augustine said in his commentary on Psalm 38, "It is your heart's desire that is your prayer; if your desire continues without interruption your prayer continues also."[2]

---

[2] Thomas A. Hand, *Saint Augustine on Prayer* (Westminster, MD: Newman Press, 1963), 90–91. Hand here quotes Augustine's commentary on Psalm (37) 38, sec. 14 (*Enarratio in Psalmum* XXXVII).

His Early Life and Conversion

Few saints are more familiar to the popular imagination than is St. Augustine. We feel like we know him; his conversion story is legendary. Still, taking a second look at a saint whom we think we know so well may put his teachings on prayer in context.

Born in Tagaste, a small town in northern Africa on the outskirts of the Roman Empire, Augustine displayed much intelligence and ambition from his youth. His parents encouraged him to seek the education that would enable him to rise to the top of Roman society. While pursuing an education, however, Augustine encountered the temptations that youth face in every age. His mother Monica, a devout Christian, was filled with dismay when Augustine began living with a woman outside of marriage, fathering a son at the age of nineteen. Around the same time, Augustine joined the Manichees, a heretical quasi-Christian group, adding to his mother's grief.

Augustine would remain a Manichee for ten long years (age 18–28) while Monica prayed daily for her son's conversion. After ten years, Augustine's search for true wisdom finally led him to reject Manichean teachings. At the age of twenty-eight, Augustine left Africa, first for Rome and then for Milan, serving as a professor of rhetoric. Having left the Manichees, Augustine was attracted to the Christian Church and persuaded by the truth of its teachings. By then only one thing prevented Augustine from being baptized into the Church: his unbridled sexual desire.

Augustine remained mired in indecision and slavery to his desires until one day in early August 386. On that day, Augustine was at home with his friend Alypius when Ponticianus, a Christian and official of the emperor's court, made an unexpected visit. Entering the house, Ponticianus was pleasantly surprised to see that Augustine had been studying a copy of the writings of St. Paul. Ponticianus had been unaware of Augustine's interest in Christianity and so he was eager to share his Christian faith. Ponticianus told Augustine about a new movement called monasticism that was spreading rapidly through the Christian world. Men and women were abandoning their occupations and possessions in order to totally dedicate themselves to a life of prayer and service to God. In fact, two of Ponticianus's friends had recently become monks, inspired by an account of the life of the monk St. Anthony (ca. 251–356).

As he listened to Ponticianus, Augustine realized that he no longer had any excuse not to be baptized as a Christian. By telling him about the monastic life, Ponticianus had given Augustine a concrete way to submit his will to the teachings of Christ. Now Augustine saw his own sinfulness clearly. He recounts this moment of conversion: "You were setting me face to face with myself . . . that I might see my iniquity and loathe it. I had known it, but I had pretended not to see it, had deliberately looked the other way and let it go from my mind."[3] Overcome with sorrow and distress, Augustine fled into a nearby garden.

In that garden, many years of search and struggle yielded to a conversion of heart amid much prayer and tears. Augustine finally resolved to completely give his life to Christ. Yet we know the story of Augustine's dramatic conversion only because he chose to write about it many years later in a work titled *Confessions*.

Confessions

Augustine's *Confessions* is a remarkable text. Most of his writings are expert treatments of very complicated subjects of theology and faith. *Confessions* is remarkable because in it we witness Augustine praying. He addresses not the reader, but God. We are allowed to observe as Augustine addresses God in terms that are intimate and awestruck, repentant and joyful. The popular view of *Confessions* is that it is a work in which Augustine confesses his sins—and that much is certainly true. But Augustine confesses something else in this work, something that ultimately turns his recollection of his past sins into an introduction to something greater. The central thing that Augustine confesses is his awestruck praise of a God who rescued him from the very precipice of despair and confusion in order to call him to a life of prayer and service. Praise of God is at the center of *Confessions* because praise is at the center of a Christian's life of prayer.

Augustine wrote *Confessions* (ca. 397–400) at a critical time in his life. He had become bishop of Hippo just a few years before (395), and he was still learning what it meant to lead the people of his flock by teaching and example. His conversion was about a dozen years past. When he had entered the Church, he had not sought ordination, although his education and speaking skills would have made him an excellent candidate. Instead, he had sought a life of prayer and ascetical

---

[3] Augustine, *Confessions*, trans. F. J. Sheed (Indianapolis: Hackett Publishing, 1993), 139.

discipline by establishing a lay religious community with some of his friends. Although he had tried to avoid ordination to the priesthood, a few years later he accepted it when the local people urged him to lead them. While writing *Confessions* he was a young bishop, and he was still finding his way. Being a bishop was a huge responsibility, a task to be approached with great fear and trembling. Being a bishop required more than just brilliant teaching. It required a personal witness. *Confessions* was Augustine's personal witness to his flock, to the people with whom he had been entrusted.

By allowing his people to witness his prayerful dialogue with God, Augustine chose to reveal himself to them in a very intimate way. Yet Augustine's intimate self-revelation was a response to God's prior self-revelation to Augustine and to us all. The intimacy with which God has chosen to reveal God's self to us is truly startling. The God of all creation chose to become one of us, die for us, and redeem us through the Resurrection.

There is no relationship without self-revelation. God reveals God's self to us and enters into relationship with us. Augustine experienced God's self-revelation in a profoundly personal way, so he was moved to lay his soul bare before God and his people. There is no relationship without self-revelation. There are, of course, a thousand caveats[4] to this statement. We have all known people who reveal too much about themselves, too quickly. This only proves the point, however; such people are usually trying desperately to enter into relationship.

If I am to enter into relationship with others, I must reveal myself to them, and if I am to enter into relationship with God in prayer, I must reveal myself to God. What could this possibly mean with a God who "knit me together in my mother's womb" (Ps 139:13) and knows my every thought? If we seek a model of self-revelation to God in prayer, we need look no further than *Confessions*. Augustine knows that God knows everything that he says, yet he still tells God. The words of prayer are for us, not God, so the self-revelation of prayer is for us, not God. Augustine claimed that in laying our souls bare before God in prayer, we not only reveal ourselves to God; God reveals ourselves to us. We see ourselves as we truly are. When this happens, we see our sinfulness, our weakness. Our reaction is to turn away. Why should I dwell on my own sinfulness?

---

[4] "Caveats" are literally things of which we should "beware."

To know God, we must know ourselves[5] (and vice versa). Augustine demonstrated that knowing and admitting that we are weak and sinful is an essential prerequisite for entering into relationship with God in prayer. Augustine admits his sinfulness in *Confessions*, and in doing so he moves past his sinfulness into prayer, into relationship with God.

The Contemplative Life and the Active Life

As a result of *Confessions*, Augustine is most often remembered for the story of his conversion. After that, Augustine is well known for being a bishop who wrote many brilliant theological treatises. It is sometimes forgotten, however, that Augustine originally sought to live the contemplative life of a monk in community.

The contemplative life meant more to Augustine than simply a quiet life of regular prayer. Through a fervent striving of the intellect and will, Augustine sought to contemplate nothing less than God, insofar as that is possible in this life. While recognizing that he could know the happiness of living in God's presence only in heaven, he nonetheless strove daily to lift his heart and mind to God in earnest prayer so as to touch, however fleetingly, the source of all truth and light, God.

About a year after his baptism, Augustine returned to his native northern Africa with some friends for the purpose of establishing a monastic community in his hometown of Tagaste. He remained in Tagaste for three years (388–91), living a common life of prayer, meditation on Scripture, good works, and fasting with his lay friends. In late 391, Augustine reluctantly agreed to be ordained a priest at the insistence of the people of Hippo. Valerius, the bishop of Hippo, agreed to allow Augustine to establish a similar community in Hippo where he could live while serving as a priest. Upon Valerius's death, Augustine succeeded him as bishop of Hippo.

Augustine accepted ordination as a priest and then as a bishop when the local people asked him to lead them. Still, he knew that the active life of a pastor must be balanced by the contemplative life of prayer and holy reading. Therefore, after his ordination as bishop Augustine gathered around himself a community of clerics with whom he could share a common life of prayer and work.

---

[5] James J. O'Donnell, *Augustine* (Boston: Twayne Publishers, 1985), 80. O'Donnell quotes Augustine's *Soliloquies* 2.1.1: "I would know myself, I would know you [God]."

In considering the proper relationship between the contemplative life and the active life, we might consider the examples of Augustine and another saint contemporary to him, St. John Chrysostom (347–407). Like Augustine, John Chrysostom lived as a monk for a while before entering into pastoral service as a bishop. Both sought to balance prayer and service as essential components of the Christian life, and both sought to avoid the same danger: egoistical self-seeking—as Luc Verheijen has observed:

> John Chrysostom, it seems, was afraid that in "pure monasticism," without pastoral responsibility, there was the danger of pernicious self-seeking. Monastic life for him would risk becoming the search for a sterile individual perfection . . . a proud and egoistic existence. . . . John Chrysostom therefore freely and deliberately opted for the pastoral ministry. But that did not prevent him from proclaiming the necessity of asceticism and of monastic life. . . . What John Chrysostom wanted to combat, around him and within him, was a solely egoistic self-seeking.
>
> All things considered, Augustine's position was identical with that of Chrysostom: it was egoism that he dreaded. But Augustine feared egoism precisely in an authoritarian and self-assertive exercise of the priesthood and the episcopate, rather than in the humble monastic way of life. That is not to say that Augustine did not see very well the dangers of a pure "contemplative life," that is, one without pastoral responsibilities. He has, among other things, left us a Sermon on the Transfiguration [Matt 17:1-6] in which he attacks Saint Peter . . . because Peter had wanted to stay close to the Lord on the top of Mount Tabor.[6]

Therefore, every vocational calling, whether primarily to the contemplative life or the active life, calls us to reject egoistical self-seeking in favor of God-seeking, as expressed in selfless prayer and service.

The Letter to Proba

Although St. Augustine was clearly a man of prayer, he never wrote a formal treatise on the subject. He did, however, write a letter about prayer to a widow named Anicia Faltonia Proba. This letter has been a

---

[6] Luc Verheijen, *Saint Augustine: Monk, Priest, Bishop* (Villanova, PA: Augustinian Historical Institute, 1978), 8–9. Verheijen is here referring to Augustine's *Sermon 78* in *Patrologia Latina*.

highly regarded commentary on prayer for centuries. For example, St. Thomas Aquinas repeatedly quoted from Augustine's letter to Proba in answering question 83 (On Prayer) in the Second Part of the Second Part of his *Summa Theologica*.

Proba was a member of the Roman family called Anicia, which was known for its wealth and influence, and also for being one of the oldest and most distinguished Christian families in Rome. Proba's husband, Sextus Anicius Petronius Probus, and all three of their sons once held the office of Roman consul, an office just below Roman emperor.

Sometime after the death of her husband in 394, Proba made a vow to live the rest of her life as a widow consecrated to God, leading a life of prayer and asceticism. The Church of her day already had a rich tradition of women dedicating their lives to God by becoming consecrated widows or virgins, and Proba chose to live this kind of religious life in Rome. Over time, other widows and virgins joined her in a life of consecrated service to God, forming a community led by Proba. When Alaric the Goth conquered Rome in 410, Proba fled Rome, accompanied by the other widows and virgins, and by her daughter Juliana and her granddaughter Demetrias. They fled across the Mediterranean Sea to northern Africa, settling in the city of Carthage.

Shortly after their arrival, they received news of the sudden death of Juliana's husband, Olybrius; Juliana decided to consecrate her widowhood to God as well. A few years later, young Demetrias surprised everyone by abandoning her marriage plans and choosing to become a consecrated virgin. Demetrias thought that her mother and grandmother would be upset with her decision, but instead they were overjoyed. Soon they began contacting their many friends, seeking advice for young Demetrias. The news that this wealthy and influential Roman family had so ardently embraced a life of prayer and ascetical moderation soon spread throughout the known world and became a source of inspiration to many Christians.

Shortly after their arrival in northern Africa, Proba and her community came into contact with Augustine who, as the bishop of Hippo, was not far from their community in Carthage. Augustine wrote several letters to the Anicia family, including his famous letter to Proba on prayer (ca. 412) and a letter to Juliana (414) titled "The Excellence of Widowhood." In it Augustine gave detailed instructions on how to live a life of consecrated widowhood and encouraged the community of widows in their pursuit of this way of life.

Augustine's letter to Proba on prayer might not seem very relevant to us today. Proba was a consecrated widow from a wealthy Roman family. We may not be widows, and we may not think of ourselves as particularly wealthy, but this letter has an important message for all Christians as we seek to become people of prayer. Indeed, as we shall see, Augustine tells Proba that worldly wealth and possessions can distract us from seeking true, eternal happiness. Therefore, when we pray we should think of ourselves as desolate widows—poor and powerless, in need of God. Widows or not, wealthy or not, we are all in the same position when we come before God in prayer.

Central to Augustine's letter to the widow Proba on prayer are two New Testament passages that speak of widows: 1 Timothy 5:5 and Luke 18:1-8 (the parable of the persistent widow). Augustine begins his letter by quoting 1 Timothy 5:5: "The real widow, left alone, has set her hope on God and continues in supplications and prayers night and day." Although Proba is indeed a widow, she is far from desolate. She is wealthy and the mother of a great family. Most people put their hope on earthly goods, on earthly pleasures, but Augustine urges Proba to despise the pleasures that money can buy. As a woman of wealth and influence, Proba has everything that this life can provide, everything that people think will bring them happiness. True happiness, however, does not come from the pleasures of this world, nor by the accumulation of worldly wealth. Indeed, "the widow who lives for pleasures is dead even while she lives" (1 Tim 5:6). Therefore, Augustine urges Proba to consider herself to be desolate and to live her life as a desolate widow—for indeed that is what she is as long as she continues in this earthly life.

The desolate widow is all alone; she has no one to protect her, no one to provide for her needs. She needs God and she knows it—and so she prays. She places her hope in God alone. This is the life that Augustine challenges Proba to live. If she lives as if she were desolate, she will persist in prayer at all times. Indeed, she has already shown her willingness to do this by asking Augustine how she should pray.

Augustine makes a clear distinction throughout this letter between earthly happiness and true happiness, between earthly life and true life. Augustine insists that true happiness is impossible in this earthly life. We will only know true happiness in heaven, where we will have true life with God. Therefore, Augustine asks, what shall we pray for? Pray for the happy life, he says; earnestly pray for it day and night, like a desolate widow who knows her only hope is in God.

This leads Augustine to explain what he means by the happy life. What is happiness? Can we know happiness in this life? These are questions with which Augustine struggled for many years. Indeed, the long process of searching and questioning through which Augustine eventually entered the Catholic Church could be described as a tireless quest for the happy life.

Augustine begins his discussion of the nature of the happy life by noting that many philosophers have asked this question and that some have suggested that happiness consists of doing one's own will. Augustine strongly rejects this idea by quoting Cicero's *Hortensius*, a work which played an important role in Augustine's first steps toward Christianity. Cicero argued that desiring that which is not proper only makes a person miserable. Furthermore, it is more miserable to obtain that which isn't proper than it is for a person to be denied what he desires.

Augustine firmly agrees with Cicero that to desire improper things makes a person miserable, not happy. Therefore, Augustine asks what it is proper to desire, and what we ought to ask of God in prayer so that we might know the happy life. Augustine notes that it is proper to desire to get married, as it is also proper to desire to live a celibate life. Still, whatever a person's state of life or age may be, all people properly seek the temporal well-being of themselves and those whom they love.

In order to be happy we need a sufficiency of the necessities of life, but only what we need and no more. We must not covet more than we need of life's necessities, for this is improper in the eyes of God and will not make us happy. It is also important to realize that we do not seek a sufficiency of the necessities of life for their own sake, but rather for the sake of bodily health and friendship. We seek health and friendship for their own sake, and properly so, for they are necessary for living a happy life. But is this all that we need to live a happy life? If I have all the necessities of life, many friends, and good health, will I be happy? Not necessarily, Augustine says. These are the things which people seek in order to be happy in this life, and yet we can successfully acquire all of these things and still not be truly happy, because true happiness is not possible in this life.

As long we live in this world, we are separated from God—in exile from the God who made us. How can we know true happiness in such a state? Without God we cannot truly be at peace. As Augustine wrote in *Confessions*, "[O]ur hearts are restless till they rest in Thee [God]."[7] Therefore, the primary thing for which we must pray—indeed, pray with ardent desire—is that we may attain the fullness of true life with God in heaven. All the other things for which we properly pray—for health and friendship, for the necessities of life—all of these are sought so that we might live this life for the sake of the life with God that is to come.

As we fix our eyes on heaven, however, our feet remain firmly on this earth. We're not in heaven yet. We must pray for that blessed day, for that truly happy life with God, but this world is full of many things that cause our hearts to grow weary and our ardent desire for God to fade. Therefore, Augustine cites Luke 18:1: "[I]t is necessary that we pray always and not give up." Augustine contrasts this assertion with the Lord's command: "In praying do not heap up empty phrases as the Gentiles do; for they think that they will be heard for their many words. Do not be like them, for your Father knows what you need before you ask him" (Matt 6:7-8). Taken together, these two passages teach us that we are to pray always, and yet not with many words.

In order to illustrate this point, Augustine reminds the widow Proba of a second Scripture passage about a widow: the parable of the persistent widow in Luke 18:1-8. Augustine summarizes the parable in this way: "[Jesus] proposed the example of a certain widow who, desiring to receive vindication from her enemy, persuaded by her entreaties the unjust judge to hear her, not because he was moved by justice or mercy, but because he was overcome by her pestering" (130.15).[8] Again, as when Augustine quoted 1 Timothy 5:5 at the beginning of his letter, the persistent widow is a model for how we should approach God in prayer. We are to pray with tireless persistence, with ardent desire for the life of true happiness with God in heaven, while asking for that which we need in this life so that we may live this life for the sake of the life to come.

But we ought not think that God needs our many words, Augustine says, "since He knows what is needful for us before we ask Him . . . God does not need to have our will made known to Him—He cannot

---

[7] Augustine, *Confessions*, 3.

[8] Augustine, *The Works of Saint Augustine: Letters 100–155*, trans. Roland Teske (New York: New City Press, 2003), 191.

but know it—but He wishes our desire to be exercised in prayer that we may be able to receive what He is preparing to give" (130.17).[9] Consequently, when we pray, "we shall receive with a greater capacity to the extent that we believe it with more fidelity, hope for it more firmly, and [desire] it more ardently" (130.17).[10]

Therefore, Augustine says, "we always pray with a continuous desire filled with faith, hope, and love" (130.18).[11] Both halves of this excerpt are important. The second half speaks of the importance of faith, hope, and love in the life of prayer. As Augustine says later in his letter, "Faith, hope, and love lead one who prays to God, that is, one who believes, hopes, desires, and considers what he asks of God in the Lord's Prayer" (130.24).[12]

Note also the first half of the excerpt above: "we always pray with a continuous desire." Prayer and desire for God are closely connected for Augustine. Thus Augustine restates St. Paul's famous dictum "Pray without ceasing" (1 Thess 5:17) as "'Desire without ceasing the happy life,' which is none but eternal life" (130.18).[13] Since it is desire for eternal life that moves us to prayer, how we keep that desire alive and strong in our hearts? The answer, Augustine says, is that we need a regular daily schedule of prayer to feed our desire for heaven. It is by praying at certain hours throughout the day that we renew the desire for heaven in our minds and hearts—a desire that can be all too easily extinguished by the cares and preoccupations of this world. One practice of praying at certain daily hours is called the Liturgy of the Hours, a practice of the Church since the earliest times (see chapter 9).

Another challenge to prayer is the tendency of the mind to wander. Augustine notes that it is necessary to sustain our alert attention during prayer. One way to do this is by the use of very brief recited prayers, such as those for which the ancient Egyptian monks were famous. Therefore, if our attention in prayer begins to wane, we can pray, "O God come to my assistance, O Lord make haste to help me" (or

[9] Augustine, *Saint Augustine: Letters 83–130*, trans. Wilfrid Parsons (New York: Fathers of the Church Inc., 1953), 389.
[10] Augustine, *The Works*, 192. Where the Teske translation used the word "love" I have here substituted "desire" as an alternative translation of the Latin *desideramus* in the phrase *desideramus ardentius*.
[11] Ibid., 192.
[12] Ibid., 195.
[13] Ibid., 192.

a similar prayer), thus stoking the fires of our desire for God and our attention to prayer.

Therefore, Augustine concludes, it is much desire—not many words—that we need in prayer. In fact, it is *we* who need words in prayer, not God. God already knows what we need and therefore need not be told. But God gives us words in prayer because they serve to rouse our desire. Thus, by praying the Lord's Prayer, the very words which Jesus gave us, we stir up our desire for those very things that God wills that we should ask for, and we ask God to prepare our hearts to receive them. In fact, Augustine holds that the Lord's Prayer contains everything for which we might properly pray. If that for which we pray is not in accord with the petitions of the Lord's Prayer, then we should not be praying for it.

We might ask Augustine: Are we to pray that we be spared the pain and afflictions of this world? Augustine addresses this issue by quoting St. Paul: "We do not know how to pray as we ought" (Rom 8:26), a passage which the widow Proba had asked Augustine to explain. Augustine insists that God can bring good out of the trials and troubles that we face in this life. For example, the troubles of this life can help cure our pride, strengthen our patience in the face of difficulties, and even help cleanse us of our sins. Nevertheless, Augustine says that it is understandable that we pray to be freed from such difficulties and pain. When we do, however, if God "does not remove [our difficulties], we are not to think that we are thereby forsaken by Him, but rather, by lovingly bearing evil, we are to hope for greater good" (130.26).[14] In this, Augustine offers us the example of Christ, who shortly before his crucifixion prayed: "Father, if it be possible, let this cup [of suffering] pass from me; nevertheless, not as I will, but as you will" (Matt 26:39).

As Augustine approaches the end of his letter to the widow Proba on prayer, he returns to the two widow passages which he commented upon earlier. As we have seen, these passages offer an image of prayer that applies not only to a widow like Proba but, indeed, to all of us. Therefore, Augustine says, "[I]n so far as every soul understands that it is poor and desolate in this world, as long as it is absent from the Lord [it prays like a widow] . . . with continual and most earnest prayer" (130.30).[15]

---

[14] Augustine, *Saint Augustine: Letters,* 396.
[15] Ibid., 400.

Finally, Augustine ends the letter by humbly asking for the prayers of Proba and her community of widows. He asks for the prayers of those whom he has just instructed in the practice of prayer. The good bishop Augustine asked for the prayers of the widow Proba, and so may we ask for his prayers for us as well: St. Augustine, in the name of our Savior Jesus Christ whom you served, intercede for us before God, that we may be filled with a constant desire for God, so that, persevering in prayer like desolate widows, we may one day know true happiness with God forever. Amen.

Further Reading

Augustine. *The City of God.* Trans. by Marcus Dods. New York: Random House, 1994.

———. *Confessions.* Trans. by F. J. Sheed. Indianapolis: Hackett Publishing, 1993.

———. *The Trinity.* Trans. by Edmund Hill. New York: New City Press, 1998.

———. *The Works of Saint Augustine.* New York: New City Press, 2003.

Butler, Dom Cuthbert. *Western Mysticism: Augustine, Gregory, and Bernard on Contemplation and the Contemplative Life.* Mineola, NY: Dover Publishers, 2003.

Chadwick, Henry. *Augustine.* New York: Oxford University Press, 2005.

Chapter 12

Lectio Divina: *Reading and Praying*

Raymond Studzinski, O.S.B.

Most of us only think of praying as saying prayers. We grew up in environments where we were taught to memorize prayers and then to say them before going to bed, before meals, or in church. To pray was to say something to God, either of our own making or something we had learned. We also read prayers out of a prayer book or worship aid. Such reading, as it were, put words in our mouths and minds that then became our prayers. But what is perhaps less familiar to us is reading itself as a fundamental way of praying. Reading sacred texts is an ancient and highly valued manner of pursuing a life of prayer. It may seem less like prayer to us because it is not talking to God that is at the heart of this approach, but reading God's Word can be at the center of a life of prayer.

The dilemma we face is what an elderly Anglican priest described: "Lots of us began by being taught by our mothers to say prayers, then shown by our teachers how to say more prayers, and so on we went, talking, talking, talking! But *praying*? . . . It is no longer a question of 'Speak, Lord, for thy servant heareth,' but 'Hear, Lord, for thy servant speaketh.'"[1] In other words, the fact that prayer includes listening as

---

[1] Ronald Blythe, *The View in Winter: Reflections on Old Age* (New York: Harcourt Brace Jovanovich, 1979), 252.

well as talking escapes many of us. Reading God's Word is a way of listening to it speak directly to us. If indeed prayer is a dialogue between ourselves and God, then we do need to hear God speak. So from earliest times, people were reminded that in prayer we talk to God and in reading God talks to us. The two activities belong together and comprise a whole which is a prayer relationship with God. Saint Cyprian and a host of others repeated the same idea and in more recent times Vatican II asserted the same thing as it quoted St. Ambrose: "We speak to [God] when we pray; we listen to [God] when we read the divine oracles."[2] More recently, Benedict XVI echoed these ancient sentiments: "Assiduous reading of sacred Scripture accompanied by prayer makes that intimate dialogue possible in which, through reading, one hears God speaking, and through prayer, one responds with a confident opening of the heart."[3] Indeed, if we look at the monastic way of life where prayer is a central element, we find that it is a life of listening to God speaking in the Scriptures and in life's events. Holy reading, called *lectio divina*, occupies a substantial portion of the monastic day.

In what follows I want to look more closely at *lectio divina* to understand how monastic practitioners went about this exercise. Who were their guides and what sort of practical guidelines did they follow? What was the place of reading in the larger spiritual enterprise of seeking God? How has the practice changed over time, and why is there interest today in retrieving the practice? Finally, what difficulties face contemporary people in appropriating the practice for themselves?

Saint Benedict (ca. 480–ca. 547) gave reading a prominent place in the life of monks in his Rule.[4] In this mid-sixth-century document (hereafter referred to as the RB), he allots more than three hours to it, varying by the time of year. Furthermore, in contrast to some other

---

[2] Ambrose, *De Officiis Ministrorum* I, 20, 88, cited in *Dei Verbum* (The Dogmatic Constitution on Divine Revelation), November 18, 1965, no. 25.

[3] Address of His Holiness Benedict XVI to the participants in the International Congress Organized to Commemorate the 40ᵗʰ Anniversary of the Dogmatic Constitution on Divine Revelation "Dei Verbum," Castel Gandolfo, September 16, 2005, http://www.vatican.va/holy_father/benedict_xvi/speeches/2005/september/documents/hf_ben-xvi_spe_20050916_40-dei-verbum_en.html.

[4] For the only contemporaneous information available on St. Benedict, see Gregory the Great, *Dialogues, Book II: Saint Benedict*, trans. Myra L. Uhlfelder (Indianapolis: Bobs-Merrill, 1967).

monastic legislators, he allocates the morning, the best time of the day, to the exercise.[5] On Sunday, apart from common exercises of the Divine Office, the Eucharist, and meals, the whole day is free for *lectio*.

Studies on the vocabulary which Benedict uses to make precise the place and nature of *lectio* in the RB show that *lectio* suggests "gathering" and "collecting" and is thus a unifying process. Indeed, the exercise of *lectio* can be seen as an effort by the monastic to draw from the Scriptures a unified vision of life.[6] Jean Leclercq observes that in the early days reading was done out loud; reading involved the mouth which formed the words and the ears which heard the sound of the words.[7] It was an acoustical performance. In using the verbs "hear" (*audire*) and "build up" (*aedificare*) with *lectio*, the RB accentuates the impact of spoken words on the reader. The Scriptures are to rejuvenate the monastic readers. So, Benedict wants the community members to be "free" (*vacare*) for reading. The practice is to be unpressured, an undistracted encounter with the Word, savored and slowly digested. *Lectio* signifies less a carefully and arduously followed routine and more a receptive and pondering attitude toward the Word and life.[8] Benedict also associates the words for "memory" and "remembering" with reading the Scriptures—the words read are to stay with the person. Memory especially comes to the fore in meditation, the practice closely associated with reading in the RB.[9]

To meditate for the ancient monastics was to repeat the words of the Scriptures until they were inscribed in the memory. The very muscles used to mouth the words and those parts in the ears that respond to the

---

[5] See Timothy Fry, *RB 1980: The Rule of St. Benedict in Latin and English with Notes* (Collegeville, MN: Liturgical Press, 1981), 48:10–23. See also Adalbert de Vogüé, *The Rule of Saint Benedict: A Doctrinal and Spiritual Commentary*, trans. John Baptist Hasbrouck (Kalamazoo, MI: Cistercian Publications, 1981), 241.

[6] See Ambrose Wathen, "Monastic *Lectio*: Some Clues from Terminology," *Monastic Studies* 12 (1976): 209; and Terrence G. Kardong, "The Vocabulary of Monastic *Lectio* in RB 48," *Cistercian Studies* 16 (1981): 171–72.

[7] Jean Leclercq, *The Love of Learning and the Desire for God: A Study of Monastic Culture*, trans. Catherine Misrahi, 3d ed. (New York: Fordham University Press, 1982), 15.

[8] See Wathen, "Monastic *Lectio*," 211–14; Kardong, "The Vocabulary of Monastic Lectio in RB 48," 175–6; idem, *Benedict's Rule: A Translation and Commentary* (Collegeville, MN: Liturgical Press, 1996), 386–87.

[9] See Wathen, "Monastic *Lectio*," 211.

spoken sound "remember" the Scriptures. Leclercq commented: "The *meditatio* consists in applying oneself with attention to this exercise in total memorization; it is, therefore, inseparable from the *lectio*. It is what inscribes, so to speak, the sacred text in the body and the soul."[10]

The content of *lectio* was in the first instance the Scriptures, but Benedict in the final chapter of the Rule mentions other works which were to be read. These other works include the patristic writings, Cassian's *Conferences* and *Institutes*, lives of the desert elders, and the Rule of St. Basil. "For observant and obedient monks, all these are nothing less than tools for the cultivation of virtues" (RB 73.6). During Lent the RB prescribes that each member is to receive a book which they are to read straight through. Commentators are in agreement that the book was a section of the Scriptures; ancient documents occasionally refer to the Bible as a library. Part of the discipline of *lectio* in this instance was staying with a particular book of the Scriptures rather than jumping around to different passages.[11]

Reading and meditation were at the service of prayer, *oratio*, the person's heartfelt response to God's Word. Although Benedict never gives a detailed description of the nature of this prayer, it clearly is of importance, for it represents a person's response to the Word which has been the focus of both the reading and the meditation. What the RB does say is that prayer should be short and pure.[12] The *oratio* focuses the self around the words read and meditated on and leads to a heartfelt response to God, often in the form of sorrow or tears.[13] At times the expressive response to God's Word makes use of the very words which were read or meditated on, enlivened with the focused commitment of the person who prays.[14] As Adalbert de Vogüé comments with regard to the psalmody sung in the oratory, "already in the psalm the human voice, praising and begging, is replying to the call of the divine voice. Thus the psalmody is both the scriptural preamble of prayer and the beginning of

---

[10] Leclercq, *The Love of Learning and the Desire for God*, 73; see also Vogüé, *The Rule of Saint Benedict*, 242–43.

[11] *RB 1980* 48:15–16.

[12] *RB 1980* 20:4.

[13] *RB 1980* 52:4.

[14] See Michael Casey, *The Undivided Heart: The Western Monastic Approach to Contemplation* (Petersham, MA: St. Bede's Publications, 1994), 163.

this prayer."[15] Reading, meditating, and praying centered on the Word of God gradually inscribed that Word in fleshly existence and transformed the monastic into a self which, like an illuminated manuscript, rendered the sacred text in a colorful, artistic way for others to "read."

Early Monastic Promoters of Reading

Both in the East and in the West, monastic writers such as Gregory the Great (ca. 540–604), Bede the Venerable (ca. 673–735), and Isaac the Syrian (d. ca. 700) passed on the tradition of reading which showed how to draw spiritual meaning from the sacred texts. Various writings from the period after the RB review and restate the wisdom inherited from Origen, Augustine, and Cassian about the literal and spiritual senses of the Scriptures. Simply put, while the literal sense set forth fact and event, the spiritual senses dealt with the deeper meaning of the passage. The text, beyond its literal message, has an allegorical sense, that is, it has something to say about the mystery of Christ as realized in the present; it has also an anagogical sense—it speaks about the goal of life found in union with God; and finally it has a tropological sense—it invites an appropriate moral response to God who speaks.[16] Because the Scriptures have these multiple layers of meaning—both literal and spiritual senses, there is always more to be gleaned from even the most familiar texts. For Benedict and for his monastic successors as well as for the early Church writers, the Scriptures speak directly to the reader in his or her particular circumstances through these various senses.

Jean Leclercq sees Gregory the Great as a transitional figure between the patristic period and the monastic culture of the Middle Ages.[17] Gregory, together with Augustine, Jerome, and Ambrose, completes a tetrad of Latin authorities who would guide the reading and understanding of the Bible in the medieval period. But Gregory, while passing on a tradition, adds his distinctive contribution. He puts emphasis on the role of the community in coming to a fuller understanding of the meaning of the Scriptures: "For I know that in the presence of my brothers and

---

[15] Vogüé, *The Rule of Saint Benedict*, 144.

[16] See Henri de Lubac, *Medieval Exegesis, Vol. 1: The Four Senses of Scripture*, trans. Mark Sebanc (Grand Rapids, MI: Eerdmans Publishing Company, 1998).

[17] Jean Leclercq, *The Love of Learning and the Desire for God*, 25.

sisters I have very often understood many things in the sacred text that I could not understand alone."[18]

Although Gregory is recognized as a master of the moral or tropological sense, he does attend to the other senses as well. Along with Augustine he was influential in disseminating the view of the Scriptures as having four senses. In one of his homilies on Ezekiel, he describes these senses as four facets or sides of a square, each revealing something distinctive—one tells of the past, another of the future, still another of what is to be done morally, and the final one of the higher or spiritual realm.[19]

Gregory's concern is always with how the Scriptures direct people in their Christian lives. The Scriptures provide the Christian with a measuring rod which can be used to assess one's progress in virtue.[20] They also serve as a mirror in which one can see oneself reflected and thus know one's true condition. "Holy Writ is set before the eyes of the mind like a kind of mirror, that we may see our inward face in it; for therein we learn the deformities, therein we learn the beauties that we possess; there we are made sensible [to] what progress we are making, there too how far we are from proficiency."[21] The Scriptures are like a spiritual trainer that could direct just the right message to the developing Christian. Thus Gregory suggests in his work on Job: "The Lord tempering in His mercy the words of Scripture, alarms us at one time with sharp excitements, comforts us at another with gentle consolations, and blends terror with comforts, and comforts with terror; in order that, while they are both tempered towards us with wonderful skill of management, we may be found neither to despair through fear, nor yet incautiously secure."[22]

[18] Gregory the Great, Homilies on Ezekiel 2.2.1 in Gregoire le Grand, *Homélies sur Ézéchiel* 2, trans. Charles Morel, Sources Chrétiennes 360 (Paris: Les Éditions du Cerf, 1990), 92–93, cited and translated in Mariano Magrassi, *Praying the Bible: An Introduction to Lectio Divina*, trans. Edward Hagman (Collegeville, MN: Liturgical Press, 1998), 10.

[19] Ibid., 2.9.8, 444–45.

[20] Ibid., 2.1.14, 78–79; see Carol Straw, *Gregory the Great: Perfection in Imperfection* (Berkeley: University of California Press, 1988), 200.

[21] Gregory the Great, *Morals* 2.1.1, *Morals on the Book of Job* (Oxford: J.H. Parker, 1844), 67.

[22] Ibid., 33.7.14, 569.

The goal of reading and understanding the Scriptures for Gregory was contemplation and a life of charity. The dynamics of reading the Scriptures led him to suggest that the Scriptural Word grows with the reader.[23] For him the Scriptures were treasures which could never be exhausted. He did his part to make sure that contact with that saving Word through reading and preaching was maintained and deepened.

Gregory's influence would be immense on those who came after him. Bede the Venerable similarly tries to bring the Word to all people.[24] He had a great pastoral concern and wanted the Scriptures to serve as a guidepost for all. His whole life was given to the study of the Scriptures. In communicating what he knew in homilies and commentaries his goal was not to present the high points of theology but rather to teach how the Scriptures addressed the spiritual lives of readers and hearers. "The priority for Bede was always the practical one of prayer: his commentaries were meditations on the Scriptures leading to conversion of life through prayer."[25]

Bede, priest, monk, and scholar, was in effect a pastor who wanted to make sure that all, even very simple souls, had access to the Word of God. In a letter written toward the end of his life to the archbishop of York, Bede argued for vernacular translations as a way of making the Word more accessible. For Bede the Scriptures were a living text which spoke to present experience and so must be available to all. "Whether you attend to the letter or seek for an allegory, in the Gospel you will always find light."[26]

Around the time that Bede was promoting the Scriptures in England, another monk by the name of Isaac was writing in Syria to encourage the reading of the Scriptures as the path to spiritual growth. For, he argued, it was reading along with prayer which would fan the love of God within one's heart. "We are transported in the direction of the love of God, whose sweetness is poured out continually in our hearts like honey in a

---

[23] Gregory the Great, Homilies on Ezekiel 1.7.8, *Homélies sur Ézéchiel* 1, trans. Charles Morel, Sources Chrétiennes 327 (Paris: Les Éditions du Cerf, 1886), 244–45.

[24] See Benedicta Ward, *The Venerable Bede*, Cistercian Studies Series 169 (Kalamazoo, MI: Cistercian Publications, 1998), 41–87.

[25] Ibid., 43.

[26] *The Explanation of the Apocalypse by Venerable Bede*, trans. E. Marshal (Oxford 1878), 33, cited in Ward, *The Venerable Bede*, 54.

honeycomb, and our souls exult at the taste which the hidden ministry of prayer and the reading of Scripture pour into our hearts."[27]

The reading Isaac was promoting was one in which a hidden or spiritual meaning was sought and came to the surface. He suggests that different parts of the Scriptures will speak to different readers and what is important is to be open and sensitive to those which touch one's heart. Faithfulness to this attuned reading will lead the reader to spiritual transformation. Isaac articulates the practical requirements for reading the Scriptures in a spiritually enriching way. Quieting the self down is essential for properly receiving the Word of God. "Let your reading be done in a stillness which nothing disturbs."[28] Prayer should preface the reading: "Do not approach the words of the mysteries contained in the divine Scriptures without prayer and beseeching God for help, but say: Lord, grant me to perceive the power in them! Reckon prayer to be the key to the true understanding of the divine Scriptures."[29]

Unfortunately, as the centuries passed, ordinary people outside monasteries, because of the lack of vernacular translations, did not have the same access to the Word that was available to more educated monastics. For these ordinary folk the Bible became a closed book. Even within monasteries and educated circles, the practice of reading as developed in the early monastic period was threatened by more academic and intellectual approaches to reading then developing. Still, the practice continued to have ardent promoters who would further delineate how it was to be done and would speak to its transformative power.

Bernard of Clairvaux

In the twelfth-century monastic milieu, despite the continued rise of Scholasticism and its intellectual approach to reading, the tradition of *lectio* was bolstered by efforts to elaborate and develop the practice. Bernard of Clairvaux (1090–1153) built on the best of the patristic

[27] Bede, *The Second Part* 29.1, cited and translated in Hilarion Alfeyev, *The Spiritual World of Isaac the Syrian*, Cistercian Studies Series 175 (Kalamazoo, MI: Cistercian Publications, 2000), 181.

[28] St. Isaac the Syrian, Homily 4 in *The Ascetical Homilies of Saint Isaac the Syrian*, trans. Holy Transfiguration Monastery (Boston: Holy Transfiguration Monastery, 1984), 34.

[29] Homily 48, in ibid., 233.

tradition to enrich *lectio*. This great Cistercian abbot gave explicit attention to the role of affectivity in the process of personal reform and return to God through *lectio*. In his theology, monastic conversion aims to restore the image of God which has been obscured by sin. The word of God illuminates areas of darkness, sinfulness, to be overcome through conversion. Scripture guides the process. "Let us . . . follow the example of Scripture, which speaks of the wisdom hidden in the mystery, but does so in words familiar to us, and which, even as it enlightens our human minds, roots our affections on God, and imparts to us the incomprehensible and invisible things of God by means of figures drawn from the likeness of things familiar to us, like precious draughts in vessels of cheap earthenware."[30]

Echoing the patristic tradition, Bernard recognized that there was more than one meaning in a given text. This focus on finding multiple meanings kept monks attentive to the text and set apart monastic reading from the reading done in the schools. Like Martha in the gospels, the search for meaning was hard work and was, in one sense, never done. Bernard indicated on a number of occasions that he was offering his listeners only one possible meaning.

Bernard hoped that the Scriptures would be assimilated in such a way that they would impact the whole person. Reading, in other words, was not for him only an intellectual activity.[31] In fact, he opposed the "learned" approach to *lectio* emerging in the wake of Scholasticism and favored a more sense-oriented or experiential way of reading.[32] He speaks of an intimate, even mystical, contact through reading.[33] He frequently speaks of "tasting" God through contact with the Scriptures.

Bernard encourages an engaged reading in which one experiences oneself present at what is being recounted. In fact, Leclercq argues that imagination was very active in monastic readers during the medieval

[30] Sermon 74, I, 2 in Bernard of Clairvaux, *On the Song of Songs IV*, trans. Irene Edmonds (Kalamazoo, MI: Cistercian Publications, 1980), 86.

[31] See Denis Farkasfalvy, "The Role of the Bible in St. Bernard's Spirituality," *Analecta Cisterciensia* 25 (1969): 8–9.

[32] See Peter Norber, "*Lectio Vere Divina*: St. Bernard and the Bible," *Monastic Studies* 3 (1965): 178–80; and G. R. Evans, *Bernard of Clairvaux* (Oxford: Oxford University Press, 2000), 56.

[33] See Bernard of Clairvaux, Sermon 32, II, 4–5, *On the Song of Songs II*, trans. Kilian Walsh (Kalamazoo, MI: Cistercian Publications, 1983), 137.

period. "[Imagination] permitted them to picture, to make present, to see beings with all the details provided by the texts: the colors and dimensions of things, the clothing, bearing and actions of the people, the complex environment in which they move."[34] The Cistercians distinguished themselves through creative imaging regarding the self; monastic readers were encouraged, much as Bernard did, to insert themselves into the scriptural event.

In Bernard's view, *lectio* provides a locus for spiritual experience which transforms monastic readers. These readers were goaded to make a connection between the text and personal experience. Commenting on the Song of Songs, Bernard invites this sort of resonance between text and experience: "Only the touch of the Spirit can inspire a song like this, and only personal experience can unfold its meaning. Let those who are versed in the mystery revel in it; let all others burn with desire rather to attain to this experience than merely to learn about it."[35]

In the pages of the Scriptures the monastic reader wanders about as in a labyrinth searching for what illuminates self and furthers conversion. Actually, the reader recovers a lost spiritual awareness in the pages of the Scriptures.[36] "For Bernard the wilderness of the text offers a mirror for the monk to find his self; the journey *is* the destiny, and exegesis becomes an invitation to conversion, to perform the monastic life as if it were a dramatic text of self-discovery."[37] This journey entails work, as Bernard illustrates in his sermons. Like Origen, he encouraged digging and diligent searching for hidden meaning. But he also noted that readers would get caught up in and even enjoy the hunt. Bernard underscores in a new and distinctive way the role of affectivity in the spiritual life of monastics. He comments in Sermon 16 on the Song of Songs: "My purpose is not so much to explain words as to move hearts."[38] In an-

[34] Jean Leclercq, *The Love of Learning and the Desire for God*, 75.

[35] Sermon 1, VI, 11, in Bernard of Clairvaux, *On the Song of Songs I*, trans. Kilian Walsh (Kalamazoo, MI: Cistercian Publications, 1971), 6.

[36] See Brian Stock, *The Implications of Literacy: Written Language and Models of Interpretation in the Eleventh and Twelfth Centuries* (Princeton, NJ: Princeton University Press, 1983), 408.

[37] Mark Burrows, "Hunters, Hounds, and Allegorical Readers: The Body of the Text and the Text of the Body in Bernard of Clairvaux's *Sermons on the Song of Songs*," *Studies in Spirituality* 14, no. 1 (2004): 123.

[38] Bernard of Clairvaux, Sermon 16, I, 1, *On the Song of Songs I*, 114.

other sermon he indicates that there is an affective evolution as people progress on the road to God. Feelings themselves become elevated and purified. "I think this is the principal reason why the invisible God willed to be seen in the flesh. . . . [God] wanted to recapture the affections of carnal men who were unable to love in any other way, by first drawing them to the salutary love of his own humanity, and then gradually to raise them to a spiritual love."[39] Contemporaries of Bernard were also proffering subtle shifts in the old approach to *lectio*. Certainly, still staunch defenders of the ancient practice, they would nuance it differently. They owe a lot to Bernard, who remained to the end the champion of reading geared primarily to nourishing the soul and not the intellect.

Hugh of St. Victor and the Didascalicon

One who joined Bernard in enlarging the *lectio* palette as people were succumbing to the lure of Scholastic approaches to reading was Hugh of St. Victor (d. 1141). Little is known of Hugh's background, but by the 1120s he was a well-established teacher and writer. He joined the canons at the Abbey of St. Victor and seems to have spent his entire life there. The *Didascalicon*, written around 1128, is his first book to deal with the art of reading.[40] Similar to Augustine's *De Doctrina Christiana*, the work attempts to draw people back to slow, meditative reading of the Scriptures while suggesting how art and science could be put at the service of understanding the scriptural text. This work was not intended to be a handbook for a teacher or preacher but a programmatic guide for a devout reader on how to restore one's personal image of God which is now distorted by sin.[41] In the Preface to the *Didascalicon*, Hugh clarifies his intention: "The things by which every [person] advances in knowledge are principally two—namely, reading and meditation. Of

---

[39] Ibid., Sermon 20, V, 6, 152.

[40] See Ivan Illich, *In the Vineyard of the Text: A Commentary to Hugh's Didascalicon* (Chicago: University of Chicago Press, 1993), 5; *The Didascalicon of Hugh of St. Victor: A Medieval Guide to the Arts*, trans. Jerome Taylor (New York: Columbia University Press, 1961).

[41] See Jerome Taylor, introduction to *The Didascalicon of Hugh of St. Victor*, 28–29.

these, reading holds first place in instruction, and it is of reading that this book treats, setting forth rules for it."[42]

In a commentary on the *Didascalicon*, Ivan Illich notes that in the very opening of Chapter 1 Hugh declares wisdom to be the goal of human striving. This Wisdom, which is Christ, will provide a remedy for the weakened human condition and will revive the dignity of the human person: "We are restored through instruction, so that we may recognize our nature and learn not to seek outside ourselves what we can find within. The highest curative in life, therefore, is the pursuit of Wisdom."[43] Wisdom illuminates the human person and, as Hugh will show, reading is the means of arriving at such illumination. Hugh underscores memory's role in storing what one reads and in the process revives ancient memory techniques.[44] "We ought, therefore, in all that we learn, to gather brief and dependable abstracts to be stored in the little chest of the memory, so that later on, when need arises, we can derive everything from them. . . . I charge you, then, my student, not to rejoice a great deal because you may have read many things, but because you have been able to retain them."[45] Hugh suggests that readers construct an ark or treasure room in their minds for the storage of scriptural events and characters.

For Hugh a reader must begin with the literal sense of the text, attending to its historical detail in order to properly position it within the order found in history. Readers grounded in history can move on to draw out the spiritual meanings of the text. Thus Hugh writes in another place:

> All exposition of divine scripture is drawn forth according to three senses: story, allegory, and "tropology," or, the exemplary sense. The story is the narrative of actions, expressed in the basic meaning of the

[42] *Didascalicon*, Preface, 44; see Illich's comments about Hugh's Preface in *In the Vineyard of the Text*, 74–78.

[43] Ibid., I, 1, 47.

[44] For Hugh's contribution to the revival of ancient memory techniques, see Hugh of St. Victor, "The Three Best Memory Aids for Learning History," in *The Medieval Craft of Memory: An Anthology of Texts and Pictures*, ed. Mary Carruthers and Jan M. Ziolkowski (Philadelphia: University of Pennsylvania Press, 2002), 32–40; Mary Carruthers, *The Book of Memory: A Study of Memory in Medieval Culture* (Cambridge: Cambridge University Press, 1990), 162–65; and Illich, *In the Vineyard of the Text*, 29–50.

[45] *Didascalicon*, III, 11, 94.

letter. Allegory is when by means of this event in the story, which we find out about in the literal meaning, another action is beckoned to [*innuitur*], belonging either to past or present or future time. Tropology is when in that action which we hear was done, we recognize what we should be doing.[46]

Hugh is careful to note that not every scriptural passage has all three senses: "It is necessary, therefore, so to handle the Sacred Scripture that we do not try to find history everywhere, nor allegory everywhere, nor tropology everywhere but rather that we assign individual things fittingly in their own places, as reason demands."[47] Furthermore, Hugh looks for meaning not only in the words of the scriptural passage but in the things referred to as well. In fact, creation is itself a book that speaks of God and the spiritual realm. Just as reading was done in accord with the ancient tradition, Hugh also suggests the reader move slowly through the text, much as a hiker moving slowly through a grove of trees. "But what shall I call Scripture if not a wood? Its thoughts, like so many sweetest fruits, we pick as we read and chew as we consider them."[48] Here is the slow, attentive encounter with the Word that the desert elders recommended and practiced. But when Hugh comes to describe meditation, the chewing and digesting of the Word which followed upon *lectio*, it is clear that a shift in understanding and practice has taken place. Meditation now has an analytical aspect to it that was not present in earlier times. "Meditation is sustained thought along planned lines: it prudently investigates the cause and the source, the manner and the utility of each thing."[49]

Soon Hugh is laying out a five-step reading process to move toward God. The first four steps are reading, meditation, prayer, and performance, putting into action what has been read and meditated upon. "It then remains for you to gird yourself for good work, so that what you have sought in prayer you may merit to receive in your practice. . . . Good performance is the road by which one travels toward life."[50] The

[46] "De Tribus Maximis Circumstaniis Gestorum," trans. Mary Carruthers, in Carruthers, *The Book of Memory*, 264.

[47] *Didascalicon*, V, 2, 121.

[48] Ibid., V, 5, 126–27.

[49] Ibid., III, 10, 92.

[50] Ibid., V, 9, 132–33.

214 Raymond Studzinski, O.S.B.

last step is contemplation, "in which, as by a sort of fruit of the preceding steps, one has a foretaste, even in this life, of what the future
reward of good work is."[51]

In the *Didascalicon* Hugh argues for preserving the ancient approach
to reading even while he moves in a somewhat new direction in keeping
with his times. Still, as underscored by Illich, for Hugh the book—both
the Scriptures and the book which is creation—is, as in centuries before,
where the reader finds the sense of all things, where "reading, far from
being an act of abstraction, is an act of incarnation."[52]

Guigo II and The Ladder of Monks

During that same historical period, another author, Guigo II (d.
1188), extolled the value of the ancient practice of *lectio* and spoke of
it as the initial part of a well-established spiritual program. His work
The Ladder of Monks (*Scala Claustralium*) was, it seems, even better
known than the *Didascalicon*.[53] Though both works relate *lectio* to other
practices (meditation, prayer, and contemplation), Guigo describes
these as rungs of the ladder which leads to God. This apparently simple
scheme could lead one to miss the nuance which Guigo interjects. As
Keith Egan observes: "Guigo is aware of the deceptions consequent upon
too superficial an interpretation of the meaning of the four steps."[54]
So Guigo, like Hugh, attempts to unpack the fullness of the reading
experience by carefully delineating the steps which for centuries had
been assumed to follow. But again like Hugh, Guigo reflects some modifications to ancient practice.

The Ladder of Monks takes the form of a letter written from one
monk to another in which Guigo shares thoughts about the spiritual
life of a monk. He outlines the comprehension of a spiritual exercise
by sketching four stages, using the visual image of a ladder with four
rungs. This image, he claims, came to him one day while he was work-

---

[51] Ibid., V, 9, 132.

[52] Illich, *In the Vineyard of the Text*, 123.

[53] *The Ladder of Monks and Twelve Meditations*, trans. Edmund Colledge and James
Walsh (New York: Doubleday, 1978). See Simon Tugwell, *Ways of Imperfection: An
Exploration of Christian Spirituality* (Springfield, IL: Templegate, 1985), 93–122.

[54] Keith Egan, "Guigo II: The Theology of the Contemplative Life," in *The Spirituality of Western Christendom*, ed. E. Rozanne Elder (Kalamazoo, MI: Cistercian
Publications, 1976), 108.

ing. He proceeds to characterize each stage, introducing subtle shifts away from earlier understandings of the connections between reading and meditation: "Reading is the careful study of the Scriptures, concentrating all one's powers on it. Meditation is the busy application of the mind to seek with the help of one's own reason for knowledge of hidden truth."[55]

Lectio in Guigo's work is no longer paired with the qualifying word *divina*.[56] In fact, "Guigo does not seem to believe that monastic or Christian reading and thinking have any special quality which distinguishes them intrinsically from anybody else's reading and thinking."[57] Furthermore, reading is decidedly less performance as envisioned by the ancients; it is edging clearly toward the more rationalized process found in the university, though the ancient concerns are there as well. For example, when Guigo writes about the function of reading, he is aware of the need for lingering with a text and penetrating to its deeper meaning beyond the letter. Using the text of the beatitude on the pure of heart, he reflects: "This is a short text of Scripture, but it is of great sweetness, like a grape that is put into the mouth filled with many senses to feed the soul. . . . So, wishing to have a fuller understanding of this [text], the soul begins to bite and chew upon this grape, as though putting it in a wine press, while it stirs up its powers of reasoning to ask what this precious purity may be and how it may be had."[58]

Whereas meditation in the tradition was simply the repetition, the chewing over, the digesting of what had been read, Guigo suggests, as he illustrates in treating the text of the beatitude on purity of heart, that meditation probes the text, in an effort to understand it by relating it to other texts. In so doing, readers encounter longings for God stirred up in their hearts. "Do you see how much juice has come from one little grape, how great a fire has been kindled from a spark, how this small piece of metal, 'Blessed are the pure in heart, for they shall see God,' has acquired a new dimension by being hammered out on the anvil of

[55] *The Ladder of Monks*, II, 82.

[56] See Charles Dumont, *Praying the Word of God: The Use of Lectio Divina* (Oxford: SLG Press, 1999), 14, where Dumont also notes: "A careful reading of this little treatise, makes it clear that we are on the way to a change of perspective."

[57] Tugwell, *Ways of Imperfection*, 94.

[58] *The Ladder of Monks*, IV, 83.

meditation?"[59] The longings stirred up by meditating may eventually be satisfied through a gift from above, a taste of the divine sweetness. Meditation, in the past always dependent on and subordinate to reading, begins to assume a prominence over reading. But meditation still needs to be linked to prayer to prove fruitful.[60]

Traditionally prayer was considered as the heartfelt response to the wisdom received in *lectio*. However, Guigo sees the function of prayer as geared to obtaining the grace of contemplation. "Prayer lifts itself up to God with all its strength, and begs for the treasure it longs for, which is the sweetness of contemplation."[61] Furthermore, there has occurred a shift in the understanding of prayer. With an increasing interest in affectivity, prayer serves less as petition and more as a welling up of devotion. In one of his summary statements, Guigo says quite simply that "prayer is concerned with desire,"[62] and in another place, "if meditation is to be fruitful, it must be followed by devoted prayer."[63]

When that happens, contemplation, the final step, the apex of the *lectio* process, is achieved:

> The [reader] who has worked in this first degree, who has pondered well in the second, who has known devotion in the third, who has raised above [self] in the fourth, goes from strength to strength by this ascent on which [the] whole heart is set, until at last [one] can see the God of gods in Sion. Blessed is the [one] to whom it is given to remain, if only for a short time, in this highest degree.[64]

This experience of God comes as gift to faithful readers; they become passive recipients of the transforming gift after the "work" of *lectio*. "In this exalted contemplation all carnal motions are so conquered and drawn out of the soul that in no way is the flesh opposed to the spirit, and [the person] becomes, as it were, wholly spiritual."[65]

[59] Ibid., V, 84–85.
[60] Ibid., XIV, 95.
[61] Ibid., XII, 92.
[62] Ibid., XII, 93.
[63] Ibid., XIII, 95.
[64] Ibid., XIII, 96.
[65] Ibid., VII, 88.

Throughout the course of his work, Guigo scatters summary descriptions of the four-step reading process. At one point he suggests that reading searches for sweetness, meditation pinpoints it, prayer requests it, and contemplation savors it.[66] Then with admirable compactness he adds: "Reading, as it were, puts food whole into the mouth, meditation chews it and breaks it up, prayer extracts its flavor, contemplation is the sweetness itself which gladdens and refreshes. Reading works on the outside, meditation on the pith; prayer asks for what we long for, contemplation gives us delight in the sweetness which we have found."[67] His succinct description of the spiritual exercise contributed to his work becoming a classic. Clarity and straightforwardness were his trademarks.

Granted that respect for the literal sense in Guigo's approach to the Scriptures is foundational, clearly his thrust moves readers beyond the literal to deeper (and more important) meaning. He himself remarks: "There is little sweetness in the study of the literal sense, unless there be a commentary, which is found in the heart, to reveal the inward sense."[68] Guigo goes further and links the steps of the reading process with the stages of a person's spiritual life. These four he calls 1) beginners, 2) proficients, 3) devotees, and 4) the blessed. Beginners, those at the first stage of reading, "an exercise of the outward senses," are more concerned with putting down a foundation for meditation through mastery of the literal text.[69] Proficients preoccupy themselves with meditation, which "digs" for treasure within the text and moves the reader to prayer. Devotees, those at the third level of spiritual development, concern themselves more properly with prayer, and, finally, the blessed, with contemplation.

Both Hugh of St. Victor and Guigo II faced the threat, as well as the challenge, that Scholastic reading posed. Each in his own way puts forth powerful statements on behalf of the classic approach to reading even though both reflect influences of the intellectual currents of their age and subscribed to some modifications in the ancient approach. The thirteenth century ushered in an even more ardent adherence to the principles and methods of Scholasticism; the older approach to reading,

---

[66] Ibid., III, 82.
[67] Ibid., III, 82–83.
[68] Ibid., VIII, 89.
[69] Ibid., XII, 92–93.

while not disappearing completely, was eclipsed. A renewed interest in the ancient practice of *lectio* among Christians emerged in only more recent times when there are still more threats and challenges to established ways of reading.

Lectio Divina *Today*

In today's postmodern world reading in the manner of the monastics goes against the tide. Postmodernism signals a breakdown in the bond established between words and reality. People are educated to be skeptics, not to believe what they read. George Steiner, among others, laments what he calls "the break of the covenant between word and world."[70] In this time of a crisis of the "word," people no longer look to texts for meaning and no longer feel they must answer to texts for the way they live. Yet what looks like liberation, no longer having to answer to texts, actually keeps one perpetually at sea with no fixed reference points.

The contemporary situation for reading is further complicated by the rise of computer technology with phenomena such as text-messaging, hyperlinks, and virtual reality. Texts on a computer screen are indeed virtual texts and easily subject to manipulation. Thus, the authority of texts in the popular mind is dealt another blow. Reading in this fast-paced world is done quickly and for the sake of the information which can be gained. Today's climate is not conducive to the slow, reverent reading associated with *lectio divina*. Yet there are increasing calls for a return to the ancient approach to reading, to reading done for formation rather than for information. Along with such calls are descriptions of a reading process in which a vital connection is made, in which the soul finds nourishment and direction. "When we read truly," George Steiner writes, "where the experience is to be that of meaning, we do so as if the text (the piece of music, the work of art) *incarnates* (the notion is grounded in the sacramental) *a real presence of significant being.*"[71]

As if in response to such desire for connection, Garcia Colombás has written about *lectio* as "reading God."[72] Such a phrase suggests that

---

[70] George Steiner, *Real Presences* (Chicago: University of Chicago Press, 1989), 93.

[71] George Steiner, "Real Presences" in *No Passion Spent: Essays 1978–1995* (New Haven, CT: Yale University Press, 1996), 35.

[72] Garcia Colombás, *Reading God*, trans. Gregory Roettger (Schuyler, NE: BMH Publications, 1993).

reading has as its goal experiencing God. In contrast to the thrust of much contemporary reading, *lectio* is not done to acquire practical bits of knowledge, but rather to bring about a life-giving connection with a real presence. For Colombás, the Bible is *the* book for God-seekers. To really read it one cannot read it passively but, rather, must read it much as a musician reads a musical score, for the Bible is something to be performed, to be lived out. To really read it is to find oneself moved to pray, to respond. "When *lectio* is attention to God and personal, intimate contact with God's Word, then prayer breaks forth spontaneously and irresistibly."[73]

Yet another contrast between contemporary secular approaches to reading and *lectio divina* has to do with extensive versus intensive reading. Extensive reading came into prominence at the end of the eighteenth century when the focus was on reading broadly and independently so as to satisfy one's curiosity. With this approach came a more casual attitude toward books and a more superficial and hasty manner of reading.[74] All this stood apart from the older intensive way of reading where the focus was on reading and rereading a small number of books of which the Bible was the centerpiece.

Introducing a term similar to intensive reading and yet going beyond it, Richard R. Niebuhr writes of "deep reading."[75] This is a way of reading the Scriptures which is attuned to the language and word patterns and leads to the innovative rather than the conventional, a way of reading that challenges rather than affirms the status quo. Reminiscent of what St. Bernard encouraged, Niebuhr endorses an experiential reading in which readers allow their experience and the passage to interconnect. Niebuhr describes it in this way: "In deep reading we do not have a text 'before' us as much as a 'presence' of voices, of living words and symbols, around us. . . . Reading of this kind is similar to living in a sprawling house, in which we climb up and down and explore adjoining rooms, halls, and yard."[76] Deep reading opens us to new images of possibility and so transforms our usual perceptions of ourselves and the world around us.

---

[73] Ibid., 50.

[74] Matei Calinescu, *Rereading* (New Haven, CT: Yale University Press, 1993), 86–87.

[75] Richard R. Niebuhr, "The Strife of Interpreting: The Moral Burden of Imagination," *Parabola* 10, no. 2 (1985): 39.

[76] Ibid., 40.

Robert Mulholland, like Niebuhr, wants to accentuate the power of the Scriptures to break into lives and to suggest new and daring possibilities.[77] He explains that the Scriptures are able to do this because they, as it were, break the crust that keeps us insulated and resistant to change. They shift our perceptual focus and thus open us to the possibility of a new slant on things.[78] Paralleling the distinction between extensive and intensive reading, Mulholland speaks of informational and formational reading. In informational reading, the text is perceived as an object to be mastered and the knowledge gained as something that will have practical benefits for us. In formational reading the reader lets the text shape him or her and work in its own way.[79] The crust that prevents the entrance of the Word into one's life is, as Mulholland sees it, the culturally reinforced tendency to approach everything from a functional, informational standpoint, to see all things in terms of what they can do for us.[80] With their crust intact, readers are imprisoned in a cold, factual world, kept from fully imagining a world filled with the surprises and innovations of grace. With their crust broken open, readers allow the Word to read them and form them in new and unexpected ways.

To read fully today is to enter into a conversation with life-giving texts which can transform our way of looking at God, the world, and ourselves. To appropriate *lectio divina* means to believe that God does indeed speak to people and then to read slowly in such a way that one connects with the God who speaks. To do *lectio* implies that we allow God's Word to address us in our unique situations and transform us as we open ourselves to its full meaning. In a recent book on reading the Scriptures titled *Eat This Book*, Eugene Peterson observes that God's Word does not force or coerce. It invites and gives space for us to answer, to participate in a conversation.[81] The answer is our prayer. In the striking expressions of André Louf, after we have chewed over and assimilated the Word, "We have become Word; we are prayer. . . .

[77] Robert Mulholland, *Shaped by the Word: The Power of Scripture in Spiritual Formation* (Nashville, TN: Upper Room Books, 1985).

[78] Ibid., 33.

[79] Ibid., 49–59.

[80] Ibid., 110–12.

[81] Eugene Peterson, *Eat This Book* (Grand Rapids, MI: Eerdmans Publishing Company, 2006), 109.

It bubbles up, it flows, it runs like living water. It is no longer we who pray, but the prayer prays itself in us."[82]

Further Reading

Bianchi, Enzo. *Praying the Word: An Introduction to Lectio Divina*. Trans. James W. Zona. Kalamazoo, MI: Cistercian Publications, 1998.

Guigo II. *The Ladder of Monks and Twelve Meditations*. Trans. Edmund Colledge and James Walsh. Garden City, NY: Doubleday, 1978.

Magrassi, Mariano. *Praying the Bible: An Introduction to Lectio Divina*. Trans. Edward Hagman. Collegeville, MN: Liturgical Press, 1998.

Pennington, M. Basil. *Lectio Divina: Renewing the Ancient Practice of Praying the Scriptures*. New York: Crossroad, 1998.

[82] André Louf, *Teach Us to Pray: Learning a Little about God,* trans. Hubert Hoskins (New York: Paulist Press, 1975), 48.

Chapter 13

Praying with Mary and the Saints

Silas Henderson, O.S.B.

Thomas Merton wrote, "All that is necessary to be a saint is to want to be one. Don't you believe that God will make you what he created you to be. . . . All you have to do is desire it."[1] This idea that sanctity is accessible to everyone is key to a balanced understanding of the place of Mary and the saints in the Christian tradition. Today, however, many reject or are embarrassed by the traditional (often sterile or over-sentimentalized) images and stories of saints treasured by generations of Catholics around the world. And yet the Church has affirmed time and again the importance of Mary and the saints in the life of the Christian. In *Lumen Gentium*, the Dogmatic Constitution on the Church of the Second Vatican Council, the council fathers declared, "Being more closely united to Christ, those who dwell in heaven consolidate the holiness of the whole church. . . . [T]hey do not cease to intercede with the Father for us, as they proffer the merits which they acquired on earth through the one mediator between God and humanity, Christ Jesus. . . . So by their familial concern is our weakness greatly helped."[2]

---

[1] Thomas Merton, *The Seven Storey Mountain* (New York: Harcourt Brace, 1998), 260.

[2] *Lumen Gentium* (Dogmatic Constitution on the Church), November 21, 1964, no. 49.

We are united to the saints in heaven and we can benefit from their intercession and the witness of their lives.

Speaking of the saints as models of virtue and sanctity, St. Anthony the Abbot (d. 356) is remembered as having encouraged his followers "to repeat by heart the commandments of the Scriptures, and to remember the deeds of the saints, that by their example the soul may train itself under the guidance of the commandments."[3] As Merton implied, each of the saints, as sanctified individuals, offers a unique witness and gift to the Church through the witness of his or her life. And in a conference given to her sisters in 1849, St. Theodore Guerin (d. 1856), foundress of the American Congregation of the Sisters of Providence of Saint Mary-of-the-Woods in Indiana, reminded her spiritual daughters of the intercessory power of the saints when she said, "They will be happy to pray for you, for like us they have been feeble, they have been tempted, they have been miserable. But they had recourse to God. God pardoned their offences and today they sing his mercies."[4] In these quotations, we have two saints offering their prophetic witness to the roles they themselves would play in the life of the Church.

The history of the development of this theology and devotion represented by these sentiments is a long and complex one and a full treatment is certainly beyond the scope of this essay.

Theological and Scriptural Foundations

Before entering into any sort of history, it seems that it would be beneficial to establish a connection between these diverse individuals who represent a two thousand year tradition that extends throughout the world. Many saints are little known outside of their own region or time while others are more universally celebrated. One might ask what the Roman virgin and martyr Agnes (d. ca. 305), the Swiss hermit-martyr Meinrad (d. 861), the Holy Roman Emperor Henry II (d. 1027), the Native American Kateri Tekakwitha (d. 1680), Pope Pius IX (d. 1878),

---

[3] Athanasius of Alexandria, *The Life of Saint Anthony the Great* (Willits, CA: Eastern Orthodox Books, n.d.), 76.

[4] Theodore Guerin, *Conference on the Eve of All Saints, 1848*. Taken from the *Positio* of the Cause for Canonization of Blessed Theodore Guerin, 832–833. Courtesy of the Sisters of Providence of Saint Mary-of-the-Woods. She was canonized on October 15, 2006.

and the Nobel Prize-winning foundress Teresa of Calcutta (d. 1997) have in common. As Professor Lawrence S. Cunningham observes, the simplest answer is that all are included in the *Roman Martyrology*, the Church's official listing of saints and blesseds.[5] Yet when we examine our understanding of the word "saint" with all its implications, we soon recognize a deeper reality that offers a name and class for those very real people who offer special witness to virtue and the Christian life.

This understanding of sanctity is, in fact, rooted in New Testament spirituality, and St. Paul frequently uses the term "saint" as a generic term for members of the Christian community.[6] In the Judeo-Christian tradition holiness is an attribute of God alone. Everything else (e.g., people, places, rituals, etc.) can be called holy only to the degree that they are joined to the holiness of God.[7] For Paul, the community of believers has become united with God by their being included as members of the Body of Christ and they, by virtue of this relationship, are themselves holy. The believer, the "saint," is holy and we can recognize the Christian community as a communion of saints and see the Church as holy because each of its composite members is united with God in Christ Jesus. This understanding has been reaffirmed in the recent teachings of the Church, most especially the Second Vatican Council, which emphasized the universal call of holiness with the witness of the diversity of the saints, proving that this holiness is accessible to all men and women.[8]

The Early Church and the Age of the Martyrs

The members of the earliest Christian communities immediately recognized some of their own as outstanding witnesses of this union with God. The early Church remembered the deacon Stephen as the first to give his life for the Gospel.[9] More generally, beginning with Nero's persecution in Rome (ca. A.D. 65), during which the apostles Peter and Paul were killed, until the Edict of Milan (313), the Christian communities

[5] Lawrence S. Cunningham, *A Brief History of Saints* (Malden, MA: Blackwell Publishing, 2005), 7.

[6] Cf. Rom 1:7; 1 Cor 1:2; Eph 1:1; 2:19; and Phil 1:1.

[7] Cunningham, *A Brief History*, 9.

[8] *Lumen Gentium*, no. 40.

[9] Cf. Acts 6:8–7:60.

throughout the Roman Empire experienced periodic persecutions. These were initially confined to certain regions and varied in their severity. It was only with the Emperor Decius that there was an empire-wide persecution (ca. 250), prompted by the Christians' refusal to participate in government-mandated religious rites. Similar persecutions occurred under the emperors Valerian and Diocletian. Christians lived outside of the religious and even political conventions of their time and were even considered atheists because of their refusal to participate in celebrations honoring the local deities.[10] They were often blamed for various natural disasters and their countercultural stance made them an easy target for their pagan neighbors. All these circumstances set the scene for the first Christian heroes: the martyrs. Deriving their title from the Greek word for "witness," the martyrs took on a cultural and theological significance that greatly contributed to the future understanding of sanctity and the place of saints in the life of the Church.

Martyrdom came to be seen as a charism of the early Church[11] and the martyrs' willingness to die for their faith was seen as a reflection of (and even a participation in) the Passion of Christ, the great Martyr of Revelation 1:5.[12] The early literature, the *passio* or *martyrium*, that described the passions of the martyrs, allowed the story of a local martyr to be spread to different regions. Because of their sharing in the Passion of Christ and their union with God in heaven, the martyrs came to be recognized as possessing a special holiness that gave them a particularly powerful relationship with God. While the faithful did not typically believe the martyr possessed any power in their own right, they were recognized as special icons (images) of Christ.

One of these accounts, *The Martyrdom of Polycarp*, recounts the events surrounding the death of Bishop Polycarp of Smyrna around 155, who was probably the first martyr to be honored universally with a special cult.[13] This second-century text recounts the death within a theological framework that constantly compares Polycarp's death to that of Christ. "These theologically charged reflections on the significance

---

[10] James P. Campbell, *Mary and the Saints: Companions on the Journey* (Chicago: Loyola Press, 2001), 24.

[11] Ibid.

[12] National Association of Pastoral Musicians Program Staff, "A Song of the Seasons: The Sanctoral Cycle—The Whole Company of Heaven," *Pastoral Music* (2005): 45.

[13] Ibid.

of the martyr's sacrifice were a kind of homily for a persecuted church: they became a 'proof' of the meaning of the life of Jesus and a model for those discipleship instructions that were in the Gospel message."[14] Other early texts such as the *Letter of Ignatius of Antioch to the Romans* and *Passion of Perpetua and Felicity* offer other martyrdom accounts that include this idea of imitating the suffering Christ and present the martyrs as models of faith.[15]

In time these texts became more fictionalized, and stock elements and themes became more common. These stories became the foundation for the tradition of hagiography (*legenda*), the composition of lives of the saints that tended to focus more on reverence than fact, a practice that was prominent in the Middle Ages and endured until the late nineteenth century.

Besides the literature that grew up around the lives of the martyrs, further proof of the esteem shown by the early Church was the veneration shown to the mortal remains and possessions (the relics) of the martyrs. Here again the text of the *Martyrdom of Polycarp* shows us a developing cult as it records that his remains were transferred to a place where they could be suitably honored on the anniversary of his death.[16] The annual celebration of the *dies natalis*, or birthday, of the martyrs was a reflection of the Roman custom of honoring the dead one day each year. Professor Peter Brown stresses, however, that the Christian motivation and understanding of this practice were a departure from that of their pagan neighbors in that the Christians broke "most of the imaginative boundaries which ancient men placed between heaven and earth, the divine and the human, the living and the dead."[17]

The careful documentation of the anniversaries of the martyrs (and later the confessors/non-martyrs) allowed the Christian community to keep these anniversaries with annual celebrations that often centered at the tomb of the saint. Early liturgical texts reveal that these celebrations might include readings (possibly from the *Acta* or *Passio* of the martyrs), psalms and prayers, and even the celebration of the Eucharist. The fourth-century *Depositio Martyrum* provides a list of those martyrs

---

[14] Cunningham, *A Brief History*, 15.

[15] Ibid.

[16] Ibid., 16.

[17] Peter Brown, *The Cult of Saints: Its Rise and Function in Latin Christianity* (Chicago: University of Chicago Press, 1981), 21.

who were commemorated each year at Rome and similar lists from other major cities, such as Antioch and Corinth, have also survived.[18]

Until the fourth century, the Christian martyrs were buried in Christian-maintained cemeteries. These were sometimes carved in underground volcanic rock (e.g., the "catacombs"). However, it is important to remember that most of the people buried in these cemeteries died of natural causes. It was an incorrect assumption by Renaissance Catholics that all those buried in these cemeteries died as martyrs and this gave rise to devotions to martyrs like St. Philomena and St. Expeditus.[19]

After the fall of the Roman Empire, the barbarian invasions that plagued Rome prompted Church leaders to rebury the martyrs inside the city walls in churches or in specially built shrines.[20] Under Emperor Constantine extravagant building campaigns helped to further glorify the remains of the martyrs.[21] It was Constantine who oversaw the construction of a large basilica over the tomb of St. Peter on the site of the shrine where his physical remains were venerated. Various traditions maintain that he was also responsible for the basilica of Saint-Paul-outside-the-Walls over the tomb of St. Paul.[22]

By the end of the fourth century (the end of the "age of the martyrs"), veneration of the martyrs was a feature of both personal devotion and liturgical celebrations. The prayers offered at the tombs of the martyrs were considered powerful and the bodies and relics of the saints were thought to be channels of sacred power.[23]

A New Kind of Martyr

When the times of persecution came to an end following the *Edict of Milan*, Christians began to look for new models of holiness. They found them in the monks and ascetics of the desert. These were the new martyrs who left behind family and society with the goal of living a

---

[18] Cunningham, *A Brief History*, 17.

[19] Ibid.

[20] Cf. John Crook, *The Architectural Setting of the Cult of the Saints in the Early Christian West: 300–1200* (Oxford: Oxford University Press, 2000).

[21] Barbara Abou-El-Haj, *The Medieval Cult of Saints: Formations and Transformations* (Cambridge: Cambridge University Press, 1997), 7–12.

[22] Abou-El-Haj, *The Medieval Cult*, 8; Cunningham, *A Brief History*, 19.

[23] Brown, *The Cult of Saints*, 10–11; Campbell, *Mary and the Saints*, 26.

life oriented completely toward the search for God.[24] *The Life of Saint Anthony*, written by his friend St. Athanasius of Alexandria (d. 373), is often credited with the rise of monasticism in the Christian tradition. Later *Vitas* of the Desert Fathers and Mothers, such as St. Pachomius (d. 346), St. Paul (the Hermit) of Thebes (d. ca. 345), and St. Macrina the Younger (d. 379), the sister of Saints Gregory of Nyssa (d. 395), and Basil the Great (d. 379), all presented the lives of these early monks and nuns as models of Christian witness (i.e., a new martyrdom).[25] Also dating from this time are collections of sayings attributed to early monastics known as the *Apophthegmata Patrum;* these continue to be an important source of study and spiritual nourishment up to our own time.

As the stories of the Desert Fathers and Mothers spread in the East, the Western Church came to honor its first non-martyr saint, Martin, bishop of Tours (d. 397). His life, written while he was still alive, presents the monk-made-bishop as a model of pastoral virtue and asceticism. His tomb became a favorite destination for pilgrims and miracle seekers.[26] One of the benefits offered by this new class of saint was that people could recognize that holiness was not limited to a chosen few. Each person could become holy through avoiding sin and seeking virtue in their own place.

Mary in the Life of the Early Church

When we consider the place and influence Mary holds over contemporary Catholic and Orthodox Christianity, we may be struck by how little biographical information about her can be found in the New Testament. Each of the four gospels and the Acts of the Apostles contains references to the Mother of Jesus, establishing a variety of theologies of Mary within the framework of the fledgling Church's developing christology and ecclesiology.

Apocryphal (i.e., unapproved) Christian writings (which appeared as early as A.D. 100) provide glimpses into the developing theologies and traditions centered on the lives of Jesus, Mary, the apostles, and others in the early Church.[27] One of the most important of these

---

[24] Campbell, *Mary and the Saints*, 27.

[25] Cunningham, *A Brief History*, 21.

[26] Campbell, *Mary and the Saints*, 29.

[27] Ibid., 14.

writings is the *Protoevangelium of James*. It is here we find accounts of the childhoods of both Jesus and Mary, as well as information about St. Joseph, the foster father of Jesus, and Mary's parents, Saints Anne and Joachim. We can also find in the *Protoevangelium* early references to belief in the immaculate conception of Mary as well as her assumption into heaven.[28]

However, as the Church continued to move into the Greco-Roman world, theologians and philosophers offered new perspectives on the person of Jesus Christ, and the place of Mary in the life of the Church began to develop beyond its Jewish roots. Writers such as St. Justin Martyr (d. ca. 165), who reflected on Mary's role as the new Eve, and St. Athanasius of Alexandria, who championed Mary's perpetual virginity, helped reinforce the belief that by giving birth to Jesus Mary played a vital role in the salvation of humankind.[29] The great St. Augustine of Hippo (d. 430) saw Mary as an integral part of understanding Christ's humanity and divinity.[30] He, with St. Ambrose of Milan (d. 397), also connected Mary with the Church, thinking of both as "mothers in charity and virginal in integrity."[31]

It was the Ecumenical Council of Ephesus (431) that proclaimed Mary to be *Theotokos* (God-bearer), teaching that Mary had truly become the Mother of God by the human conception of God in her womb. "Mother of God, not that the nature of the Word of his divinity received the beginning of its existence from the holy Virgin, but that, since the holy body, animated by a rational soul, which the Word of God united to himself according to the hypostasis [union of the humanity and divinity of Jesus], was born from her, the Word is said to be born according to the flesh."[32] At Ephesus, the council fathers raised the Church's understanding of Mary from the obedient handmaiden of the

---

[28] Luigi Gambero, S.M., *Mary and the Fathers of the Church: The Blessed Virgin Mary in Patristic Thought* (San Francisco: Ignatius Press, 1999), 33–41.

[29] Ibid., 46–47, 103–5.

[30] *Mary Most Holy: Meditating with the Early Cistercians* (Kalamazoo, MI: Cistercian Publications, 2003), xiv.

[31] Ibid.

[32] Council of Ephesus as quoted in United States Conference of Catholic Bishops, excerpt from the English translation of the *Catechism of the Catholic Church* for use in the United States of America. Copyright © 1997. United States Catholic Conference, Inc.—*Liberia Editrice Vaticana*. Used with permission.

Scriptures and early traditions to the royal status of Mother of God. In response to this teaching new churches and shrines dedicated to her appeared in both the Eastern and Western Churches and devotion to Mary increased universally. We see this beautifully expressed in the writings of St. Cyril of Alexandria (d. 444):

> I see the assembly of the saints, all zealously gathered together, invited by the holy Mother of God, Mary, ever-virgin . . . Now the sweet words of the hymnographer David have been fulfilled in our presence: "Behold how fair, and how pleasant it is, when brothers dwell together as one!" (Ps 133:1). Hail, we say, O holy and mystic Trinity, who have called us together in this church dedicated to Mary, Mother of God. We hail you, O Mary Mother of God, venerable treasure of the entire world, inextinguishable lamp, crown of virginity, scepter of orthodoxy, imperishable temple, container of him who cannot be contained.[33]

Only after the Council of Ephesus do we see the development of the first liturgical celebrations honoring Mary. The first of these seems to have been a celebration at Jerusalem honoring her *Dormition* (falling asleep) sometime around the year 450. This feast made its way to the West where it was celebrated at Rome in the seventh century. This Eastern celebration combined the motherhood of Mary with her "falling asleep," which in the Western Church, came to be called the Assumption. However, this does not mean that there was no devotion to Mary at Rome prior to this. In the year 432, Pope Sixtus III dedicated the Basilica of Saint Mary-Major and added the name of Mary to the *Roman Canon*. The seventh century also saw the addition of three other Marian feasts, each celebrated with solemn processions and the Eucharist: the Annunciation (March 25), the Presentation of the Lord in the Temple (February 2), and the Nativity of the Blessed Virgin (September 8).[34] The anniversary of the dedication of the first church honoring Mary at Jerusalem in 543 forms the basis of the Memorial of the Presentation of Mary, celebrated on November 21.[35] The sixth and

---

[33] Gambero, *Mary and the Fathers*, 247.

[34] J. D. Crichton, *Our Lady in the Liturgy* (Collegeville, MN: Liturgical Press, 1997), 24–25.

[35] Ibid., 81.

seventh centuries also saw the celebration of more localized Marian feasts in Spain and Gaul.

Saints in the Middle Ages

The period following the decline of the Roman Empire saw Christianity spread as far as the British Isles. This period also saw the continued rise in monasticism in both the Eastern and Western Churches during which time monks, particularly from Ireland, began the work of evangelizing on the continent, spreading their unique brand of spirituality. Devotion to the saints served to ensure orthodoxy in the face of Arianism and other persistent heresies that plagued the Church.[36]

The intercessory power of the saints continued to be emphasized and they filled the ever-widening gap between Christ, the Judge of Revelation, and humanity. In an effort to promote a sense of obedience in a culture that had little use for philosophical and theological truths, the spiritual wrath of a distant and vengeful God was used to capture the attention of both the rich and poor.[37] It was the saints who came to be the special protectors and intercessors for individuals, communities, and countries. Men and women of all classes flocked to their shrines in ever-increasing numbers, helping create some of the great abbeys and pilgrimage centers. The power of the saints was celebrated in wondrous tales of healing. These writings offered witness to the power of the Church in overcoming the world by teaching that the saints are ready and able to assist in any earthly or spiritual need, however great. Saints defended those dedicated to them and supported those who sought their help.

One of the most important elements in the spread and permanence of any saint's cult was the performance of miracles during his or her life, and, more important, after death. Ever more elaborate shrines, the focus of pilgrims and those hoping for miracles, provided a link between heaven and earth. The *Dialogues* of St. Gregory the Great (d. 604), written around 593, illustrate the great emphasis placed on miracles during this time.[38] The *Dialogues* also show an understanding of the power of the relics of the saints. As Professor Cunningham states: "Gregory's interlocutor in the *Dialogues* asks why relics sometimes are

---

[36] Ibid., 25–26.
[37] Campbell, *Mary and the Saints*, 32.
[38] Cunningham, *A Brief History*, 23.

the occasion of greater miracles than those performed at the tomb of a saint. Gregory explains that a person praying before distant relics of a saint 'earns all the more merit by his faith, for he realizes that the martyrs are present to hear his prayers even though their bodies happened to be buried elsewhere.'"[39]

This appreciation (and even obsession) with miracles and relics helped spur the great pilgrimage movements that characterized the Middle Ages. Rome, Tours, Canterbury, Santiago de Compostela, and even the Holy Land became the goal for generations of Christian pilgrims seeking forgiveness and miracles. Pilgrimage ultimately became such a common phenomenon that, with time, it lost much of its penitential and spiritual appeal. For contemporary proof of this, we need only read Chaucer's story of a group of pilgrims traveling to the shrine of St. Thomas à Becket (d. 1170) in *The Canterbury Tales*.

As the centuries passed and the cult of the saints became ever more popular and even secularized, the *legenda* of the saints, their lives and accounts of their miracles, became more standardized and fanciful. There developed a tendency to supplement the sometimes sparse biographical information available for a given saint. It was this period that saw stories of nameless New Testament characters embellished. While St. Veronica and St. Dismas (the "Good Thief") are never named in the New Testament, they became fixtures of Medieval piety and meditations on the Passion.[40] The cults of other biblical personages, such as Joseph of Arimathea, Mary Magdalene, Martha, Luke, Barnabas, and Silas, all benefited from this practice with both the Eastern and Western Churches seeking to further glorify these individuals who captured the Christian imagination. In other places the lives of more popular saints were blended with the characters from local folktales; St. Nicholas of Myra (d. ca. 342) became Santa Claus, and St. Patrick's (d. 461) intercession was offered as the explanation of why there are no snakes in Ireland.

Collections of these legends grew and the most important of these, *The Golden Legend*, was compiled by a Dominican friar around 1260. This work brought together numerous pious stories spanning the entire

---

[39] Ibid., 24. Cf. Gregory the Great, *The Life and Miracles of Saint Benedict (Book Two of the Dialogues)*, trans. Odo Zimmerman et al. (Collegeville, MN: Liturgical Press, n.d.), 77.

[40] Cunningham, *A Brief History*, 32.

medieval period. It became enormously popular, and there are over one thousand surviving manuscript copies. No other book was reprinted more often between 1470 and 1530.[41] It was *The Golden Legend* that assured a permanent place in Christian piety for SS. Christopher, George, Catherine, and many others. These *legenda* also provided a useful tool for preachers who used the lives and legends of the saints to reinforce moral and devotional standards.

It is important to remember that until this period there was no formal process of canonization. Many communities and dioceses honored local saints, and it was the memory of the people and the manifestation of miracles that ensured the cult of the saint. Elaborate legends served only to ensure the perseverance of a particular cult, even if it remained as only a local observance.

Mary in the Middle Ages

As the monastic movement continued to grow and spread throughout the medieval period, it carried with it not only the surviving elements of Greco-Roman culture but also the stories of the saints. It was in this movement, with its emphasis on contemplation and personal sanctification that a new piety honoring Mary began to emerge.[42] At the Abbey of Reichenau, Blessed Herman "the Cripple" (d. 1054) composed the *Alma Redemptoris Mater* and other devotional hymns and prayers dedicated to Mary which became part of the daily life of the great Benedictine Abbey of Cluny and its daughter-monasteries.[43] By the eleventh century Mary had come to be regarded as unique not only for her role in salvation history but also, "because of her singular privilege of merits," she came to be considered superior to all the saints and even the angels.[44]

Monastic writers, such as Blessed Guerric of Igny (d. 1151) and St. Bernard of Clairvaux (d. 1153), emphasized Mary's care and solicitude for believers who were encouraged to seek her protection and patronage. As St. Bernard writes: "Take away Mary, this star of the sea, the sea truly great and wide: what is left but enveloping darkness and the shadow of death and the densest blackness? With the very core of our

---

[41] Ibid., 33.
[42] Campbell, *Mary and the Saints,* 39.
[43] *Mary Most Holy,* xxii.
[44] Ibid., xxiii.

being then, with all the affections of our hearts and with all our prayers let us honor Mary, because this is the will of Him who wills that we possess all things through Mary."[45]

The eleventh century saw the rapid growth of cities throughout Europe. Universities began to replace monastery schools and expanding humanist sentiments helped bring education to the new middle classes.[46] These innovations allowed for a new, non-monastic spirituality. The mendicant orders of Franciscans and Dominicans began to travel throughout Europe spreading their unique devotions and theologies. These new communities brought a more human and earthy spirituality to the masses. Images of Mary became less theologically oriented and focused on images of Mary at the crèche of the nativity or standing at the cross. She became more than the intercessor and model of obedience and faith she had been for centuries and came to be seen as a tender and caring mother. Liturgical celebrations honoring Mary's conception (December 8), which appeared as early as 700, spread throughout Europe during this period, emphasizing not only Mary's purity and special place in salvation history but also her humanity.[47]

As the Black Death ravaged Europe during the thirteenth and fourteenth centuries and the Church faced schism, the lowly virgin of Nazareth came to be seen as the Queen of Heaven and the Refuge of Sinners. She represented the promise of God fulfilled: a lowly peasant shared the very heart of God; the Lord had lifted up, and would continue to lift up, the lowly.[48] She came to be recognized as one who could mediate God's mercy, and many forms of devotion expressed this hope in her loving care. It was during this period that the devotion we know as the rosary developed as a "Psalter of the unlettered."[49] Beginning as a simple way for people to imitate the monks who prayed the 150 psalms each week as part of the Divine Office, the rosary later took on a decidedly Marian character and over time it became a tool for meditation on specific events in the lives of Jesus and Mary. Eventually the Dominican Order became the champions of this devotion and it remains a great icon of

---

[45] Bernard of Clairvaux, *Sermon for the Feast of the Nativity of Mary,* from *Mary Most Holy,* 349.

[46] Campbell, *Mary and the Saints,* 40.

[47] Crichton, *Our Lady in the Liturgy,* 64–68.

[48] Campbell, *Mary and the Saints,* 42. Cf. Luke 1:52.

[49] Ibid., 46.

Catholic culture and piety. In 1573, Pope Gregory XIII named October 7 the Feast of the Most Holy Rosary at Rome; this was extended to the universal Church by Pope Clement XI in 1716.[50]

The Late Middle Ages

The thirteenth and fourteenth centuries saw many innovations in the Church's understanding of the cult of the saints. Interest in the saints had become practical and almost every aspect of public life was permeated by the stories and symbols of the saints. Reflecting the strongly feudalistic structure of society, the idea of "patron" saints became commonplace and saints became associated with given occupations or needs. For instance the French hermit Fiacre (d. 671) came to be invoked as the patron not only of gardeners but also of cab drivers and those suffering from hemorrhoids; Benedict of Nursia (d. 547) was invoked against poisoning; and the French Abbess Odilia (d. ca. 720) joined St. Lucy (d. ca. 304) as patroness of the blind. Every trade guild, town, and parish had its favorite saint and even down to our time children still take the name of a patron saint at the time of their confirmation.[51]

As the Church became more institutionalized, the papacy assumed sole right to name saints (i.e., to *canonize*, or officially list, them). The first saint canonized by papal decree was actually St. Ulrich, bishop of Augsburg (d. 983), in 993.[52] The publication of the Decretals of Pope Gregory IX in 1234 asserted the right of the pope to have absolute authority in naming those worthy of veneration as saints.[53] This was based on the notion that saints were models of the universal Church, not simply the objects of local veneration.[54]

During the Avignon Papacy (1309–77) the process of canonization took the form of a legal trial "in which candidates for canonization were represented by their petitioners and presented before the court by an

---

[50] Crichton, *Our Lady in the Liturgy*, 88–91, and Campbell, *Mary and the Saints*, 46–47. On October 16, 2002, Pope John Paul II issued the Apostolic Letter *Rosarium Virginis Mariae* (On the Most Holy Rosary), in which he reemphasized the special place Marian devotion, particularly the rosary, holds in the Church in the present day.

[51] Cunningham, *A Brief History*, 47.

[52] Ibid., 38.

[53] Campbell, *Mary and the Saints*, 50.

[54] Kenneth L. Woodward, *Making Saints* (New York: Touchstone Books, 1996), 17–18.

official procurator or prosecutor of the cause."[55] The process even allowed for a "Promoter of the Faith" (commonly known as the "Devil's Advocate") who investigated any questions raised that might lead to a rejection of beatification or canonization.[56]

However, in spite of this developing bureaucracy, the saints continued to hold the imagination of the common people. Pilgrimages continued and modern studies indicate that in the year 1400 there were nearly 1,500 shrines throughout Europe.[57] The institution of the Jubilee Years by Pope Boniface VIII in 1300 gave further endorsement to this practice as pilgrims traveled to Rome and other major shrines in order to gain special Jubilee indulgences.[58]

An examination of the saints canonized and popularized during this time reveals a set of common characteristics among candidates. While the manifestation of miracles was still considered an important part of the process, holiness of life and virtue were given the most emphasis.[59] Saints from this period were primarily clerics and religious (the majority of them men) with very few lay saints. Among those few men and women who were not bishops, priests, monks, or nuns, there are practically no saints from among the lowest classes; most were nobles or royalty.[60] This practice reflected a changing popular belief that a life of moral discipline and an intense interior life necessary for true sanctity was available for only a few. Saints like Francis of Assisi (d. 1226), Clare of Assisi (d. 1253), and King Louis IX of France (d. 1279) came to be seen as measures of holiness, not as the exceptions we now recognize them to have been.

Reformation and Counter-Reformation

By the beginning of the sixteenth century the cult of saints had become clouded with abuses, particularly concerning the devotions

---

[55] Campbell, *Mary and the Saints*, 51.

[56] Ibid. The beatification of a candidate (often considered the first "step" to sainthood) allows for local veneration, while canonization recognizes the individual as a model of holiness for the universal Church.

[57] Cunningham, *A Brief History*, 49.

[58] Ibid., 50.

[59] Campbell, *Mary and the Saints*, 52.

[60] Cunningham, *A Brief History*, 46–48. Two notable exceptions to this are St. Isidore the Farmer (d. 1130) and Blessed Joan of Aza (d. ca. 1190), the mother of the Dominican Order's founder, St. Dominic Guzman (d. 1221).

surrounding relics. Pilgrimage had begun to take the form of a vacation and holy days had become holidays.[61] At times devotion to the saints became little more than superstition.[62] One of the most popular devotions in Italy and Germany was the "Fourteen Holy Helpers." This group of fourteen saints, mostly early martyrs, arose in response to the many dangers and challenges faced by medieval peasants. Invoked against the plague, drought, epilepsy, storms, and war, these saints (many of whom are fictional) were credited with almost divine power.[63] Complicating the situation further were the abuses surrounding the trafficking of relics and the sale of indulgences.

The time was ripe for church reform. Under the influence of reformers such as Martin Luther, Ulrich Zwingli, and John Calvin, the cult of saints was abandoned in favor of an ecclesiology that reemphasized that all members of the Church (both those in heaven and who were promised heaven) were saints. Images, relics, shrines, and devotions were ultimately rejected by their followers.[64] This change in ideology frequently resulted in acts of desecration and destruction. Many of the popular shrines throughout Europe were dismantled, the relics of the saints desecrated, their images destroyed, and their altars burned or broken.

In response to what we now know as the Protestant Reformation, the Catholic Church underwent a Counter-Reformation which centered around the Council of Trent (1545–63). The final session of the council was dedicated to the question of the saints. The bishops agreed to uphold the Church's traditional teachings on the saints and the veneration of relics and the legitimate use of images.[65] They also recognized the need to abolish all previous abuses. In 1564, Pope Pius IV issued a profession of faith to be made by every bishop and all wishing to enter the Roman Catholic Church. It included a declaration that "the saints are to be venerated and invoked; that they offer prayers to God for us and that their relics are to be venerated. I firmly assert that the images of Christ and the ever-Virgin Mother of God, as also those of the other

[61] Ibid., 54–56.
[62] Ibid., 56–57.
[63] Ibid., 58.
[64] Ibid., 59–63. See also Campbell, *Mary and the Saints*, 55.
[65] Cunningham, *A Brief History*, 61.

saints, are to be kept and retained, and that due honor and veneration are to be paid them."[66]

The saints canonized during this time also reflect (and even contributed to) this process of Catholic reform. The great saints Ignatius Loyola (d. 1556), Francis Xavier (d. 1552), Philip Neri (d. 1595), and Teresa of Avila (d. 1582) were canonized together in a single ceremony by Pope Gregory XV in 1622.[67] Each of these saints, in his or her own way, represents various aspects of the Catholic Counter-Reformation and were the first of a number of reformers and founders who have been canonized in more recent history. From that point on, canonization took on a greater political and sociological aspect: the Church was setting a new standard of holiness and orthodoxy, represented by the men and women it chose to put forward for universal veneration.[68] The Catholic Counter-Reformation also saw a new group of martyrs, representing the Church's growing missionary endeavors.[69]

It was Pope Urban VIII (1623–44) who defined the canonical process,[70] a set procedure controlled by the papacy and the Congregation of Rites (established in 1588). Many of the criteria and policies established then still govern the process of canonization today.

Mary and the Saints in the Modern Era

Following the Age of Reformation, European life changed drastically. The colonization of the New World as well as conquests in Africa and Asia flooded Europe with new products and ideas and offered new mission fields for both Catholics and Protestants. Political change was unavoidable and the Age of the Enlightenment, the French Revolution, other European revolutions and civil wars, and finally the nineteenth-century Industrial Revolution impacted peoples all over the globe.

---

[66] Ibid., 62. The full text can be found in *Creeds and Confessions of Faith in the Christian Tradition*, eds. Jaroslav Pelikan and Valerie Hotchkiss, vol. 2 (New Haven, CT: Yale University Press, 2003), 873.

[67] Ibid., 63–64. It was in the same ceremony that St. Isidore the Farmer (mentioned above) was canonized.

[68] Ibid., 66.

[69] These martyrs represent missions to re-evangelize those nations where Protestantism had taken root and include the Church's new mission fields in Africa, Asia, and the Americas. Cf. Cunningham, *A Brief History*, 70–71.

[70] Campbell, *Mary and the Saints*, 56–57.

Within the Catholic Church a large number of new religious communities appeared. Francis de Sales (d. 1622), Vincent de Paul (d. 1664), Alphonsus Liguori (d. 1790), and Anthony Claret (d. 1870), established new communities of missionaries (men and women). Others, such as Angela Merici (d. 1540), Joseph Calasanz (d. 1648), John Baptist de la Salle (d. 1726), and Lucy Filippini (d. 1732), founded communities of teachers.

This period also saw a renewal of the contemplative life as monastic communities began to rebuild following the devastation brought by European political unrest. These communities eventually sent their missionaries to the mission fields, establishing the Catholic monastic tradition in fertile soil. The Church also canonized contemplative men and women of this period and among them we find Mary Magdalene de Pazzi (d. 1607) and Margaret Mary Alocoque (d. 1690). Along with these contemplatives, there is an abundance of canonized priests and religious representing a wide variety of charisms and ministries. Among these are a group of young religious who, until the Second Vatican Council, were honored as models of holiness for young Christians: Rose of Lima (d. 1617), Stanislaus Kostka (d. 1568), Aloysius Gonzaga (d. 1591), John Berchmans (d. 1621), and Gerard Majella (d. 1755).

Probably most important, this period of expansion also became a new age of martyrs. North America, Korea, Japan, Vietnam, China, the Philippines, Thailand, the Pacific Islands, and Africa all claim their martyr-missionaries. Finally, we may recall the countless canonized men and women who lost their lives as a direct result of the Protestant Reformation and the political upheavals of this era. Even in our day the causes of canonization for these martyrs remain active and hundreds of them have been beatified and canonized.

It can be said that the saints of this period following the Counter-Reformation represent the sociological, political, and theological emphases of the Church at that time. The legacies of these saints continue to immediately impact our time as members of their religious families or adherents to their particular school of spirituality remain active in the Church today.

The Nineteenth and Twentieth Centuries

The late nineteenth century brought new challenges to the structures of the Catholic Church. Faced with ever-growing tides of European nationalism, the papacy sought to retain its voice and influence in an increasingly secularized Europe. The First Vatican Council, convoked by Pope Pius IX in 1870, reaffirmed the power of the papacy. It was Pope Pius IX who, in 1854, solemnly declared the long-held doctrine of the Immaculate Conception, declaring that Mary, from the first moment of her conception, was kept free from the stain of original sin.[71] This declaration came at a time of global spiritual awakening in reaction to a culture that had come to value reason above all. Christians tried to reconnect with their God, and it fell to preachers to try to reignite the faith of their people.[72] It was at this time that reports of Marian apparitions became more and more common.

To date, the Church has granted official recognition to only eight Marian apparitions.[73] The first of these, and one with particular importance in the Americas, occurred at Guadalupe, Mexico, in 1531. Juan Diego (d. 1549) presented to his astonished bishop an image of the Virgin Mary imprinted on his cloak after a series of apparitions during which Mary requested that a chapel be built in her honor.[74] This image is still preserved in the Basilica of Our Lady of Guadalupe in Mexico City. The other, more recent, approved Marian apparitions were recorded in France, Portugal, Belgium, and Ireland. The Church carefully investigates reported apparitions and follows an exhaustive process.[75] These apparitions, and the miracles associated with them, helped spur a new wave of Marian devotion that continues to the present day, and these sites remain major centers of pilgrimage for hundreds of thousands each year. This renewed devotion to Mary was further enhanced in 1950 when Pope Pius XII officially proclaimed as dogma the long-held belief of the Assumption.[76]

The nineteenth century also saw the first saints in the United States. Elizabeth Seton (d. 1821), Theodore Guerin (d. 1856), John Neumann (d. 1860), Francis Seelos (d. 1867), and Damian de Veuster (d.

[71] United States Conference of Catholic Bishops, *Catholic Catechism*, 490–93; Crichton, *Our Lady in the Liturgy*, 64–65.

[72] Campbell, *Mary and the Saints*, 61.

[73] Ibid., 62.

[74] Ibid., 62–63.

[75] Ibid., 70–71.

[76] United States Catholic Conference of Bishops, *Catholic Catechism*, 996; Crichton, *Our Lady in the Liturgy*, 52.

1889) all spoke of the growing faith of the (then-missionary) American Church. The twentieth century also had its American models of holiness: Frances Cabrini (d. 1917), Marianne Cope (d. 1918), and Katharine Drexel (d. 1955).

The Church in the twentieth century benefited from the teachings and witness of some of the more recent saints in the Church's history. The young Carmelite nun, Thérèsè (Martin) of Lisieux (d. 1897), left a spirituality that has earned her a place with the Church's greatest teachers. Another Carmelite, Teresa Benedicta of the Cross (Edith Stein; d. 1942), a philosopher convert from Judaism, was murdered by the Nazis at Auschwitz as was the Franciscan priest Maximilian Kolbe (d. 1941). Josephine Bakhita (d. 1947), a Sudanese woman sold into slavery as a child, eventually became a nun in Italy and is remembered for her charity and simplicity. The Capuchin priest and stigmatist, Pio of Pietrelcina (d. 1968), is especially remembered for his dedication to the poor and miracles.

The Second Vatican Council (1961–65) inspired great changes in every corner of the Catholic world. New emphases on ecumenism and religious dialogue, with changes in the role of the laity, redefinition of the duties of priests and religious, and liturgical reform, affected the lives of Catholics in countless ways. The ripples of these reforms were felt in society at large. Among the liturgical reforms of the council was a revision of the Church's liturgical calendar and a reexamination of the cult of the saints. The period following the Council of Trent had witnessed a proliferation of saints' days in the liturgical calendar and, as part of the reforms, a number of these feast days were "dropped" or removed from universal observance.[77] While the council clearly recommitted the Church to its traditional teachings on the role of the saints, for perhaps the first time in Church history interest in the saints began to wane as Catholics abandoned many of the traditional devotions of past centuries.[78] The council fathers praised the life of Mary as a "pilgrimage of faith," reemphasizing Mary as a model of faith and obedience: "She

[77] See Adolf Adam, *Foundations of Liturgy: An Introduction to Its History and Practice* (Collegeville, MN: Liturgical Press, 1985), 209–10.

[78] National Association of Pastoral Musicians, 45.

stands out among the poor and humble of the Lord, who confidently hope for and receive salvation from him."[79]

The 1970s and '80s saw a Catholic world still adjusting to what was considered a new identity and mission. However, the Church remained true to its teachings on Mary and the saints. In 1974, Pope Paul VI issued the apostolic exhortation *Marialis Cultus*, on devotion to the Virgin Mary. It put before the faithful the witness of Mary's faith and invited them to remain dedicated to traditional Marian devotions while seeking the positive ways Mary might speak to the modern world.[80]

In 1978, Karol Wojtyla (d. 2005) was elected Pope John Paul II. A native of Poland, he grew up under communist and socialist regimes. In 1983, sensitive to the growing diversity of the Church, he issued *Divinus Perfectionis Magister* (The Divine Teacher of Perfection). In it, he radically modified the process of canonization and beatification. Among the changes was a decision to place the investigation of a given candidate in the hands of the local bishop.[81] This decision was a deliberate attempt to make the local church more directly involved in the "saint-making" process, although still only the pope can actually proclaim a beatification or canonization.[82] Pope John Paul II made great use of this new streamlined process and in his twenty-five years as pope he beatified and canonized more men and women than all his predecessors combined. It was his intention to convey the message that holiness was truly accessible to men and women of all times and places.

Conclusion

As we have seen, the theologies and devotion to Mary and the saints have a rich history, closely connected with the very history of the Church itself. No age in the Church's history has been without its models of holiness, and today the Church continues to beatify and canonize men and women from all over the world, celebrating their holiness, teachings, and virtues.

---

[79] *Lumen Gentium* (Dogmatic Constitution on the Church), November 21, 1964, no. 55.

[80] Campbell, *Mary and the Saints*, 77–78.

[81] Cunningham, *A Brief History*, 120.

[82] Ibid., 121.

In his first encyclical letter, *Deus Caritas Est* (God Is Love), Pope Benedict XVI wrote, "The lives of the saints are not limited to their earthly biographies but also include their being and working in God after death. In the saints one thing becomes clear: those who draw near to God do not withdraw from men, but rather become truly close to them."[83] This "closeness" is founded on a relationship that is beautifully expressed in the doctrine of the communion of saints. This realization of our union with those who have gone before remains an essential part of the Church's teaching. As such, devotion to Mary and the saints remains one of the most beautiful aspects of Christian life and spirituality. The idea of praying with the saints is not merely a relic of past ages but is a manifestation of a relationship rooted in love. The Church celebrates this today in its liturgy, devotions, and popular piety, and our understanding of this mystery is an important tool for finding our individual places in the Church and in God's creation. In our prayer with the saints and meditation on their lives we connect with those who have gone before us, and we invite them to teach us and to pray for and with us. In establishing and developing these relationships, we open ourselves to their witness and the power of their intercession.

As we come to know them as individuals, as brothers and sisters who in their day experienced the same temptations and weaknesses we do today, we recognize men and women who, in faith and trust in Providence, were found worthy of hearing the words, "Well done, my good and faithful servant. . . . Come, share your master's joy" (Matt 25:21 NAB).

This essay opened with Thomas Merton's declaration that the only thing necessary to be a saint is the desire to be one. This is a true reality that the everyday Christian should always remember. In fact, to become a saint is really all that matters.

Further Reading

Campbell, James P. *Mary and the Saints: Companions on the Journey*. Chicago: Loyola Press, 2002.

[83] Pope Benedict XVI, Encyclical Letter *Deus Caritas Est* (Boston: Pauline Books and Media, 2006), 57–58.

Cunningham, Lawrence S. *A Brief History of the Saints*. Malden, MA: Blackwell Publishing, 2005.

McBrien, Richard. *Lives of the Saints: From Mary and St. Francis of Assisi to John XXIII and Mother Teresa*. San Francisco: Harper San Francisco, 2003.

Woodward, Kenneth L. *Making Saints: How the Catholic Church Determines Who Becomes a Saint, Who Doesn't, and Why*. New York: Touchstone Books, 1996.

Chapter 14

From Lectio to Video: Praying with Images of Jesus

Guerric DeBona, O.S.B.

Come and see.
John 1:39

I have somewhat mischievously titled this reflection on the importance of religious images "From *Lectio* to Video" in order to underline what almost everyone knows: in the last hundred years or so, the West has moved dramatically from a written to a visual culture. In so doing, I certainly do not wish to diminish the importance of the written expression in prayer. We know that there is a venerable tradition of *lectio divina*, the practice which savors the written Word of God in Scripture and leads to prayer and contemplation; that legacy continues to be a vital and influential component in the history of spirituality. Indeed, words will always play a crucial, primary role in shaping the human subject as communicative and formative features of our environment. Nevertheless, we live in a world that has been shaped, irrevocably, by the visual. Walk down the street of a major city in almost any country on the planet and you will find a cascade of fascinating architecture, pulsating lights, and aggressive advertisements aimed at an unimaginable array of human desires. We live and walk and breathe by the delight of our eyes.

Visually Speaking: A Religious Tradition

Catholic culture has long known the power of the visual imagination to transform the faith community. Christian art depicts episodes in the life of Mary, the Mother of God, the saints, and, of course, Jesus himself. These portraits have ranged from the symbolic to the realistic, from highly expressive to shockingly abstract. All have tried to capture the religious spirit of the holy in some way or other. The great cathedrals in Western Europe, such as Notre Dame of Paris or Chartres, beckon us with their formidable Gothic arches, their dazzling stained-glass windows, their inspirational stone statuary. Enter the front doors of the baroque church of St. Gall in Switzerland and the colors—bright blue, pink, gold—virtually leap off the ceiling. Here is passionate Christianity representing God and creation full of life and power. To paraphrase St. Thomas Aquinas, we know God by analogy and apprehend the holy by our senses. Visual expression is part of the identity of the Catholic Christian community, often accessed by scholars and saints over the centuries for the purposes of prayer. Saint Ignatius Loyola, for instance, enjoined his retreatants making the *Spiritual Exercises* to use their imagination to experience the passion, death, and resurrection of the Lord. In evoking specific details and images in the life of Jesus, Ignatius was drawing on his Basque and Spanish culture and, more broadly, on the world of the Renaissance, with its burgeoning depictions of nature and dramatized human form to reveal God's presence in the world.

The visual remains linked to Catholic sacramental and liturgical life as well. Consider the visual aspects of the preeminent expression of Catholic Christianity in the Church, the Eucharistic Liturgy. The Eucharist expresses the Lord's tangible, passionate care for the whole person. The celebration of the Eucharist is a prayer that communicates profoundly the human capacity to engage the holy through the senses. Our eyes behold the wonder of mystery unfolding: the celebrant and the sanctuary are lavishly decorated with the colors of the liturgical year and this is only one of the many reminders that the action of the liturgy itself participates in a reality greater than itself. We imagine the heavenly banquet unfolding before us: "Behold the Lamb of God who takes away the sin of the world."

Catholic popular culture has evangelized in a visual piety all its own. From statues of Mary and the saints in the local church or home, to images of Jesus as the Sacred Heart or the Crucified Lord, Catholic culture has expressed itself in images—often quite dramatically. When Mel Gibson's *The Passion of the Christ* was released during Lent 2004, the film exceeded all box office expectations. Images provoke us, evangelize us, and convert us. Praying with images of Jesus, then, participates in our contemporary situation and reminds us of a long tradition in the Church. What better way to think about God than by contemplating the artistic expressions given to us over the years on canvas, stone, and film? After all, don't we profess that the Word was made visible?

In confronting a work that depicts Jesus, I would like to suggest that we are entering a world that invites us to think about at least three distinct encounters that might enliven and nourish our prayer. First, we are most obviously meeting the *artistic expression* itself. Every work of art must be accessed for what it is and what it is doing as a piece of art. How am I invited into the work? Where am I in relationship to the painting, sculpture, or film? Second, we also meet the *artist*. A human being with or without some level of faith commitment fashioned this piece of religious expression. What does the work of art tell me about the artist and his or her interests or theological stance? How do I relate to the artist? Is this artistic expression a testimony of faith or not? How so? Last, with any work of art, we meet a particular historically defined *culture* that also helped produce it. A specific culture is more or less responsible for its artistic inspiration, religious or not; the artifact emerges from a specific time and place. In a secular culture like ours, we are more apt to see the contrasts between artistic renderings which come from a highly religious milieu and our irreligiously defined world. Does the artistic piece say something about its own age that might speak to our time? How does interfacing with other cultures through art change my preconceived notions of who Jesus is? We will return to these considerations of artifact, artist, and culture later in this chapter. I would like to explore briefly the history and theology of images before attending to their practical application.

Seeing Is Believing

Chances are that sometime during the past several weeks you have prayed through some kind of artistic rendering. That image may have been just a glance at a wooden crucifix in a church depicting the suffering Jesus. Perhaps it was a painting of the Lord at the Last Supper, or maybe a sculpture of the infant Christ in the arms of his mother. We all have stored favorite images of our Lord in our mind's eye and refer to them often in our prayer. As St. Thomas suggests in his *Summa Theologiae* (II-II, q.175., 3) when he speaks of divine "rapture," we tend to rely on images of God in order to fill our prayer with meaning, feeling, and devotion; contemplation comes through imagining pictures of the holy. Despite the fact that the first commandment enjoined the people of Israel not to construct "graven images" of God, for most of its history the Christian tradition has done just that—and sometimes with brazen and lavish abandon. In attempting to capture the image of God, Christian artists have not claimed to establish what God really looks like. God is beyond all our reckoning. In a certain sense, however, artistic modeling of Almighty God is an expression of the work of the Incarnation. That mystery tells us that God has a human face and entered into human history. Our central claim as a Christian people is that we have already encountered the living God—in Christ Jesus. As Paul wrote in his Letter to the Colossians, "[Christ] is the image of the invisible God, the firstborn of all creation; for in him all things in heaven and on earth were created, things visible and invisible" (1:15-16a). Through Christ, God has become flesh and has been made manifest to all humanity.

The faith experience of the Christian community for over two thousand years has been a prayerful and artistic discovery of the face of God in Christ in all manner of expressions. The gospels are our first substantial evidence of a faith community rendering a "portrait" of God's face on earth. Although there is no physical description of Jesus in either the Synoptics or John's Gospel, that does not seem to be the point. One thing is perfectly clear: Jesus' actual physical appearance is less important than how he is grasped through the eyes of faith. When Christ rose from the dead, some of the disciples later proclaimed that "we have seen the Lord!" That is the visionary encounter with God made possible only by a faith-filled witness. That the eyes of faith determine the way in which we see the Lord is clear when Jesus confronts Thomas, his erstwhile doubting disciple. "Blessed are those who have not seen and yet have come to believe," says the Lord (John 20:29). Indeed, St. Paul reckons himself an apostle, not by being historically present to witness Jesus' physical presence, but through an appearance of the risen Lord: "Last of all, as to one untimely born, he appeared also to me" (1 Cor 15:8). It was the vision of the risen Lord which gave Paul the confidence and the credibility not only to preach but also to establish a unique bond

Figure 1. Detail of the Orans: a veiled woman in the traditional posture of prayer, A.D. 250–300. Catacombs of St. Priscilla, Rome. See ch. 1, pg. 14.
© Scala/Art Resource, NY. Used with permission.

Figure 2. Since the 14th century, pilgrims have come to pray before the statue of our Lady at the Abbey of Einsiedeln in Switzerland, the place of the hermitage of St. Meinrad. In 1854 monks of Einsiedeln came to Indiana and founded Saint Meinrad Archabbey, which carries on their tradition of prayer. See ch. 5, pg. 76.
© 2007, Kloster Einsiedeln, photo Bruno Greis, O.S.B. Used with permission.

Figure 3: Deesis Mosaic of Christ, 12th to 13th century A.D., Hagia Sofia, Istanbul, Turkey. See ch. 14, pg. 258.

Figure 4. Detail from Christ on the Cross, the Isenheim Altarpiece, by Matthias Grünwald, 1515, Musée d'Unterlinden. See ch. 14, pg. 259.
© Musée d'Unterlinden Colmar, photo O. Zimmermann. Used with permission.

Figure 5. The Supper at Emmaus by Caravaggio, 1600–1601, National Gallery, London. See ch. 14, pg. 259.
© The National Gallery, London. Used with permission.

Figure 6. Jesus in the Garden of Gethsemane by Heinrich Hofmann, 1890, Riverside Church. See ch. 14, pg. 260.
© New York Graphic Society. Used with permission.

Figure 7. The Incredulity of Thomas by Nicholas Mynheer, 1991, private collection. See ch. 14, pg. 260.
© Nicholas Mynheer. Used with permission.

with the Lord Jesus and to proclaim that resurrected Lord throughout the ancient Mediterranean world. When we see a portrait of Jesus, we grasp that vision with the eyes of faith—a communication of a reality beyond reason that only the heart can tell.

Two Traditions

Christian theology and its understanding of God in images evolved in complicated ways over the centuries and had important implications on the use of images in spirituality. Briefly, we might say that in the history of spirituality, two divergent ways of understanding the risen Lord emerged that directly influenced the way in which images of Christ are understood and prayerfully comprehended. On the one hand, there is an imagistic theology which has dominated the West and flourished, especially in Catholic and some Reformed traditions. This is a spirituality that is called *kataphatic*—or one that relies on affirmations of what God is like. This theological strand is imagistic, endorsing a vigorous and imaginative rainbow of how God might look, act, and reveal himself in the world. Images of Jesus are *kataphatic* by definition; they claim to represent a way of knowing God through our senses and by analogy. Numerous prayer traditions have grown up around the *kataphatic* tradition as well, among the most popular of which remains Ignatian prayer, which, as I have already suggested, fosters imaginative and highly personal depictions of Jesus during prayer.

In contrast to the *kataphatic*, the *apophatic* tradition seeks to deconstruct images of God in order to grasp the mystery of the transcendent. Harkening back to the early tradition of Israel and the first commandment, this latter spirituality has mostly been an element in the Eastern Orthodox tradition, with some notable practitioners—mostly monastics—in the West. The *apophatic* tradition does not deny the theological claims of God working in the world or an incarnational or sacramental imagination. But the *apophatic* approach to spirituality is committed to an imageless understanding of God, reminding us what God is *not*—though God became human, God is *not* entirely like human beings; though God entered history, God is *not* contained in history, and so on. Hence, images have no place in the *apophatic* tradition, which focuses its spirituality on self-emptying and an encounter with a God who cannot be named. The most well-known work of *apophatic* prayer is *The Cloud of Unknowing* and its current practice today is found in the use of "Centering Prayer." Much of the imageless prayer recommended in this tradition draws from Scripture and turns our attention to the unknowable, transcendent God, before whom we stand empty, still and lost, like Moses, in a cloud of mystery.

These two traditions, the *kataphatic* and the *apophatic*, have a violent history as well. Although we take images of God for granted today, the so-called iconoclasts of the eighth and ninth centuries in the East fought bitterly to erase all images of Christ; Christ alone was a unique being and shared in the Father's unimaginable glory and so was not able to be represented by any image. And, indeed, a version of these two traditions surfaces in one way or another within the contours of Christian history. After the Protestant Reformation, many images were smashed or stripped from churches. Some groups, like the Anabaptists, favored no representation of God of any kind. Underlying much of the dispute over images are dense theological issues, such as those concerning the theology of the Incarnation and Mary's place as the Mother of God. Yet despite the war over images throughout Christianity, the *kataphatic* tradition has overwhelmingly shaped our understanding of prayer, especially in American culture. Representations of the Savior have been a window into his person and an avenue to prayer. Perhaps the most popular portrait ever sold of any kind was Warner Sallman's *The Head of Christ* (1940). Indeed, Sallman's various portraits of Jesus, such as *Christ in Gethsemane* (1941), *Christ at Heart's Door* (1942), or *The Lord Is My Shepherd* (1943), became a substantial backbone for American Protestant visual piety during the troubled years of World War II. During the mid-twentieth century, it would be hard *not* to find a picture of Jesus in a pious Christian household. Sallman's *Head of Christ* has been imitated many times, even turned into a paint by number kit for would-be artists. Like Zaccheus, the short tax collector in the sycamore tree, we want to see Jesus; we want a glimpse of the holy.

The Triumph of the Visual

Religious visual culture, already theologically shaped by the *kataphatic* tradition, influences the way we understand God. Just how significant is this religious visual culture? We could point to the unfathomable riches of precious museum pieces that have been amassed over the centuries. Virtually every major museum in the world has a good deal of its collection devoted to Christian religious art, depicting divine mysteries or biblical scenes. These visual depictions of God are, of course, necessarily contextualized by the historical period in which these representations were made. We have only to take a cursory look at a difference between a baroque crucifixion, with its characteristic ornament, extravagant color, and attendant kinetic bodily and emotional freight and, say, a more modern depiction of "Christ on the Cross" by Georges Rouault to know that depictions of Jesus are culturally influenced. Although Rouault was highly influenced by Cezanne and was a devout Catholic, his portrait of Christ's death on the cross is uniquely modern and contemporary in its use of color and composition. Then again, we might contrast a more contemporary portrait of *Jesus Praying in the Garden* by Frank Carter (1987), in which Jesus is depicted with distinctly African features and sweating blood, with Sallman's strictly Anglo-faced Messiah at midcentury: both lay claim to a faith tradition that has seen the Lord, albeit in different ways. Carter's representation of the Lord was informed by a growing awareness of racial tensions that erupted in the mid-twentieth century. It seems that every age makes God over in its own image.

If the voracious consumption of reproduced images of Jesus over the last century is any indication, we might consider the way in which popular culture has deployed images of Jesus in our day. We can see the importance that our culture places on representations of Jesus from pictures of the Sacred Heart over the fireplace and representations of the crowning of thorns on T-shirts, to blockbuster films like *The Passion of the Christ*. Not all these images of Jesus are destined for prayer. With the help of technology that is still developing, some have begun to dismantle or deconstruct the most stable and traditional sacred images. Now in the age of digital computers, Jesus has been morphed and patched into all sorts of modern designs and animations. Not too long ago, I received a book catalogue from a well-known company, the cover of which had a traditional picture of the Sacred Heart with one alteration: the head was Elvis Presley's! Parody, burlesque, pastiche—all are available, even when representing our most cherished images, especially in our contemporary age where the use of irony and sarcasm are ubiquitous. It is therefore all the more important for us to be able to "read" these images of God so that we can understand the kind of faith they represent. Jesus is not just a prayerful icon for the pious. In the modern age, the Savior has become, according to Stephen Prothero's *American*

Jesus (2003), a "national icon" as well. Thus, images necessarily require interpretation: the truth is that we stand poised between the visual and the unrepresentable, between the *kataphatic* and the *apophatic*. As Plato reminded us long ago, the shadows projected onto the cave wall are only representations—false ones at that—which we sometimes take to be the real thing. We pray then with images to understand and comprehend the divine reality they seek to represent, all the while knowing that the merciful Father is shrouded in mystery, incarnate in Christ, and ever new in the Holy Spirit.

"Reading" Five Portraits of Jesus

Jesus Christ has been represented in Western art and culture in various ways over the years, as the examples in figures 3–7 on pages 252–254 demonstrate. Again, we can remind ourselves that when we encounter these works we meet the artistic piece itself, the artist, and the world from which they emerged.

"Deesis Mosaic of Christ" (fig. 3, pg. 252)

This fabulous Byzantine mosaic, taken from the church of Hagia Sophia in Constantinople, Turkey, was the center of a larger depiction that included Mary on one side and John the Baptist on the other. The three portraits together depict that the Word of God has been promised, fulfilled, and remains living and active in God's people. The portrait of Christ suggests a strong teacher, intuitively aware of himself and his divinity. Majestically, he holds two fingers up as if to bless the congregation, signifying his place as the second person of the Blessed Trinity. We have no idea of the identity of the artist, but we can be sure that the artist(s) represented a strong religious sentiment at the time, dating back to the founding of Constantinople and the Council of Nicaea: that the second person of the Blessed Trinity, begotten, not made, guides creation from the beginning. Typical of Byzantine art, this depiction of Christ has absorbed much of the technique of classical Greece, with its attention to symmetry and detail. Christ is a glorified and victorious leader. We can see that the commanding presence of Christ demands all our attention, even gathering the Christian assembly into a unified fold.

"Christ on the Cross" from the Isenheim Altarpiece by Matthias Grünewald (fig. 4, pg. 253)

This depiction of Christ, like figure 3, is taken from an ecclesial space, but it has a much different emotional effect. It was painted around 1515 for the Order of St. Anthony, a religious sect that cared for the sick, especially those suffering from skin diseases. We immediately sense in this image the overwhelming pain and anguish of Jesus. Interestingly, the portrait places us as somewhat distant spectators, once again in contrast to the triumphant Byzantine Christ, who holds us fast with his wondrous gaze. Here we are witnesses to the end of cruelty, injustice, and the violent fate of the Suffering Servant. In the full image (fig. 4 is a detail) the figure of Christ is flanked by other panels; together they make a polyptych. The painting is loaded with symbolism: a lamb holds a cross and fills a cup with blood; John the Baptist points to Scripture. Grünewald, a popular German painter on the edge of the Protestant Reformation, aggressively states the humanity of Christ and the intense feeling and passion involved in the crucifixion. As is well known, the religious fervor that erupted during the Reformation grew out of theological concerns regarding the grace God has given through Christ's death on the cross. The painting foregrounds such religious sentiment and becomes a prophetic voice for the monumental changes that would soon occur in Germany and throughout the world.

"The Supper at Emmaus" by Michelangelo M. da Caravaggio (fig. 5, pg. 253)

Space itself is perhaps the feature that confronts us most immediately in this 1601 depiction of Jesus and the disciples at Emmaus (cf. Luke 24:13-35). The table breaks into our own viewing area, and the disciple on the right reaches out to us as if to draw us closer. We have been invited to share an intimate moment of table fellowship. At the same time, the disciple on the left appears to be jumping out of his chair in amazement. All three disciples are focused on Jesus as a center point, further accentuating a kind of gravity that draws us into the painting. Caravaggio's masterful use of light and shadow creates an almost three-dimensional look to the painting, heightening the realism. The painting has taken into itself all the important characteristics of the Renaissance, while anticipating the lavishness of the Baroque: the balance of composition; the interest in the human body and its proportionate, realistic details; the dramatic setting achieved by characters in motion. Even the fruit on the table seems to have a life of its own. Caravaggio was known as a man of passion, and his paintings often reveal a drama buried in the biblical narratives. Moreover, the early seventeenth century world of Caravaggio in southern Italy was theologically rich with discourses on the Eucharist. The Council of Trent and the Counter-Reformation enlivened a discussion on transubstantiation, a debate this painting intends to provoke.

"Jesus in the Garden of Gethsemane" by Heinrich Hofmann (fig. 6, pg. 254)

This is truly a popular image of Jesus that has become commonplace among the (mostly Protestant) faithful for over a century. Instantly recognizable as the seminal moment when Jesus prays in the Garden of Gethsemane to be delivered from his coming passion (Luke 22:41-44), Hofmann's painting (1890) has been the inspiration for countless moments of religious devotion and is often duplicated on holy cards, Bibles, and stained-glass windows. Shrouded in darkness, with the sleeping disciples in the background, the painting accentuates Jesus' face through the use of a halo. The light that enters the painting comes from above, as if it were a spotlight shining on a special subject. In a way, the painting is theatrical, even melodramatic, in its showcasing Jesus' prayer with the Father as a dramatic moment like none other. Hofmann was part of a German neo-Romantic revival in the late nineteenth century, a movement that tended to emotionalize religious experience toward highly devotional sentiments. It is striking that the face of Jesus, although bearded, appears delicate. Such emotional encounters with Jesus and the biblical text might be seen more broadly as part of the evangelistic revival in America. Like Sallman's portraits (see pg. 256 above), which also emphasized an emotional side to the Savior, Hofmann's depictions of Jesus certainly played an important role against the backdrop of an increasingly secular, rational society.

"The Incredulity of Thomas" by Nicholas Mynheer (fig. 7, pg. 254)

This contemporary rendering of Jesus' postresurrection appearance to Thomas and the disciples captures the moment when the apostle makes his profession of faith (John 20:28). Notable are the Savior's very large hands and the nail marks, which are prominent in the gospel text as well. In a way, Thomas's desire to probe Jesus' hands and side become our desire, since the wounds are so outstanding to the viewer. Also, the composition suggests Jesus as a maternal figure, about to gather his followers in his arms. Far from rebuking Thomas for his unbelief, Jesus appears about to embrace him. The strong lines and radiant colors are especially notable. Finally, Mynheer, who lived a rather secular life early on, worked in advertising, and was then converted to Christianity, manages to express a good deal of emotion in the exaggerated and truncated features of the characters in this scene. The mouths agape give us a sense of the wonder of the moment when someone comes to believe. Such a bold expression in both pigment and technique transcends conventional stereotyping of religious images. Painted for Lady Margaret Hall of Oxford in 1992, this painting is a wonderful contribution to contemporary religious art and showcases the apostle who has become an icon for the age of skepticism.

Chapter 15

Prayer and Conversion

Mark O'Keefe, O.S.B.

Once, while teaching a class on fundamental moral theology, I asked my class to tell me the "first principle of the natural law" (that is, the most basic, natural moral rule) which had been discussed in the assigned reading for that day's class. The correct response, of course, is: "Do good and avoid evil." One of the smart alecks in the class, however, promptly blurted out: "If it feels good, do it." And then he quickly added: "And don't forget its corollary: 'You got a problem? Take a pill.'"

Of course (at least I have always profoundly hoped), the student was joking. One of the things that makes his smart-aleck remark sadly funny, however, is the fact that our society does sometimes convey both messages, almost as basic laws of nature: "If it feels good, do it" and "Got a problem? Take a pill." A lot of contemporary consumer products and advertising is aimed at maximizing good feelings and easy fixes. Have a typical sort of weight problem? Don't bother with exercise or trouble yourself with watching your diet! Take a carbohydrate blocker or a fat burner or a metabolism booster! Don't cook from scratch! Buy it frozen. Don't use it if you have to wash it later! Buy disposable!

Perhaps it is not so surprising that such "easy-fix" thinking can encroach even into our spiritual lives. And, of course, it is natural enough. We want "good" prayer experiences, and we want them now. We want good feelings in prayer. We would all like to find just the "right" prayer technique that would make our prayer easy, sweet, and consistent. We would like to think that if we attend the right workshop on prayer, we could learn to become instant contemplatives.

Now, it is a great thing to have good feelings in prayer and to experience moments that feel like real, quiet, wordless prayer. Recently, for example, many people are rediscovering the beauty of eucharistic adoration. The incense, the pageantry of the ritual, the music, the people gathered for periods of silence—all of these can lead us into a real sense of communion with the Lord, a real experience of a type of contemplative prayer. Oh, if only we could experience prayer like this all the time!

Would that it were that easy! But, for the vast majority of us, in the vast majority of times, it isn't that easy at all. Both our experience, over time, and the recorded experience and wisdom of prayerful saints tell us that real and consistent prayer isn't easy at all. Feelings in prayer—even good feelings in prayer—aren't a reliable measure of "good" prayer. And real contemplative prayer, beyond a special moment or a special grace, is fleeting at best without consistent effort and time.

There is no "easy fix" when it comes to prayer. There isn't a pill that can be taken when we have a problem with our prayer to make it magically better. If we lived by a "if it feels good, do it" mentality in prayer, we would quickly find that we wouldn't be praying very often at all.

The great spiritual masters of our tradition, and our own experience after even a little trying, tell us that building up a habit of prayer is hard work. But, what's more, growth in real prayer, entering into deeper prayer, is not just about praying more often or more consistently. Growth and deepening in prayer requires making our whole life, day in and day out, fertile ground for prayer. Our daily life must become increasingly consistent with our growing life of prayer in order to support that prayer and as a manifestation of a true growth in prayer.

Would that growth in prayer was just about praying! But it isn't! It is also about living—how we live, as consistent with our prayer.

It is no accident that one of the classic works of the great teacher of our spiritual tradition, St. John of the Cross (d. 1591), is titled *The Ascent of Mt. Carmel*. We can't reach the heights of prayer without the difficult climb through a life-changing and a lifelong conversion. Spirituality before the Second Vatican Council (1962–65) was often taught in two sections: "Mystical Theology" and "Ascetical Theology." We didn't study the heights of prayer in mystical theology until we had studied the steps in prayer and conversion that necessarily precede it. There is no authentic mysticism without true asceticism. This pattern reflects the experience and the teaching of holy men and women throughout our spiritual tradition.

Prayer Requires Conversion

Real growth and authentic deepening of prayer requires an ongoing conversion of life. Sin stands in the way of prayer. Mortal sin, of course, separates us from the life of grace; but all sin, any sin, the roots of sin in our hearts, pull us away from prayer. Sinful thoughts distract us. Sinful desires tempt us away from praying at all. Sinful habits keep us from making time for praying. The selfishness that is at the heart of all sin focuses attention on self and on our selfish desires rather than on increasing surrender to God that is at the heart of any deepening life of prayer.

In order to grow, the seed of prayer requires the fertile soil of a life consistent with and open to God. Or to use an image of St. John of the Cross: A soul in sin is like a glass window covered with grime and dirt. The light of God's presence, always inviting us into a deeper prayer, cannot penetrate the opaque obstacle of sin. We need to clean the window to let the divine light into our souls and in our lives. We need conversion.

The experience of praying itself makes it obvious to us that we need to change. The more time that we spend with the Lord and the more time that we spend meditating on the Scriptures, the more we see that our living is not entirely consistent with the ways and the will of God. As we draw closer to God in prayer, we see that we need to live in ways that are more consistent with God's will. The very act of praying is a statement that the person who prays wants to be united with God. We see increasingly that such union is not only about praying but also about living—and about the ongoing conversion through which such consistency must necessarily develop and mature.

As we bring any object closer to the light, we begin more clearly to see its flaws. At a distance, in the shadows, it can look flawless, but in a brightening light we see better the object's reality. Drawing closer to God in prayer has the same effect. So, the regular refrain of the great saints is: "Oh, I am the greatest sinner of all!" Their sinfulness is not so obvious to us, and we would overlook in ourselves the minor faults that remain in them. But they have drawn close to God in prayer, and in that Light they see the reality of themselves more deeply. They see their need to change, to be ever more deeply converted. Deeper prayer always reveals the greater need for conversion.

In a particular ministry assignment, I was a regular confessor to a woman who took great pride in telling me that she was reading St. Teresa of Avila, St. John of the Cross, and the works of the mystics. She felt that she had made great strides in her prayer. But, in confession, she could think of nothing to confess. But how could that be, if she was truly growing closer to the Lord in authentic prayer? Perhaps it was quite true that she could think of no particular acts of sin—at least of any serious nature—but how can one draw close to the God of Infinite Love and not see more deeply one's own failure to love through a greater spirit of generosity, patience, hospitality, or service?

It is easy to think that we can judge the quality or health of our prayer by how it feels. But feelings in prayer are notoriously fleeting and unreliable. The wisdom of our tradition tells us that we should judge the quality of our prayer not by how it feels, but by how it is changing our living. We judge the health of a tree by the fruit it bears. If our prayer is converting us by making us more loving, more patient, more generous, more forgiving, then we can be sure that our prayer is good; because real prayer is always and necessarily linked to conversion of life.

Conversion Requires Prayer

Of course, if it is true that prayer requires conversion, it is no less true that conversion requires prayer. Our daily efforts to live consistently as disciples of Jesus, according to his example and teaching, reveals this truth to us immediately. Conversion, like prayer, is hard work, but hard work is not enough. Our experience of failing at the task so often tells us so. We need grace, God's help, God's presence, and God's infinite patience with us. Ongoing conversion requires the grace that is available to us, that we become open to receive, in prayer.

Jesus tells us in the Gospel of John (10:3-5) that he is the Good Shepherd, and his sheep recognize his voice and follow him. Following Jesus is the lifelong task of Christians, becoming more and more like him, living consistently with his teaching and example. This is the path of ongoing conversion. No wonder that we so often speak of the Christian life as a "way" or a "journey." But it is a path that requires us to listen to the Lord, to recognize God's voice in the midst of the noise and distraction that so often surround us. The path of true conversion can only be walked by the person of prayer who recognizes and listens attentively to the voice of the True Shepherd. Those sheep who do not or cannot listen attentively become easy victims of the wolves along the path who masquerade as sheep and of the false shepherds who would lead them astray.

Responding to the Good News

In the Gospel of Mark, Jesus begins his public ministry with the announcement: "The time is fulfilled, and the kingdom of God has come near; repent, and believe in the good news" (1:15). Jesus came to announce good news. His life, death, and resurrection for our salvation is good news. Christian faith is belief and trust in that good news. And Christian life and prayer are a response to the Good News.

In Jesus Christ, God offers himself, gives himself, to sinners. Prayer and the ongoing conversion of our lives in order to give ourselves to God in return are simply two manners of response to God's amazing self-giving. In prayer, personal and communal, we respond to the continual offering of communion that God is making to us in the Spirit. In a life of ongoing conversion, we strive, with the help of grace, to grow in an ever more authentic conformity to God's will and ways.

It is ultimately gratitude, then, that fuels both growth in prayer and ongoing conversion. God offers himself to sinners! God offers eternal life to sinners. Prayer, in whatever form, is the grateful response to the offer that God has first made to us. It is no surprise, then, that the Eucharist, the celebration in which God offers himself to us again in the body and blood of his Son, is the height of Christian prayer in which we respond in gratitude by giving ourselves and our daily efforts to be conformed to him.

A Single Journey of Surrender

Ultimately, at heart, both the life of Christian prayer and the life of ongoing conversion lead us beyond ourselves, to surrendering ourselves to God. That is the path of authentic human development. Both prayer and conversion are our response and imitation of God's gift of himself to us through Christ.

It is true that we must strive to know and accept ourselves, to develop our gifts and talents, possess ourselves as mature adults. But it is no less true that, created in the image of a God who *is* self-giving love and baptized into a Savior who gave himself in love on the Cross, our ultimate fulfillment and fullest development as human beings lies in giving ourselves in love to God and to other persons.

Our self-giving is always invited and made possible by God's prior self-offering in the crucifixion and resurrection. Even the smallest impulse to pray is the action of God's gracious invitation at work in us. Any awareness of God's constant presence is made possible by this action. Any and all prayer begins with God's initiative. God invites sinners into conversation, into relationship, into communion, into union with him. God's self-giving love, which is the model and foundation of all loving, seeks reciprocity, mutuality, return. Our prayer is precisely our response.

On our part, then, every act of prayer is an act of giving ourselves in return, surrendering to the one who first gave himself to us. This is so, no matter what form the prayer takes. Our tradition tells us that prayer can be said to be of four types: petition, repentance, thanksgiving, and adoration. To ask God for something in *petition* is to acknowledge our need for God, to place our need into the hands of God, and ultimately to surrender it in trust. Prayer of *repentance* is an acknowledgment of our sin, a recognition of our complete need for God's mercy and aid, and a surrender in trust to the mercy that has been assured us in Christ Jesus. To *thank* God in prayer is to acknowledge that every good gift comes from God's provident hand and to surrender ourselves to that sure embrace once again. *Adoration* is a prayer of receiving God's offer of Jesus Christ and giving ourselves to God in silent, wordless response. All of these are present in Eucharist where God gives himself, and, united with Christ, we give ourselves to God in petition, repentance, thanksgiving, and adoration. And this dynamic of giving and receiving in prayer, this mutuality, anticipates and even allows us to participate now in the inner life of the Triune God.

Perhaps the characteristic of prayer as surrender and self-transcendence is most apparent in what St. John of the Cross described as the "Dark Night of the Soul." The person who has traveled consistently on the path of prayer and conversion reaches a point in the journey where all seems dark, in which it feels that God is absent (though, in fact, God is so close that the person is blinded to his presence, like someone blinded by closeness to an intense light). If the person is to advance to the highest form of prayer, says St. John of the Cross, he or she must surrender in trust, believing that God is present in the darkness and in the experience of seeming absence. And there, in the Dark Night, the person must surrender even precious images and supposed certainties about God. (In fact, to pray faithfully when there are no pleasant feelings is, in a more humble way, also a surrender to the presence of God as God chooses to manifest himself to us at that moment, whether in good feelings or in dryness.)

Conversion too is ultimately about self-surrender and self-transcendence. The central teaching of Jesus, the challenge for our ongoing growth and maturity as his disciples, is love. In fact, our tradition has taught that the most perfect flowering of the Christian life is not, as we might think, in the heights of mystical prayer. Rather, the "perfection" of the Christian life, it was said, is in the "perfection of charity." We reach fully developed and mature, authentic humanity by becoming fully loving.

But real love—and the ongoing effort to become more loving through a life of conversion—is always about self-transcendence. Authentic love always involves looking to others rather than to oneself. It involves serving others, rather than being self-serving. The true meaning of love, of course, is manifest by Jesus on the Cross. Although he was being ridiculed, abused, betrayed, abandoned, and unjustly put to death, nonetheless, he gave himself for those who were acting against him. At that moment when any other human being would have thought first of self, he thought of others. He forgave; he gave himself; he surrendered. In short, he loved.

Just as good feelings are not to be mistaken for good prayer, warm feelings for other people are not to be mistaken for real love. Real love acts on behalf of others whether we feel warmly for them or not. And, as we know from our own experience, the ability to overcome the deep-seated selfishness of sin that lives in us, fueling every selfish act of sin, is a lifelong task of transcending our selfish desires and self-serving. This is the self-transcending task of Christian conversion, to give ourselves more freely and more completely in love.

"The kingdom of God is at hand." God's ruling is present. It is manifest whenever we surrender to God's will, whenever we act according to God's ways, whenever we give ourselves to the Lord. Both prayer and conversion, then, are a response to the breaking in of God's kingdom. Both are a surrender to God and a living affirmation of the statement that "Jesus is Lord." To pray and to remain faithful to the daily path of conversion is our response to the invitation of Jesus: "The kingdom of God is at hand. Repent and believe the Good News."

The "Three Ways"

The fundamental insight into the dynamic and unified nature of prayer and conversion has been manifest in a classic description of progress in the Christian life called the "Three Ways." Beginning with early Christian writers such as Evagrius Ponticus (d. 399), St. John Climacus (d. 606), and Pseudo-Dionysius (fifth century), through St. Thomas Aquinas (d. 1274), and into the pre-Vatican II manuals of ascetical and mystical theology, spiritual writers have described stages in the development of the Christian life. Eventually, these stages were usually called purgative, illuminative, and unitive. Each stage is characterized by growth both in prayer and in ongoing conversion of life.

The beginning stage of the Christian life is marked by vocal prayers and by the effort to develop a real, consistent habit of prayer. At the same time, the person is striving to overcome serious sin. As we have seen, these two tasks are interconnected. Growth in prayer requires overcoming the sinful tendencies that pull us away from prayer, and the effort to overcome habits of sin requires the powerful help of grace that becomes available to us through prayer. This stage is called "purgative," because the beginner is struggling (the root meaning of "asceticism") to purge himself or herself of sinful acts and habits and of the sinful inclinations that keep us from surrendering fully to God both in praying and in loving.

As the Christian's prayer develops and the path of conversion becomes more secure, the Christian enters into the "illuminative" way. Prayer becomes less wordy and more silent, more a resting in God. The person of prayer learns to listen rather than just talk in prayer, and the person's spirit is increasingly "illuminated" by the divine light. But this stage is described as "illuminative" also because the person's life is increasingly enlightened by love. The task is less the effort to overcome sinful acts; rather, there is the deeper work of removing the roots of sin. In fact, the work of conversion becomes more positive—developing virtues and growing in love, rather than just the negative work of fighting sin.

It is at this point, as the person passes from the second to the third stage, that St. John of the Cross describes the "Dark Night of the Soul." As we said above, the Christian has made good progress in the spiritual and moral journey. He or she has surrendered more and more of self to God in prayer and in loving. But the Lord wants a total surrender; so the doorway into the final stage requires a surrender of our precious images of God and of our supposed certainties about how God does and should act. Like Jesus, praying in the darkness of Gethsemane and in the seeming abandonment of the Cross, the Christian is challenged to let go, to trust, and to abandon self into the hands of an unseen and ultimately incomprehensible God. Jesus' surrender in prayer in the Garden is one with his surrender in love on the Cross.

In the final stage, the Christian attains, by God's gift, an experience of consistent union with God in prayer and in loving—the deepest communion available in this life. At this stage, those who have surrendered totally to God in prayer are finally able to live the challenge of St. Augustine (d. 371): "Love, and do what you will" because their own wills, after years of prayer and conversion, have become united with the loving will of God.

Each of the three stages is marked by a deeper integration of prayer and ongoing conversion. Each successive stage is marked by a more complete surrender as the person becomes increasingly free of sin and of its roots in selfishness. So the person is increasingly able to surrender in prayer and in love.

Saint Benedict provides us with a simple but deeply insightful teaching about the central importance of ongoing conversion united with a life of prayer. Benedictines take a vow of *conversatio morum*, a vow of ongoing conversion. This conversion is realized precisely in the ordinary, daily, and most usually humble effort to be faithful and attentive to prayer and to be generous in serving, forgiving, and accepting one's brothers or sisters in the monastery. For Saint Benedict this path of conversion, faithfully lived, leads ultimately to "purity of heart"—a heart that is free of selfish desires and self-serving, and so truly free to love.

Prayer and Conversion as Communal Acts

But to speak of either prayer or conversion as if they were completely personal or solely individual would be at least incomplete and perhaps even false. Both prayer and conversion are ultimately also social and communal.

The First Letter of John (4:7-21) reminds us of the intimate connection between love of God and love of neighbor. We cannot truly love God without loving our brother or sister. We might also add that truly loving one's neighbor is an implicit act of loving the God who is creator of all human life. The deepening love of God experienced in prayer, if authentic, must be manifest in a growing love of neighbor that is also the mark of a deepening conversion. As we have seen, we tell the health of the tree by the fruit it bears. In like manner, to truly love our neighbor, wholly and completely, leads us to love God who is their source, their protector, their father.

Prayer can be deeply personal, but it can never be completely individual. Every Christian is united with all of the other baptized in the life of the Church, and the prayer of every Christian is united in the prayer of Christ to the Father. Further, prayer draws us into the heart of God where God holds in existence, embraces in existence, every human being, whether Christian or not. In the end, deeper communion with God always leads to a deeper sense of connectedness, communion with, and commitment to others in God.

True conversion, for its part, begins a new way of viewing reality: Jesus—his teaching, example, life, death, and resurrection—becomes the lens through which we view ourselves, our world, other people, our relationships, our priorities, and our vision of how the world "should be." A deepening life of prayer, then, fueled by ongoing conversion, allows us to cut through the barriers that separate us from one another; it frees us from the blindness to our true relationship with other men and women as brothers and sisters; it reveals the true preciousness of every human life and the terrible affront to human dignity of every form and structure of injustice. So the challenge of Jesus (Matt 5:23-24) becomes obvious to us: If we come to prayer and realize that we are alienated from our sister or brother, we must leave our gift at the altar and first seek reconciliation.

Authentic prayer leads to a deeper social conversion, a deeper turning to other persons in need, and a clearer repugnance toward every structure that oppresses them. This reality explains the seeming paradox of contemplatives and mystics who were also social activists. In viewing popular images of St. Francis of Assisi (d. 1226), surrounded by sweet little animals, we can forget that he was a mystic with a deep, almost fanatic commitment to serve the poor. In recent memory, there is perhaps no better witness than Blessed Mother Teresa (d. 1997), who was surely a woman of deep prayer as well as a courageous and sometimes outspoken servant of the poor. Thomas Merton (d. 1968) was both a contemplative monk and a social critic who described the Christian life as a journey to discover one's true self in God where one discovers as well one's relationship with others in God. The patron of the monastery to which the authors of this volume belong is St. Meinrad, a hermit who was also paradoxically a "martyr of hospitality." His legend describes a Christian who went into the wilderness to be alone with God in deep, silent prayer. Saint Meinrad welcomed death at the hands of murderers to whom he had extended hospitality, knowing they had come to kill him.

If prayer is authentic, it leads to a "social conversion," a conversion to the needs of others, one's brothers and sisters. And a deep commitment to other people leads to prayer on their behalf when human efforts are insufficient, and to prayer of praise and wonder at the giftedness of other people, especially those whose gifts are rarely acknowledged by those in "normal" society.

Conclusion

The late Bernard Lonergan (d. 1984) described religious conversion as "an other-worldly falling in love . . . a total and permanent self-surrender without conditions, qualifications, reservations . . . not as an act, but as a dynamic state."[1] But this "other-worldly falling in love" flows out into moral conversion as a deeper commitment to true values that serve persons and into an affective conversion which is a growing ability in love to place others before self.

Conversion is a falling in love with God—not as a one-time event but as an ever-deepening relationship. Prayer is the language of this conversion. Prayer is the language of an other-worldly falling in love, whether it is sung or recited, personal or communal, eloquently spoken or silent and wordless. Prayer is the language of one who has fallen in love, even though this love is, at first, weak and tender and not yet complete. But it is always a language that must be expressed in living. So prayer is grounded in conversion even as it fuels conversion. Conversion seeks the

---

[1] Bernard Lonergan, *Method in Theology* (New York: Seabury, 1972).

expression of prayer and of love lived out more authentically in thought, word, deed—and in relationships and commitments.

Prayer requires conversion, and conversion requires prayer because they are different manifestations of love—the loving response to a divine love given and ever more gratefully received.

Further Reading

Billy, Dennis J., and James F. Keating. *Conscience and Prayer: The Spirit of Catholic Moral Theology*. Collegeville, MN: Liturgical Press, Michael Glazier, 2001.

Billy, Dennis J., and Donna Lynn Orsuto, eds. *Spirituality and Morality: Integrating Prayer and Action*. Mahwah, NJ: Paulist Press, 1996.

Garrigou-Lagrange, Reginald. *The Three Ways of the Spiritual Life*. Westminster, MD: Newman Press, 1950.

Lonergan, Bernard. *Method in Theology*. New York: Seabury, 1972.

O'Keefe, Mark. *Becoming Good, Becoming Holy: On the Relationship of Christian Ethics and Spirituality*. Mahwah, NJ: Paulist, 1995.

Rahner, Karl. *The Love of Jesus and the Love of Neighbor*. Trans. Robert Barr. New York: Crossroad, 1983.

Tastard, Terry. *The Spark in the Soul: Four Mystics on Justice*. Mahwah, NJ: Paulist, 1989.

Our Call to Prayer: An Afterword

Archbishop Daniel M. Buechlein, O.S.B.

In his apostolic letter setting the Church's course for the third millennium, the late Pope John Paul II reminded us that our major task is evangelization, but he went further and made it more personal. He said just as in the days of Jesus when some Greeks came to Philip and the disciples and said, "We want to see Jesus," so in our day people want to see Jesus. The Holy Father said people do not want us just to talk about Jesus. They want to *see* the compassionate Jesus. Ours is the task to show Jesus to our world. The pope reminded us that if we are to show the face of Jesus to the world, we must contemplate the face of Jesus—in the gospel, in prayer, and in contemplation.[1]

The call to prayer is fundamental to our Christian vocation. When I was ordained a bishop in Memphis in 1987, I stated that the greatest gift I brought to my ministry as a bishop from my monastic roots was the fact that I was schooled in the habit of prayer. I promised to be a man of prayer, and I was so happy to learn that my promise meant a great deal to the people of the diocese. To be people of prayer is not only for priests and religious, however, but is for all of us baptized in Christ. How else, except in personal prayer, do any of us remember

---

[1] Pope John Paul II, *Novo Millennio Ineunte:* Apostolic Letter, esp. Section II: A Face to Contemplate, no. 16–28.

and keep on wanting to remember and seek and show the face of Jesus to each other?

We cannot guarantee each other much about life, but we can guarantee this: if we are faithful in prayer day in and day out, everything will be okay, and we will find peace and joy. Like Mama Dora, my elderly African American friend in Memphis would tell me, "My feets is tired, but my spirit is happy." Remaining faithful in prayer liberates us in our quest for what truly matters in life.

As I reflect on the Christian call to prayer the words of two other important leaders of faith come to mind. Blessed Teresa of Calcutta said:

> I don't think there is anyone who needs God's help and grace as much as I do. Sometimes I feel so helpless and so weak. I think this is why God uses me. Because I cannot depend on my own strength, I rely on him twenty-four hours a day. All of us must cling to God through prayer. My secret is simple: I pray. Through prayer I become one in love with Christ. I realize that praying to him is loving him. [2]

Mother Teresa is justly famous for her work among the poorest of the poor, but she does not see this as *her* work but as *God's* work. Through her prayer she joins what she does to the love of God. Mother Teresa goes on to say:

> We cannot find God in noise or agitation. Nature: trees, flowers and grass grow in silence. The stars, the moon, and the sun move in silence. What is essential is not what we say but what God tells others through us. In silence He listens to us; in silence He speaks to our souls. In silence we are granted the privilege of listening to His voice.
> Silence of our eyes,
> Silence of our ears,
> Silence of our minds,
> . . . In the silence of the heart God will speak." [3]

---

[2] Mother Teresa of Calcutta, as cited in *The Power of Prayer* (New York: MJF Books, 1998), 3, 7-8, taken from *United States Catholic Catechism for Adults* (Washington, D.C.: USCCB, 2006), 479–80.

[3] Ibid.

Ironically, Mother Teresa lived in a very noisy and busy city: modern Calcutta. She was involved in a work that was endless and endlessly complicated. Still, she was able to create in the midst of this noise and busyness a place of silence where she could be with her God in order to carry out more clearly the ministry of Christ.

In his encyclical *Deus Caritas Est (God Is Love)*, Pope Benedict XVI underlines this idea and points specifically to Mother Teresa:

> Prayer, as a means of drawing ever new strength from Christ, is con-cretely and urgently needed. People who pray are not wasting their time, even though the situation appears desperate and seems to call for action alone. Piety does not undermine the struggle against the poverty of our neighbors, however extreme. In the example of Blessed Teresa of Calcutta we have a clear illustration of the fact that time devoted to God in prayer not only does not detract from effective and loving service of our neighbor but is in fact an inexhaustible source of that service. In her letter for Lent, 1996, Blessed Teresa wrote to her lay co-workers: "We need this deep connection with God in our daily life. How can we obtain it? By prayer."[4]

Pope Benedict urges us to answer the call to prayer as a way of avoiding a growing secular activism in our charitable works as Christians.[5]

The Holy Father also addressed one of the inevitable temptations that one can encounter in prayer: the temptation to doubt the good-ness of God.

> Often we cannot understand why God refrains from intervening (in the face of suffering). Yet he does not prevent us from crying out like Jesus on the Cross: "My God, my God why have you forsaken me?" We should continue asking the question in prayerful dialogue before his face: "Lord, holy and true, how long will it be?" . . . Even in their bewilderment and failure to understand the world around them, Christians continue to believe in the goodness and loving kindness of God.[6]

I have a simple story about trust in God. On some evenings toward the end of her life, my mother and I would pray the rosary together.

---

[4] Pope Benedict XVI, *Deus Caritas Est* (Washington, D.C.: USCCB, 2006), no. 36.
[5] Ibid., no. 37.
[6] Ibid., no. 38.

Toward the end she was feeling too weak to pray aloud. As she prayed silently in her wheelchair, I would sit by and do the same. One evening she suddenly straightened up, stretched out her rosary and asked, "Do you think this does any good?" Imagine my surprise. Then she said, "Don't answer that!" And she kept on praying. Did my mother doubt God? No, I don't think so because she kept on praying. I think she may have wondered if her prayer was good enough. But she kept on praying. The message I learned from her that evening was the reminder that it is the Holy Spirit who makes something good of our prayer, not us. Our part is to do it—to remain faithful in praying. That was my mom's last great gift to me—the witness of trusting in God. It is what the call to prayer is about.

Praying need not be complicated. The holy priest John Vianney told an anecdote about an elderly man who would come into the parish church at Ars every day without fail, rain or shine. He would spend time there. One day the Curé asked the gentleman, "You come here every day. What happens?" The man answered, "I look at Jesus and he looks at me"[7]

Archbishop Fulton Sheen was an insistent promoter of prayer before the Blessed Sacrament. "We become like that which we gaze upon. Looking into a sunset the face takes on a golden glow. Looking at the Eucharistic Lord for an hour transforms the heart in a mysterious way."[8] I believe it.

The Eucharist is the greatest of all prayers, and by our baptism we have both the responsibility and the great privilege to participate in this perfect prayer of Christ. We are also called to pray with the Word of God, that eternal font of prayer. Beyond that, each one of us is called in our own way to pray. The way that we express our trust in God will differ from person to person because it must truly be our own. The prayer may be short or long. It may be with words that come at the moment or with prayers learned long ago and recited over and over. However we pray, our common call is simply to do it.

---

[7] *Catechism of the Catholic Church* (Washington, D.C.: United States Catholic Conference, 1994), no. 2715.

[8] *United States Catholic Catechism for Adults,* 462.

Contributors

(Listed according to seniority as found in the monastic ordo)

Archabbot Justin DuVall, O.S.B., M.Div., A.M.L.S.
Archabbot Justin professed his vows as a monk of Saint Meinrad in 1974, was ordained a priest in 1978, and was elected ninth abbot and sixth archabbot of Saint Meinrad Archabbey in 2004. He also serves as the chair of the Board of Trustees for Saint Meinrad School of Theology. After holding several jobs in the library and monastery, he was appointed prior of the monastery, a position that he held from 1984 to 1995. In 1995 he joined the staff of the School of Theology, becoming provost-vice rector from 1996 until his election. Widely respected both for his spiritual insight and his ability to put his thoughts into words, Father Archabbot wrote the introduction to this book.

Archbishop Daniel M. Buechlein, O.S.B., D.D., S.T.L.
Archbishop Daniel made his profession as a monk of Saint Meinrad Archabbey in 1959 and was ordained a priest in 1964. After his college and theology at Saint Meinrad, he received a license in theology at Collegio di Sant' Anselmo and then was called home for administration. In 1971 he was appointed president-rector of Saint Meinrad School of Theology, and president-rector also for Saint Meinrad College in 1982. In 1987 he was ordained the Bishop of Memphis, and in 1992 he was

installed as Archbishop of Indianapolis. Archbishop Daniel serves as a consultor to the Vatican's Congregation for the Clergy and as co-moderator of the Disciples of Christ-Roman Catholic International Dialogue. He has published two volumes collecting his weekly columns for the archdiocesan newspaper: *Seeking the Face of the Lord* (1999) and *Still Seeking the Face of the Lord* (2006). Archbishop Daniel wrote a call to prayer that concludes this book.

Cyprian Davis, O.S.B., Dr.Sci.Hist.

Father Cyprian professed his vows as a monk of Saint Meinrad Archabbey in 1951 and was ordained in 1956. After completing his college and theology at Saint Meinrad, he did an S.T.L. at the Catholic University of America and his doctoral studies at the University of Louvain. He joined the School of Theology faculty in 1963 and is professor of church history. He also teaches in the Institute for Black Catholic Studies at Xavier University of Louisiana in New Orleans and has been a visiting professor for many Benedictine and Cistercian monasteries in West Africa. He has written extensively in the area of monastic history and the history and spirituality of African American Catholics in the United States. In 1990, he published *The History of Black Catholics in the United States* (New York: Crossroad, 1990). This volume received the John Gilmary Shea Award in 1991. Father Cyprian served on the subcommittee for the preliminary drafts of the Bishops' Pastoral Letter "Brothers and Sisters to Us" (1979) and the Black Bishops' Pastoral Letter "What We Have Seen and Heard" (1984). He serves as the archivist of Saint Meinrad Archabbey and the Swiss-American Benedictine Congregation. For his work he has received honorary degrees from the University of Notre Dame and the Catholic Theological Union, St. Vincent College and the Catholic University of America. He is also the recipient of the Johannes Quasten Medal for excellence in scholarship and leadership in religious studies. He is a past honorary vice president of the American Catholic Historical Association and the Society of American Archivists. For this volume, Father Cyprian wrote a chapter on the monastic contribution to prayer.

Matthias Neuman, O.S.B., S.T.D.

Father Matthias professed his first vows as a monk of Saint Meinrad Archabbey in 1962 and was ordained to the priesthood in 1967. He did his doctoral studies at the Collegio di Sant' Anselmo in Rome. He has held numerous positions at Saint Meinrad College and Saint Meinrad School of Theology and is currently chaplain for Our Lady of Grace Monastery in Beech Grove, IN. Widely published in the areas of theology, monasticism, and spirituality, he is the author of *Christology: True God, True Man*. Father Matthias wrote the chapter on prayer in the early Christian centuries for this book.

Raymond Studzinski, O.S.B., Ph.D.

Father Raymond professed his vows as a monk of Saint Meinrad Archabbey in 1964 and was ordained a priest in 1969. After finishing his college and theology at Saint Meinrad, he did his doctorate at Fordham University. He is associate professor of religion and culture at Catholic University of America. He has published research articles in *Horizons*, *Louvain Studies*, *Bulletin of the Menninger Clinic*, *Social Thought*, *The Psychotherapy Patient*, and *Concilium*. He is presently working on a book on *lectio divina*, which is also the topic of the chapter he contributed to this volume.

Harry Hagan, O.S.B., S.S.D.

Father Harry professed his vows as a monk of Saint Meinrad in 1972 and was ordained a priest in 1986. After college and theology at Saint Meinrad, he did his doctoral studies in Scripture at the Pontifical Biblical Institute in Rome. He is associate professor of Scripture at Saint Meinrad School of Theology. He was provost-vice rector from 1986–1996. Since 1996, he has served as the novice and junior master. In 2002, Oregon Catholic Press published *Awake, My Soul*, a collection of his hymns. Father Harry is a coeditor of this book and he wrote the chapter on prayer in the Old Testament and coauthored chapters on the liturgical year, the Liturgy of the Hours, and prayer in the modern period.

Eugene Hensell, O.S.B., Ph.D.

Father Eugene was ordained for the Diocese of Lafayette-in-Indiana in 1969 and professed his vows as a monk of Saint Meinrad Archabbey in 1979. After doing his college and theology at Saint Meinrad, he completed his doctorate at St. Louis University. From 1987–1996 he served as president-rector of Saint Meinrad College and School of Theology. Father Eugene sees himself primarily as a teacher and knows his craft well. While continuing as associate professor of Scripture at

Saint Meinrad School of Theology, he is much sought after for retreats and workshops. In addition, he is the past president of The American Benedictine Academy, and serves on the advisory board of the journal *Review for Religious*. For the past twenty years Father Eugene has been a contributing writer for Weekday and Sunday Homily Hints, a service published by St. Anthony Messenger Press. A voracious reader, he regularly contributes book reviews to *The Catholic Biblical Quarterly, The Review of Biblical Literature, Cistercian Studies*, and other scholarly journals. He also is an associate editor for *The American Benedictine Review*. Father Eugene offered his reflections on prayer in the New Testament for this work.

Kurt Stasiak, O.S.B., S.T.D.

Father Kurt professed his vows as a monk of Saint Meinrad Archabbey in 1975 and was ordained a priest in 1980. After finishing his college and theology at Saint Meinrad, he worked in spiritual formation before pursuing his doctoral studies in sacramental theology at the Collegio di Sant' Anselmo in Rome. He is now associate professor of sacramental/liturgical theology at Saint Meinrad School of Theology. A spiritual director of many years, he served as director of spiritual formation and is presently the provost-vice rector of the School of Theology. Father Kurt is the author of several books, including *Sacramental Theology: Means of Grace, Ways of Life* (Loyola, 2002); *A Confessor's Handbook* (Paulist, 1999); and *Return to Grace: A Theology for Infant Baptism* (Liturgical Press-A Pueblo Book, 1996). He has published numerous articles and book reviews appearing in a variety of publications. In this book, Father Kurt authored the chapter on the Eucharist.

Mark O'Keefe, O.S.B., S.T.D.

Father Mark professed his vows as a monk of Saint Meinrad Archabbey in 1979 and was ordained a priest in 1983. After college and theology at Saint Meinrad, he did his doctoral studies at the Catholic University of America in moral theology. He is associate professor of moral theology at Saint Meinrad School of Theology. After serving as academic dean, he was elected president-rector and is serving his third term. Father Mark is the author of a series of five books on the Catholic priesthood. They include *Priestly Wisdom: Insights from St. Benedict; Priestly Prayer: Reflections on Prayer in the Life of the Priest; Priestly Virtues: Reflec-*

tions on the Moral Virtues in the Life of the Priest; The Ordination of a Priest: Reflections on the Priesthood in the Rite of Ordination; and *In Persona Christi: Reflections on Priestly Identity and Holiness.* His other books include *Becoming Good, Becoming Holy: On the Relationship of Christian Ethics and Spirituality* and *What Are They Saying About Social Sin?* His articles have appeared in academic and popular journals, and he is a frequent speaker at gatherings of priests, seminarians, and parish groups. Father Mark authored the chapter in this work on prayer and conversion.

Guerric DeBona, O.S.B., Ph.D.
Father Guerric professed his vows as a monk of Saint Meinrad Archabbey in 1981 and was ordained a priest in 1986. Before coming to the monastery he completed his M.A. in English at Indiana University. After his theology at Saint Meinrad, he taught English at Saint Meinrad College before finishing his Ph.D. in English at Indiana University with a focus on film. Currently, he is associate professor of homiletics and also serves as director of spiritual formation at Saint Meinrad School of Theology. He is a joint author of *Savior on the Silver Screen*, which explores the image of Jesus in film. He is the author of *Praying with the Benedictines: A Window on the Cloister; Fulfilled in Our Hearing: History and Method of Christian Preaching;* and he coauthored *Lift Up Your Hearts*, a three-volume set of homilies for the three-year cycle of Sunday readings. Father Guerric authored the chapter on praying with the images of Jesus.

Godfrey Mullen, O.S.B., Ph.D.
Father Godfrey professed his vows as a monk of Saint Meinrad Archabbey in 1989 and was ordained a priest in 1994. After finishing his college and theology at Saint Meinrad, he completed his doctoral studies in the area of liturgy at the Catholic University of America. He is now assistant professor of sacramental/liturgical theology and director of permanent deacon formation at Saint Meinrad School of Theology. In the past he has served as an associate pastor, as the choirmaster of the Archabbey, and as the chaplain to the monastery of the Benedictine Sisters of Virginia. He continues to give parish workshops, retreats, and missions in the areas of liturgy and liturgical spirituality. Father Godfrey coauthored chapters on the Liturgy of the Hours and the liturgical year for this book.

Denis Robinson, O.S.B., S.T.D.

Father Denis was ordained a priest for the Diocese of Memphis in 1993 and professed his vows as a monk of Saint Meinrad Archabbey in 1997. He finished his college and theology at Saint Meinrad and has just defended his doctoral dissertation on John Henry Newman at the University of Leuven. He is assistant professor of systematic theology at Saint Meinrad School of Theology. He is particularly interested in the work of John Henry Newman, but also teaches and writes in the areas of reformation theology, Anglican studies, theology and literature, and priesthood. Father Denis formerly served the School of Theology as director of continuing education and began the school's program for the formation of permanent deacons. Here, Father Denis authored the chapter on prayer in the counter-reformation.

Paul Nord, O.S.B., M.A., M.Div.

Father Paul professed his vows as a monk at Saint Meinrad Archabbey in 2003. He did his undergraduate studies in chemical engineering at Rose-Hulman Institute of Technology (1997) and then did graduate studies in theology at Saint Meinrad School of Theology, receiving his M.A. in 2001 and his M.Div. in 2005. He was ordained a priest in 2007. He currently serves as assistant director of supervised ministry at Saint Meinrad School of Theology and studies ancient languages. Father Paul contributed a chapter on St. Augustine to this volume.

Silas Henderson, O.S.B., B.A.

Brother Silas professed his vows as a monk of Saint Meinrad Archabbey in 2004. He received his bachelor's degree from Saint Joseph Seminary College in 2006. A bright young monk, Br. Silas has both a scholarly and a devotional interest in Mary and the saints and has presented many talks for young people on devotion to the saints. He is currently studying for the priesthood at Saint Meinrad School of Theology. Brother Silas contributed the chapter on praying to Mary and the saints.

Christian Raab, O.S.B., M.A.

Brother Christian professed his vows as a monk of Saint Meinrad Arch-abbey in 2005. He did his undergraduate studies in history and religion at Indiana University and holds a master's degree in pastoral studies from Loyola University in Chicago, where he wrote his final project on *lectio divina*. Before coming to the monastery, Brother Christian earned five years' experience as a high school religion teacher and campus minister. He is currently studying for the priesthood at Saint Meinrad School of Theology. Brother Christian wrote the chapter on prayer in the medieval Church, and coauthored the chapter on prayer in the modern period. He is coeditor of the book.

Thomas Gricoski, O.S.B., Ph.L./M.A.

Brother Thomas professed his vows as a monk of Saint Meinrad Arch-abbey in 2006. He did his undergraduate studies in philosophy and theology at the University of Scranton and in 2004 completed the master's program (Ph.L.) in philosophy at the Katholieke Universiteit Leuven, Belgium. He wrote his master's thesis on Rahner's philosophy of religion and Heidegger's critique of metaphysics as onto-theology. He is currently studying for the priesthood at Saint Meinrad School of Theology. He is interested in philosophy as a helper of theology, which can lead the way to a deeper appreciation for the mysteries of life and the faith. Brother Thomas coauthored the chapter on prayer in the modern period for this volume.

Scripture Index

Old Testament

Genesis

1	4
2:2-3	16
32:31	19

Exodus

12:1-8	139
12:11-14	139
14	10
15	10
15:1-18, 19-21	23
24:15-18	63
24:18	138
31:16-17	16
33:18-23	18, 63
34:6-9	63
34:28	138

Leviticus

23:3	16

Deuteronomy

34:10	19

Judges

4	10
5	10
5:1-31	23
6:22	19
9	10
13:22	19
16	10

1 Samuel

1–2	10
2	10
2:1-10	23

1 Kings

8:22	14
19:8	138
19:12	19

Psalms

6:1-7, 8-10	9
13:1-5, 6	9
22	9, 11, 25
22:21a	9
22:21b	9

New Testament

Subjects and Names Index